Also by A.J. Jacobs

The Know-It-All
The Year of Living Biblically
My Life as an Experiment
Drop Dead Healthy
It's All Relative
Thanks a Thousand

The Puzzler

THE Puzzler

ONE MAN'S QUEST TO SOLVE THE MOST BAFFLING PUZZLES EVER, FROM CROSSWORDS TO JIGSAWS TO THE MEANING OF LIFE

CROWN

NEW YORK

A.J. Jacobs

with puzzles by Greg Pliska

Published in the United States by Crown, an imprint of Random House, a division of Penguin Random House LLC, New York.

CROWN and the Crown colophon are registered trademarks of Penguin Random House LLC.

LIBRARY OF CONGRESS CATALOGING-IN-PUBLICATION DATA
Names: Jacobs, A. J., author.
Title: The puzzler : one man's quest to solve the most baffling puzzles ever,
    from crosswords to jigsaws to the meaning of life / AJ Jacobs.
Description: First edition. | New York : Crown, 2022.
Identifiers: LCCN 2021053376 (print) | LCCN 2021053377 (ebook) |
    ISBN 9780593136713 (hardcover) | ISBN 9780593136720 (ebook)
Subjects: LCSH: Puzzles. | Cognition. | Thought and thinking.
Classification: LCC GV1493 .J34 2022 (print) | LCC GV1493 (ebook) |
    DDC 793.73—dc23/eng/20211206
LC record available at https://lccn.loc.gov/2021053376
LC ebook record available at https://lccn.loc.gov/2021053377

Printed in the United States of America on acid-free paper

crownpublishing.com

9 8 7 6 5 4 3 2 1

FIRST EDITION

Book design by Simon M. Sullivan

To my favorite co-solvers: Julie, Jasper, Zane, and Lucas

Contents

Introduction   xi

1 *Crosswords*   3

2 *The Puzzle of Puzzles*   21

3 *The Rubik's Cube*   27

4 *Anagrams*   43

5 *Rebuses*   58

6 *Jigsaws*   68

7 *Mazes*   93

8 *Math and Logic Puzzles*   110

9 *Ciphers and Secret Codes*   127

10 *Visual Puzzles*   142

11 *Sudoku and KenKen*   161

12 *Chess Puzzles (Chess Problems)*   174

13 *Riddles*   190

14 *Japanese Puzzle Boxes*   203

15 *Controversial Puzzles*   212

16 *Cryptics*   218

17 *Scavenger Hunts and Puzzle Hunts*   228

18 *Infinite Puzzles*   241

The Puzzler Contest   251

An Original Puzzle Hunt by Greg Pliska   253

Puzzle Resources   289

Solutions   301

Hints to the Original Puzzle Hunt by Greg Pliska   319

Solutions to the Original Puzzle Hunt by Greg Pliska   323

Acknowledgments   337

Image Credits   341

Introduction

One winter morning several years ago, I got an email with some ridiculously exciting news. Or so I thought.

The email was from a friend who informed me that the answer to 1-Down in that day's *New York Times* crossword puzzle was . . . me.

The clue was "A.J. _____, author of *The Know-It-All.*"

My first reaction was *This is the greatest moment of my life.* My marriage and the births of my kids, yes, those were pretty good. But this! As a word nerd since childhood, this was the holy grail!

And then, a couple of hours later, I got another email that changed everything. It came from my brother-in-law. He congratulated me but went out of his way to point out that my name was featured in the Saturday edition of the *New York Times* puzzle. As crossword fans know, Saturday is the hardest puzzle of the week. Monday's is the easiest, with each day's grid getting more and more difficult until Saturday, when the puzzle reaches peak impenetrability.

Saturday is the killer, the one with the most obscure clues, harder than Sunday. We're talking clues like Francisco Goya's ethnic heritage (Aragonese). Or the voice of the car in the sitcom *My Mother the Car* (Ann Sothern). Stuff no normal person knows.

So my brother-in-law's implication—or at least my interpretation—was that my Saturday appearance was the *opposite* of a compliment. Unlike a Monday or Tuesday mention, it's actually proof that I'm totally obscure, the very embodiment of irrelevance.

Dammit. I could see his point. No doubt this wasn't the most charitable interpretation, and my rational side knew I shouldn't let it tarnish my elation. But I couldn't help it. I'm a master of focusing on the negative once it's shown to me. It's like the arrow in the FedEx logo. I can't unsee it. My life's highlight now had a galling asterisk.

Then, a couple of years later, my crossword adventure took another twist. I was on a podcast, and I told the tale of my emotional roller coaster.

Well, it turns out one of the people listening to the podcast was a *New York Times* crossword creator. God bless him, he decided to take pity on me and save me from my end-of-the-week shadows. He wrote a puzzle with me as the answer to 1-Across, and submitted it to run on a Tuesday. Legendary crossword editor Will Shortz let it through.

And *that* became the true greatest moment of my life. I know full well I don't belong in a Tuesday puzzle. It's where truly famous names like Biden and Gaga make their home. I was thrilled to sneak in as an interloper. I mean, it's not Monday, but it's more than I could have hoped.

I emailed the crossword creator, who has since become a friend, and thanked him. He said it was no problem. Though he admitted that, to compensate, he had to make the corresponding down clues super-easy, like *TV Guide*-crossword-puzzle easy. I'm okay with that.

As I hinted, there's a reason my crossword cameos made me ecstatic beyond what is appropriate. Namely, I've been crazy for puzzles all my life.

Partly I inherited this passion from my family. When my dad was in the army in Korea and my mom was stateside, they'd keep in touch by sending a puzzle back and forth, each filling out a clue or two per turn. Not the most efficient method but certainly romantic.

So I was introduced to crosswords early. But I wasn't monogamous when it came to puzzles. I embraced all kinds: mazes, secret codes, riddles, logic puzzles. As a kid who was not in danger of being recruited to varsity teams, nor burdened with a time-consuming dating schedule, I spent my spare time on puzzles. My bookshelf was filled with titles like "Brain-busters" or "Brain-twisters" or "Brain-teasers"— anything involving mental sadism. I programmed mazes on my school's Radio Shack computer. I did hundreds of mix-and-matches in *Games* magazine. Puzzles were my solace.

My enthusiasm didn't wane as I grew older. Like my parents, I married a fellow puzzle lover. It's her job, in fact. My wife, Julie, works at a company that puts on scavenger hunts for corporations, as well as private events. Our weekends often involve escape rooms or games of Mastermind with our three sons. For my birthday a couple of years ago, my son Zane created an elaborate mental obstacle course that included Sudoku, Rubik's Cubes, and anagrams. It took me two weeks to crack, which didn't impress him. I've even tried to recruit our dog, Stella, into the puzzle cult. I buy her these "doggie puzzles" where she has to flip open a latch to get her doggie treat. The manufacturer claims it will keep her canine brain stimulated, though I'm guessing Stella's brain is mostly thinking "Next time, asshole, just give me the peanut butter on a spoon."

After my appearance as 1-Down a few years back, I went from being an occasional crossword solver to a frequent one, perhaps unconsciously hoping I'd reappear. I did the *Times* crossword every day. At first, I only solved a smattering of words in the harder puzzles. But eventually, after years of practice, I could reliably finish Saturday's puzzles.

My addiction became a problem. One day, I decided I wasn't getting enough accomplished in my life and I should quit all puzzles. I figured it would free up several hours every week. Who knows what I could get done? Maybe I'd start a podcast or run a triathlon or build a barn!

The experiment was a failure. After two months, I relapsed, and I relapsed hard. Puzzles once again began to mark the start and end of my day. Now, as soon as I wake up, I check my iPhone for the *New York Times* Spelling Bee, a find-a-word game that is both compelling and maddening (What?! You're telling me "ottomen" isn't a word? Then what's the plural of "ottoman"?!). Before going to sleep, I do Wordle and the *Times* crossword puzzle.

Since my relapse, I've come to two important realizations about puzzles.

1) I'm not a great puzzler.

I mean, I'm okay. But as I started to meet real puzzlers, I got an insight into a whole other league. I realized I'm like the guy who plays decent intramural basketball, but is no match for the LeBron Jameses and Kevin Durants.

2) Puzzles can make us better people.

Okay, there's a pretty good chance this is more of a rationalization than a realization—a way to justify all the mental energy I spend on puzzles. But rationalization or not, I believe it deeply: puzzles are not a waste of time. Doing puzzles can make us better thinkers, more creative, more incisive, more persistent.

I'm not just talking about staving off dementia and keeping our minds sharp. Yes, there's some mild evidence that doing crossword puzzles might help delay cognitive decline (it's probably not just puzzles that help—any mental challenge might delay dementia, whether it's puzzles or learning a new language).

I'm talking about something more global. It's been my experience that puzzles can shift our worldview. They can nudge us to adopt the puzzle mindset—a mindset of ceaseless curiosity about everything in the world, from politics to science to human relationships—and a desire to find solutions.

These insights sparked the idea for the book you are holding now. I decided to embrace my passion and do a deep dive into the puzzle world. I pledged to embed myself with the world's greatest puzzle solvers, creators, and collectors and learn their secrets. I'd try to crack the hardest puzzles in each genre, from jigsaws to crosswords to Sudoku.

My hope is that the adventures and revelations I had will be entertaining and useful, whether you are a puzzle fanatic, a puzzle skeptic, or a full-on puzzlephobe.

I can tell you that when I started, I wouldn't have predicted the fascinating trip to come. I certainly didn't know that I'd be researching part of my book during the Covid crisis. With all of us stuck inside, puzzles had a spike in popularity not seen since the Great Depression. As Ross Trudeau, a *New York Times* crossword creator, wrote during the depths of the pandemic, puzzles and the puzzle community provided him a "balm against anxiety, anger, depression." He added, "I love y'all. We'll get through this."

When I was able to travel, I went anywhere great puzzles took me. My family and I competed in the World Jigsaw Puzzle Championship in Spain. I visited the artists at the base of Mount Fuji in Japan who make intricate wooden puzzle boxes that sell for thousands of dollars.

I learned the surprising history of puzzles, perhaps the oldest form of entertainment. I learned how they've played a part in religion, love, and war. How the British secret service used a crossword puzzle in *The Daily Telegraph* to recruit codebreakers against the Nazis. How Benedict Arnold sent secret messages encoded in publicly available books (a method that is still used today, with slight variations).

I met the man who holds a record for solving the Rubik's Cube with his feet. I got a lesson on solving chess puzzles from Garry Kasparov and visited the CIA to see the infamous unsolved Kryptos sculpture. I grappled with a puzzle that has 641,453,134,591,872,261,694,522, 936,731,324,693 possible arrangements, but only one solution.

I've seen the dark side of puzzles, how they can overlap with paranoia and obsession. And I grew to love types of puzzles that never appealed to me before. I talked to scientists about why we're so drawn to puzzles, why an estimated 50 million people do crosswords every day and more than 450 million Rubik's Cubes have been sold.

In the end, I've come to a conclusion that may seem overly bold, but I'm going to try to convince you of it by the time you finish this book. The conclusion is that puzzles can save the world. Or at least help save the world.

Puzzles can teach us lessons about fresh perspectives, compassion, and cooperation. If we see the world as a series of puzzles instead of a series of battles, we will come up with more and better solutions, and we need solutions more than ever.

But this isn't just a book *about* puzzles. It's also a book *of* puzzles. Within these pages, I have included my favorite puzzles from history. Why just read about the first-ever crossword puzzle from 1913, when you can solve it? The book contains dozens of historical puzzles spanning all genres.

Since puzzles are all about ingenuity, I also wanted some new puzzles. I considered creating them myself, but I soon realized that making great brainteasers is an art that requires years to master. So I teamed up with Greg Pliska, one of the most talented puzzlemakers in the world and founder of the delightfully named Exaltation of Larks puzzle company. He created twenty puzzles, each one related to a different chapter of the book, which can be found starting on page 253.

And one final but important point: In this introduction you are reading now, Greg and I have hidden a secret puzzle. Or more precisely, a secret passcode that will give you access to a series of puzzles on the website thepuzzlerbook.com. The first reader to find and solve the puzzles on the website will get a prize of $10,000.*

I figured I couldn't write a book on puzzles that didn't contain a secret one itself. As a kid, one of my favorite books was *Masquerade*, published in 1979 by a British artist named Kit Williams. The gorgeous illustrations contained clues to a golden rabbit sculpture buried somewhere in England. The book kicked off a frenzy—and not in an entirely good way. Thousands of treasure hunters dug up yards and gardens all over the United Kingdom. Williams received death threats and unwelcome 3 A.M. visits from desperate solvers.

I'm hoping to avoid these pitfalls. The prize is not buried, for starters, so please don't tear up any lawns. And whether or not you claim the prize, I hope you enjoy the rest of the book—except for some of the harder puzzles, which I hope cause you just the right amount of anguish, followed by well-deserved aha moments.

---

* NO PURCHASE NECESSARY. The contest begins May 3, 2022, and ends when the first correct answer is submitted or May 3, 2023, whichever comes first. Open to U.S. residents 18 and older. Void where prohibited or restricted by law. See official rules and more details at thepuzzlerbook.com.

The Puzzler

Crosswords

E very night at 10:01 P.M., the next day's *New York Times* cross-word puzzle appears online. I know this because at 10:00 P.M., I begin furiously refreshing my browser like the helpless addict I am.

What may surprise non-puzzlers is that the ensuing twenty minutes (or so) aren't just an intellectual exercise. They're an emotional experience, sometimes exhaustingly so. Those black and white squares, at least for me, have all the drama of a telenovela, all the comedy of a Chris Rock stand-up special (especially if it's a really hard puzzle).

There's frustration, of course.

Even anger. I'm not proud to admit this, but I sometimes give my computer the middle finger *(I despise you, unnamed Eastern European river!)*.

There's the catharsis when a clue finally reveals itself. Especially if it involves a paradigm shift—*ah, it's "trunk" as in torso, not "trunk" as in elephant's nose.* There's a sense of giddy connectedness, like I've had a Vulcan mind meld with the puzzlemaker (whom I flipped off moments ago).

There's pride in my ability to resist temptation. Like that time the clue was "The key above Caps Lock" and I stopped myself from looking at my laptop keyboard for the answer. You can call me a hero if you want, but that's your word, not mine. (The answer was TAB, by the way.)

There's shame when I fall for the puzzlemakers' traps. And for my own biases—last week, the clue was about boxers, and I searched my mental catalog for every male boxer I knew. The answer was LAILA ALI, a female boxer.

There's humility at the huge gaps in my knowledge, from 1930s baseball players to types of Italian cheeses. There's awe at the sheer variety of microscopic and giant, ancient and new, sublime and ridiculous stuff that makes up our world.

There's despair *(I've looked at fourteen clues in a row and know none of them!)* that can suddenly flip to delusional optimism *(I got 12-Across, I can get anything!)*.

And sometimes there's terror. If I'm struggling to finish a puzzle, I feel a creeping fear that this is the moment when I finally have proof that my aging brain is turning to tapioca. The fear motivates me. I refuse to stop solving until the grid breaks open, even if I have to cycle through hundreds of letter combinations. (When I said it takes me twenty minutes "or so," the "or so" can last till late at night.)

After which, sweet relief. I can tell myself that my mind is still intact for now. Mostly, anyway: I often get a couple of letters wrong, but let's keep that between us.

All this is why I figure I should start this puzzle journey by exploring crosswords, my first love. Later, I'll be investigating puzzles of all kinds—number puzzles, metal wire puzzles, "Vintage French Entanglement Puzzles," whatever those may be (I saw them on a list of puzzle types and my interest was piqued by the vaguely salacious name).

But let's begin with crosswords.

MEETING MY HERO

I arrange my first stop, a visit to my savior: the crossword maker who wrote the Tuesday *New York Times* puzzle that featured me as an answer. His name is Peter Gordon. It turns out I got lucky: Peter isn't just your everyday crossword maker. He's a legend in the puzzle world, known for his creativity and deviousness.

He puts out a weekly puzzle for subscribers called Fireball Crosswords. This is a hard puzzle. Harder than the *Times*'s Saturday crossword. Its slogan is "How hard? If you have to ask, too hard for you."

I want to get inside Peter's mind. What can one of the best puzzlemakers teach me about being a better solver? A better thinker? Can he explain why I'm so obsessed with those squares with the little numbers in the corner?

I take a train to Great Neck, a suburb of New York City. Peter picks me up at the station in his Mini Cooper. He's got brown glasses, strawberry blond hair, a short beard—and a surplus of energy (he talks quickly and frequently cracks his knuckles).

"You ready for some cruciverbal magic?" he asks.

I am. We arrive at his house, and he gives me a tour. There are stacks of wonderfully specific reference books: one contains the closing lines of three thousand movies, another is a guide to weird brand names called *How Do You Spell Häagen-Dazs?*

On the wall in the family room there's a quilt of a giant crossword puzzle.

"That's a reproduction of the puzzle where I proposed to my wife," Peter says. "My sister-in-law turned it into a quilt."

The original version was published in the Long Island newspaper *Newsday*. It's filled with clues about his now-wife, such as her favorite beverage (Diet Coke) and Peter's pet name for her ("Honeybun").

The most important part, of course, is 48-Across, with the answer WILL YOU MARRY ME. It's clued simply as "Proposal." Peter's wife responded (verbally) that yes, she would.

We sit down in Peter's office, a room near the kitchen piled high with newspapers and notepads. He turns on his desktop computer and opens a database that contains all the clues Peter has written or edited in his years as a crossword constructor and editor: 232,974 of them.

The first entry, alphabetically, is AAA, which is clued as "Small battery size."

The last is "ZZZQUILPUREZZZS" (a nighttime cough remedy).

"What's the favorite clue you've ever written?" I ask.

"Fuck off," Peter says, gleefully.

"Pardon me?"

"The answer was 'ahem,' and the clue was 'fuck off.' "

I'm not getting it.

" 'Ahem' is the sound you make to indicate a fake cough," Peter explains. "So the clue is *faux cough*. I wrote it specifically so that when someone asked me for my favorite clue, I could say 'faux cough.' And they would hear what they hear."

As I mentioned: devious. I ask Peter why he thinks people—he, I, and millions of others—are so addicted to crosswords.

"Well, life is a puzzle," he says. "Who should you marry? That's a puzzle. What job should you take? That's a puzzle. With those puzzles, it's hard to know if you got the best answer. But with crosswords, there is one correct answer. So that's comforting."

I nod: puzzles provide a level of certainty you don't get in this confusing real world. It's a solid theory, though not the only one, as I'll discuss next chapter.

Peter pushes his glasses up on top of his forehead, leans in, and opens an empty grid on the crossword-making software. He starts by double-clicking some squares, turning them black. Then he fills in some potential answers, beginning with the theme words. Today's puzzle is a news-related crossword, so the theme words are names of scandal-tarred politicians and just-released movies.

One thing becomes clear very quickly. As hard as it is to solve puzzles, it's even harder to create them. Especially good ones, like Peter's. So many constraints, so many traps, so much pressure to be original. Among the guidelines you have to keep in mind:

- Avoid crosswordese. If you've done some crosswords, you've no doubt seen a lot of crosswordese. Words like OONA (as in actress Oona Chaplin). Or ELAND (an African antelope). These words have a huge advantage for puzzlemakers: They are loaded with vowels and common consonants. But they're also awkward and obscure, so you only use them if you need the vowels to create a more captivating intersecting word. "Like everything in life," Peter says, "crosswords are about trade-offs."
- Steer clear of the dreaded "Natick." A "Natick" is one of the gravest sins in crossword-making. It's when two relatively obscure clues cross each other, making it hard to guess either one. The Natick is named for a 2008 *Times* puzzle that had the answer N. C. WYETH (an early twentieth-century American realist painter) that crossed with NATICK—a little-known Boston suburb (sorry, readers from Natick).
- Be super-accurate. Solvers are unforgiving about typos. Peter once clued a John Wayne movie as " 'Neath Arizona Skies" instead of " 'Neath *the* Arizona Skies." The horror!

All these answers must fit in a symmetrical 15-by-15 grid with no more than seventy-eight words. If art is all about creativity within constraints, crosswords go above and beyond, with more constraints than haiku or Broadway musicals.

WORD-CROSSES

We take a break for lunch, and Peter shows me the first *Times* puzzle he ever published. It's from 1989. "Back then," he says, "they didn't have bylines for the puzzles, so I didn't know it was mine till I started doing it."

Which raises the question: What was the first puzzle ever? Who was the original Peter Gordon?

It turns out the crossword is a surprisingly recent invention—the first official crossword puzzle was written by a former concert violinist named Arthur Wynne and appeared in 1913 in *The New York World* (a newspaper that also gifted us with the less delightful legacy of yellow journalism).

Later that week, after my visit to Peter's house, I printed that first crossword—or actually word-cross, as it was called then, and I gave it a try. I encountered an unpleasant surprise: it gave me a lot of trouble.

In case you want to attempt it, here it is (for solution see page 301):

Why was it so challenging? I came up with a face-saving excuse. I decided the problem was

FUN'S Word-Cross Puzzle.

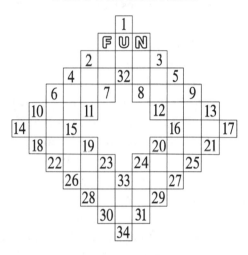

Fill in the small squares with words which agree with the following definitions:

2-3. What bargain hunters enjoy.
4-5. A written acknowledgement.
6-7. Such and nothing more.
10-11. A bird.
14-15. Opposed to less.
18-19. What this puzzle is.
22-23. An animal of prey.
26-27. The close of a day.
28-29. To elude.
30-31. The plural of is.
8-9. To cultivate.
12-13. A bar of wood or iron.
16-17. What artists learn to do.
20-21. Fastened.
24-25. Found on the seashore.
10-18. The fibre of the gomuti palm.
6-22. What we all should be.
4-26. A day dream.

2-11. A talon.
19-28. A pigeon.
F-7. Part of your head.
23-30. A river in Russia.
1-32. To govern.
33-34. An aromatic plant.
N-8. A fist.
24-31. To agree with.
3-12. Part of a ship.
20-29. One.
5-27. Exchanging.
9-25. Sunk in mud.
13-21. A boy.

not with *me*, it's with the *puzzle*. It's a pretty lame puzzle, at least by modern standards. It commits several crossword sins, including:

- The answer DOVE appears twice in the same puzzle, which is a crossword no-no.
- There are too many ridiculously arcane clues, such as "The fibre of the gomuti palm." The answer is DOH (as current solvers know, the proper clue for DOH is "Homer Simpson outburst," but apparently 1913 was even before the premiere of *The Simpsons*).
- Most clues lack cleverness.

Yet I shouldn't be so harsh on Arthur Wynne. The man created something I love, after all. And the first-ever attempt at any art form is rarely a shining example of the genre. I wouldn't expect to play Atari's Pong and be blown away by the graphics.

The important thing is that Wynne's creation took off. Crosswords became a fad, appearing in hundreds of newspapers and bestselling books. You could see a 1925 Broadway play about crosswords or listen to a hit song called "Cross-word Mamma, You Puzzle Me (But Papa's Gonna Figure You Out)."

However, one newspaper at the time did NOT print crosswords: *The New York Times*. The *Times* considered crosswords too lowbrow, too frivolous.

Instead, the *Times* made it a habit to print articles about the evils of crosswords. Here are just a sample of headlines from the 1920s and 1930s about this menace to society.

PITTSBURGH PASTOR SAYS CROSSWORDS ARE "THE MARK OF A CHILDISH MENTALITY."

HUSBAND SHOOTS WIFE, THEN KILLS HIMSELF WHEN SHE WON'T HELP DO CROSS-WORD PUZZLE.

CROSS-WORD HEADACHE BOOMS OPTICAL TRADE: NEW STRAIN ON EYES REVEALS DEFECTS IN VISION.

There are stories of dictionaries stolen from libraries, children ne-glected by puzzle-obsessed parents, athletes forgoing their training to fill in the squares. Those crosswords are a dangerous vice! They're in the same category as gambling and prostitution! The headlines make my nerdy pastime seem edgy and dangerous, which is kind of thrilling. And they bring up a question that I'll be exploring in the book: Are puzzles an addictive peril? Or are they crucial mind-sharpening tools?

Finally, on February 15, 1942, *The New York Times* buckled to popular pressure and printed their first crossword puzzle. It was under the guidance of the founding *Times* crossword editor, the extraordinary Margaret Petherbridge Farrar. Margaret introduced several key improvements, including making the puzzles symmetrical, fixing the inaccuracies, and banning two-letter words.

The *Times* crossword has flourished ever since, now with millions of solvers a day. For the past three decades, the *Times* crossword has been overseen by Will Shortz, the most famous person in puzzling (I'll be talking about Will at length in Chapter 5). The first crossword of the Shortz era? It was by Peter Gordon.

Back at Peter's office, it's early evening, and he's finally finished making the crossword. He sends it off to a couple of friends to test it out. I pack up to go. I've learned a lot about the art of crossword making, as well as important information such as Arnold Schwarzenegger's middle name (it's Alois).

As I say goodbye, I ask Peter if he'd email me his hardest Fireball ever.

FIREBALL #9

The next day, Peter emails me Fireball Year 4, Puzzle #9. Only nine of his hundreds of subscribers cracked it, he says.

I show the printout to my wife, Julie.

"You sure you want to do that? I've got plenty of hard puzzles that need solving. How to get the kids to hang up their wet towels, for instance. That could be a good use of your time."

True. But why do I, nevertheless, stubbornly want to try Puzzle #9?

Partly it's a nerdy version of the reason to climb Everest: because it's there.

Partly it's because I believe the hardest puzzles will teach me the most insightful lessons about how to think differently, and partly because it will provide me with even more of an emotional wallop if I solve it.

I'm also genetically predisposed to attempt absurd and time-consuming feats. My dad is a lawyer, and many years ago, he wrote a law review article with 4,824 footnotes, the most ever in a law review article. The article consisted almost entirely of footnotes, in fact. It gave him boasting rights to a very niche group of people who care about such matters (the niche consists of himself).

On a Thursday afternoon, I lay the puzzle on my desk, and dive in.

I stare at it and stare at it. It's not giving way. Not a single answer jumps out at me. It's much harder than the first-ever crossword. And this time I can't blame the puzzle.

I remind myself of three of my favorite strategies for any kind of problem solving.

1) Find the toehold.

When faced with a stumper of a puzzle, I often think of something Bill Clinton said in the crossword documentary *Wordplay*. "You have to go at a problem the way I go at a complicated crossword puzzle. Sometimes I'd pick up the Saturday *New York Times* crossword puzzle and I'd go through way over half the clues before I'll know the answer to one. And then you start with what you know the answer to. And you just build on it. And eventually you can unravel the whole puzzle."

It's a good strategy for almost any knotty problem. I use it whenever I can. When I'm working on an article, I start with the easiest section to write—the most vivid anecdote or crucial quote—and build out from there.

I force myself to stay optimistic. I need optimism, even if it's a bit delusional. And I need a toehold. After a couple of minutes, I zero in on one possible weak spot: 65-Across. "Ben-_____".

The answer is three letters. It's probably HUR, as in *Ben-Hur,* the cheesy but classic Charlton Heston chariot movie.

And I'm off!

And then I'm stuck!

It takes me another three minutes to get the next one.

This will be slow going. Some clues are obscure trivia, or at least obscure to me, such as the capital of Zambia (it's LUSAKA). Some are tricky wordplay such as "Pigeon English?" (the answer turns out to be COO). None is a gimme.

2) Embrace the eraser.

I'm using a pencil, and the eraser is getting a nice workout. Which is fine. More than fine.

I once met a crossword fan wearing a T-shirt that read "Real Solvers Do It in Pen." Sure, it's a macho slogan that no doubt got him lots of dates with the ladies, but I couldn't disagree more with the sentiment.

During our meeting, Peter told me one of the keys to solving crosswords is to keep your mind flexible. Keep it open to new perspectives. Don't fall in love with your hypothesis. Good advice for both life and puzzles.

Consider my epic struggle with 27-Down.

The clue is "Bee relative," four letters. I know the middle two letters from the crossing answers, so I have:

_PI_

My hypothesis: The first letter is probably an A. Because API is the prefix relating to bees, as in apiary, a collection of beehives. I figure the answer is probably something like APIN, a word I'd never heard of but sounds reasonable.

Unfortunately, the API isn't working with the across clues.

Frustrated, I step away from the puzzle to answer some emails. This is another absolutely key strategy Peter and I discussed. When stuck, take a break. Let the problem marinate in the back corner of your brain. Loosen your grip. Puzzle fan Leonardo da Vinci knew this long ago. As he said about painting, "Every now and then go away, have a little relaxation, for when you come back to your work your judgment will be surer."

When I return to the puzzle, I have a mini-revelation: What if API isn't correct at all? What if the answer starts OPI?

And then it clicks. My paradigm shifts.

The Bee in the clue is not the buzzing, stinging kind of bee. The bee is Aunt Bee, the matronly character from *The Andy Griffith Show*! Her great-nephew, played by Ron Howard as a child actor, is OPIE.

As usual, I'm angry at myself for not seeing it sooner. I'm annoyed at myself for being too attached to my entomological etymology. But at least I got it eventually.

I give thanks to my glorious eraser.

What a great invention, the eraser. Crosswords have made me a huge eraser-head. Let us also praise the Delete key, since I solve most of the *Times* puzzles online. I love them both.

I see erasers as a guiding symbol for my life: Embrace the Way of the Eraser. As the saying goes, "Everyone makes mistakes. That's why there is an eraser on the end of every pencil" (the quote's origin is either Japanese folklore or Dodgers' manager Tommy Lasorda, depending on which source you believe).

The Way of the Eraser is about being okay with mistakes, okay with tentative beliefs, okay with flexibility. I could be wrong, of course, but I believe that my years of crossword solving have made me more flexible in every part of my life, from parenting to writing to marriage.

I have one core belief: don't be an asshole; be kind to others. That one's written in pen. The rest of my beliefs are all in pencil. They are hypotheses waiting for updating on new evidence, ready for the eraser.

As the great philosopher Bertrand Russell said, certitude is a dangerous thing. "The fundamental cause of the trouble is that in the modern world the stupid are cocksure while the intelligent are full of doubt."

I even talk in probabilities.

"When will you be home?" Julie will text me.

"There's a 70 percent chance I'll be home at 6:30 P.M."

There's a 90 percent chance she rolls her eyes at this. But I stand by it.

3) No multitasking.

My mom hates multitasking. Sometimes she'll lecture me on the dangers of multitasking during our phone calls. "So true," I'll say, as I scroll through my emails.

But puzzles have made me realize she's right. If I work on a difficult puzzle with the TV on in the background, I often get stuck. As soon as I turn off the TV, the answers miraculously appear. So when solving Peter's puzzle, I make sure to close my door and put my phone in a drawer.

THE SUMMIT

It took me nine days to finish Fireball Year 4, Puzzle #9, the longest I've ever spent on a single crossword.

But I don't fetishize speed. Some solvers do. Some solvers fill out the grids so fast, it's as if they are taking dictation at a board meeting. At the annual American Crossword Puzzle Tournament in Connecticut, you can witness this in action. Peter told me that he sometimes both constructs puzzles and competes in the tournament. And the crazy thing is, he is slower at filling out the answers to puzzles he *himself had written.*

I'm okay with being a tortoise, slow and steady. The point is, I finished. I'm elated. I'm one of an elite cadre who solved it!

I look at the answer key that Peter has sent me. Yes! All correct. Except . . . the answer key also contains a paragraph about how the Greek letters in the puzzle spell out a word.

I'm confused. I email Peter.

"Oops," he writes back. "Sorry." Apparently, when he sent me the puzzle, he forgot to send the instructions about the meta-puzzle.

A meta-puzzle is an additional puzzle within the puzzle. Like a hidden word or a theme you have to decode. This meta-puzzle was about

Greek letters. Some of the answers could be anagrammed into Greek letters (PINE-SOL turns into EPSILON). If you put the Greek letters together they spell the word "Phoenix." Which was the ultimate answer that only nine people got.

Huh. So I'd climbed Mount Everest—only to discover I'd reached the camp near the summit, not the summit itself. On the one hand, I'm disappointed. On the other, I tell myself that even being within sight of the summit is an accomplishment.

AN EVEN HIGHER SUMMIT

A few weeks later, I'm interviewing another crossword constructor—the brilliant, big-bearded Brendan Emmett Quigley—and I tell him that I've wrestled with one of the hardest crosswords ever.

He nods.

"I don't really solve a lot of American puzzles anymore," he says. "It's not that I don't think that people are doing good work. I just wasn't having any fun anymore."

Instead, he says, "I like borderline unfair British cryptic puzzles."

Ah yes. British cryptics. These are puzzles you find in UK newspapers that live up to their names. They are on another level of trickiness. The answers are often ridiculously obscure words, like a Scottish dagger ("skean"). But the real challenge is that the clues are all about complex wordplay—homophones, puns, anagrams, coded language. The clues are nonsensical to the uninitiated, such as this one: "Discharge by beak in Australia accepted by sheila."

"There's just a bunch of these batshit crazy-ass hard clues," says Brendan. "It's almost like a hair shirt, you know? That's how I describe it. You feel like, 'Why on earth am I doing this to myself?' Some of these things are like war crimes."

In other words, I may have climbed an American mountain, but the United Kingdom has a whole other mountain range, and this one is far steeper.

Brendan tells me he recently finished a puzzle in *The Spectator* that was perhaps the hardest he'd ever tried. Too inscrutable, even for Brendan.

"You got the impression that they were trying to murder the idea of making puzzles," he says. He needed a day to recover from the experience. "It felt like an organ transplant coupled with a colonoscopy or something. It was just so invasively terrible."

I laugh.

Brendan continues: "But then yesterday the new *Spectator* came out. I'm a lemming. I just printed this thing out and dove in."

"Well, now I have to do that puzzle," I say.

"Oh no, don't bother. There is literally nothing redeemable about it."

I get out my to-do list and make a note: *Spectator* cryptic.

Four Crossword Puzzles from History

At the end of most chapters of this book, I will feature a handful of notable puzzles from the genre I just discussed, along with some historical and cultural context. Here are four crossword puzzles I hope you find interesting. The solutions can be found starting on page 301.

1) A More Diverse Crossword

In recent years, there's been increasing criticism that crossword puzzles in mainstream newspapers lack diversity. Many say that crosswords need to boost the representation of people of color, women, and the LGBTQ+ community—both in the content of the clues and in those making and editing the puzzles.

"Like any art form, crosswords should engage in what's happening in culture and politics," says Laura Braunstein, a crossword constructor and librarian at Dartmouth. She was one of nearly six hundred puzzlemakers who signed an open letter in 2020 to *The New York Times* urging them to diversify.

Laura says far too many of the puzzle answers are the names of men or are male-centric. And when there is an answer about women, it's often sexualized. "You see a lot of clues about G-Spot, but rarely see something like 'Pap Smear,'" she says. People of color are similarly overlooked, she and others say.

The *Times* does seem to be trying to address this. They have recently hired a more diverse staff of puzzle editors. There's an uptick in the clues that are more inclusive of women and the LGBTQ+ community. For instance, one recent clue was "Like some monogrammed towels." The answer was: "His and his."

Laura says some strides have been made, but mainstream newspapers still have a long way to go. More women contributed to the *Times* last year than in previous years, but they still make up a minority of constructors.

Laura cofounded a subscription service called *The Inkubator* (inkubatorcrosswords.com), which features women and nonbinary constructors. Here's a sample puzzle from *The Inkubator:*

SECRET SHARERS

Tracy Bennett and Laura Braunstein

Across

1. Wilderness pack snack
5. Some families have two
10. Dropped letters?
13. Architect Lin or poet Angelou
14. Moon-shaped
15. She played Mia in "Pulp Fiction"
16. Where the Raven was rapping and tapping, in a Poe poem
18. 87% of *New York Times* crossword constructors, in 2017
19. Straw hats and parasols, e.g.
20. Rocky beach particle
22. Camping spot for an Airstream
25. Some sacred winter songs
26. Met Gala, for one
30. Waters who sang "Stormy Weather"
31. Storm and Metro maker
32. "I like the cut of your ___"
35. Flowed
38. T. S. Eliot's internal debate about eating a peach
41. "___-dollar Founding Father without a father..."
42. Go on the ___ (skedaddle)
44. Some matriarchs
45. Lime, for a certain pie
50. A-line or maxi, for a skirt
52. Monetary unit of Iceland
53. Gertrude Stein's beloved Alice B.
55. Joan Watson portrayer in "Elementary"
59. Former Texas governor Richards
60. Julia Child had one for hollandaise
63. Make like Mikaela Shiffrin or Picabo Street
64. Tread lightly
65. Give consent
66. Cloche or pillbox
67. Stands out like a queen, in modern parlance
68. Unites legally

Down

1. Some SUVs
2. Site of Queen Lili'uokalani's palace
3. Jeri of "Star Trek" and "Boston Public"
4. She was Foxy Brown
5. 18th-century American feminist Judith Sargent ___
6. Plus
7. Jiang Qing, Madame ___
8. On
9. ___ Slam (rare achievement in tennis)
10. She's quite a feller
11. Febreze target
12. Karen Blixen and Connie Nielsen, for two
14. Bounded
17. Angles, as on a jewel
21. "Sk8er ___" (Avril Lavigne hit)
23. On the ___ (derogatory term for menstruation)
24. Britney's ex
26. The Shakers were one
27. Plains people
28. Like a cowl made on size 15 needles
29. "Learn to Fly" band ___ Fighters
33. Shirin Ebadi's country
34. Defeat
36. Priest who blessed Hannah
37. Like some memes or basements
39. Bring about, as labor
40. Holstein who's udderly productive
43. She's the one in charge: Abbr.
46. First in line?
47. Agents working in bread and beer
48. Log-rolling competitions for a 10-Down
49. Accustom
50. Cannabis supply
51. Name on a little girl's front end loader, perhaps
54. Spinnaker, mizzen or 32-Across, e.g.
56. Click the heart icon
57. Tablet that's hard to swallow
58. On-the-road roll reversals?
61. Cook ___ storm
62. State division with a seat: Abbr.

2) Crosswords and World War II

The puzzle below—and four that followed in ensuing days—caused a national security crisis during World War II. The puzzles appeared in *The Telegraph* in the days preceding D-Day. The problem? The answers contained a series of code words related to the top-secret invasion. UTAH is the code name for one of the beaches the Allies planned to storm. Other crosswords contained OMAHA (another beach), MULBERRY (a harbor), NEPTUNE (the code name for the naval phase), and most suspicious of all, OVERLORD, clued as "Bigwig," which was the code name for D-Day itself.

The British intelligence agency became alarmed and arrested the crossword maker—a school headmaster named Leonard Dawe. Dawe was interrogated extensively, but he was eventually released after the government apparently decided it was just an odd coincidence. Years later, there was speculation it wasn't a coincidence after all. One the-

ACROSS

1 A cause of postscripts (13)
10 Very attentive commonly (two words-3,4)
11 A fool's weapon (7)
12 But this isn't to be bought at this shop (6)
15 Foils start thus (two words-3,3)
16 Definite (7)
18 Achievement that the guardians of the Tower always have at heart (4)
19 Proper behaviour (7)
20 But cook has a practical use for this old weapon (4)
22 Part of one's last will and testament (4)
24 This knight of old had a fair start (7)
26 Little Samuel has got something from the pantry to make a boat (6)
27 The ceremonious tart (6)
30 Fifty fifty (7)
31 White wine (7)
33 "Intense matter"

DOWN

2 This probably has a lateen sail (7)
3 What all will be when the cease fire sounds (6)
4 Try the clue for 22 across (4)
5 Derby winner or preposition (4)
6 Systematically sorted (6)
7 When this loses its tail it doesn't grow another (7)
8 He rations the port among those who want it (13)
9 The ups and downs of business (three words-6,3,4)
13 Conference centre lately (7)
14 "Sleep rough" (7)
15 Lay (7)
21 Assess (7)
23 "Having drink taken" (7)
24 Many an oak-tree has this measurement (6)
25 This might make mad, sir (6)
28 This German Island sounds of alluvial origin (4)
29 The last Alice saw of the White Rabbit (4)

ory claims Dawe's students, who helped him construct the crosswords, overheard the words when chatting with soldiers stationed nearby.

While we're talking about World War II, I should mention that the Nazis tried to use crosswords for evil. According to a 1945 *New York Times* article, the Nazis sent aircraft over London to drop leaflets that contained propaganda-filled crosswords. The article described the clues as "rather feeble and heavy-handed." For instance, the answer to "He wants all you've got" turned out to be ROOSEVELT.

A few years later, during the Cold War, the Soviets also used crosswords for propaganda purposes. A 1950 *New York Times* article described a Soviet crossword with an anti-American theme. For instance: "What is General MacArthur's concept of a courtesy call." The answer was Russian for "raid."

3) A Scandinavian Crossword

The American crossword format is the most famous, but other formats exist. Here's an example of a Swedish-style crossword, where the clues are embedded within the grid itself. (They are also sometimes called Arrow Word puzzles.) I like the clean design. So Scandinavian.

Couple ▼	Lofty ▼	Rating unit ▼	Spring flower ▼	
▶ Flour box	You're looking at it ▼	African cobras ▼	Way in, way out ▼	
▶ Fruit farms	Cave-man's weapon	Part of a poem	Clump ▼	Russo or Clair ▼
Artist, master of shapes ▶				
Spare time	Get some air	Mole-cule part ▼	Choir song ▼	
Food fish ↖	Clear soup	Update	Butter-fly ▼	Power of a number ▼
↙	Not here ▼	Hen tracks on paper ▼	Celtic cat	Picture puzzle ▼
▶ Furry feet	Egypt's capital ▶		School tool ▶	
▶ Mouse clicker	Pueblo brick ▶		Sky shiner ▶	
▶ Chilly powder	Mini-mum ▶			

To solve the puzzle simply write your answers in the direction of the arrows. (For bigger images of this and other puzzles, visit thepuzzlerbook.com).

4) A Fireball Crossword by Peter Gordon

And finally, here's an example of a fiendishly difficult crossword puzzle by my hero.

IN RETIREMENT

BY PETER GORDON

FIREBALL Crosswords

What number is the final answer to this puzzle?

ACROSS
1 Monkey or ape
6 Purple Pantone color
10 "Band of Brothers" event
14 "Manner of sitting," in Sanskrit
15 Reject with disdain
16 Due
17 Hope for good luck
20 Like Tourette syndrome awareness ribbons
21 Punt's lack
22 Side from a wok
27 Georgia's state wildflower
30 The Gaels of collegiate sports
31 Gruyère alternative
33 Fails to keep
34 Brand of Scotch whisky
36 It's often close to a grand
38 Birthday cards?
39 He never met his brother Seth
41 Sister brand of Calvin Klein
42 Parent
43 Impersonates
44 Flight sergeant's org.
47 Bright yellow Crayola color
51 1988 Summer Olympics host city
53 Affectedly playful
54 On the subject of

55 Thing under a fermata
56 Estrange bedfellows?
58 Animal whose thick fur turns white in the winter
62 Kamchatka's setting
63 Place for a runner
64 1962 Olivia de Havilland film
72 Sidle
73 Purity measure
74 Get around
75 Papillons, e.g.
76 Got on
77 Oceans, to poets

DOWN
1 Cosmetics brand with dots between the letters of its logo
2 Nazarene's home: Abbr.
3 "Political power grows out of the barrel of a gun" writer
4 As a substitute
5 Considered for a job?
6 Squishee seller of Springfield
7 Heel
8 Pound sound
9 Jamaican reggae singer with the hit "Here Comes the Hotstepper"
10 Turned down, in a way
11 Linger over
12 ___ Lingus (carrier to Dublin)
13 HB stat
15 Recital high points
18 "Star Trek: The Next Generation" character Tasha ___
19 M. Patate piece

22 Suva is its capital
23 Word with race or rage
24 Cozy stopovers
25 Don't leave topless, as a room
26 "How to Survive Parenthood" author LeShan
28 Space-saving abbr.
29 Bat wood
32 Negatively charged particle
35 Boxer who defeated Schmeling at Yankee Stadium in 1933
36 1994 Peace co-Nobelist with Arafat and Rabin
37 Person with fire power?
40 It has a triangular body

42 Goes over again
43 Opportunity, metaphorically
44 Part of the mouth
45 Camera setting
46 Contract
47 ___ Palmas (Spanish province)
48 A father of Dada
49 Unlike bodybuilders
50 1959 hit with the lyric "He may ride forever 'neath the streets of Boston"
52 Land in a foreign country, of sorts
57 Cleverly humorous person
59 Jazz trumpeter Baker who was played by Ethan Hawke in the movie "Born to Be Blue"
60 Obtain resources from
61 It's a long story
64 Abated, with "up"
65 Reply to a bailiff
66 Unlikely favorite in a horse race
67 2% of centocinquanta
68 Ate
69 Ballet-loving Muppet
70 Nada
71 Annoyances of free apps

Solutions to historical crossword puzzles begin on page 301. For Greg's original crossword puzzle, see page 257. You'll find his other puzzles in the immediate vicinity.

The Puzzle of Puzzles

Before I move on to more puzzle genres (I have my eyes on Rubik's Cubes, also known as twisty puzzles), let's take a step back to wrestle with an overarching puzzle: What the heck is a puzzle? And why do we like them?

Okay, that's two puzzles, I suppose.

I've been researching these questions for some time, and I have come to some tentative answers.

Starting with the first: What is a puzzle?

Puzzles vary wildly in format, but almost all seem to share this: They cause the solver to experience a period of difficulty and struggle, followed by relief. They provide an aha moment. Tension leading to an almost, well, orgasmic ending

The late Japanese puzzlemaker Maki Kaji expresses it in a beautifully succinct and poetic way:

$$? \rightarrow !$$

Bafflement, wrestling, solution! That is the arc of puzzling—as well as much of art and life itself. (Side note: Has there ever been more brilliantly designed punctuation than the question mark and the exclamation point? The question mark is all twists and turns and mystery. The exclamation point—so assertive and aggressive and final!)

A puzzle's exclamation point can be reached in two ways, often in combination. First, there's plain old hard work. The grinding, the brute force, trial and error. Think of solving a maze by trying every path till you get the right one. Or with a jigsaw puzzle, when you sort out all the edge pieces.

But the best puzzles involve a second parallel method: insight. The solution is revealed only after a sudden shift in paradigm. An unexpected way of looking at it. You see the problem in a new light.

Wait! It's not letters, it's Roman numerals!

Those chocolate chips aren't random—they are Braille!

Consider *New York Times* crossword editor Will Shortz's favorite clue: "It turns into a different story." You need to defy your first instinct and realize the "story" is not the once-upon-a-time story, it's the stories in a house! The answer is SPIRAL STAIRCASE.

To me, this emphasis on ingenuity is what distinguishes a puzzle from a problem. It's a fuzzy line—a spectrum, to be sure. But consider a math *problem:*

Find the number to make this equation true:

$$21 \div \_ = 7$$

The answer is 3.

Versus a math *puzzle:*

Move one digit to make this equation true.

$$30-33 = 3$$

(Pause here if you want to try to solve it yourself.)

The answer is that you shift one of the threes upward so it turns into an exponent. And three cubed is 27, so you get:

$$30-3^3 = 3$$

Moving on to the second stumper: Why do I—and millions of others—love puzzles? Why would anyone bother frustrating themselves so much? I don't consider myself a masochist, at least not in the literal sense. I don't like physical pain. I have no moral problem with

S&M, though I do find the prospect of it tiring. It involves too much equipment for me. It's the same reason I don't like skiing.

But I love the psychological pain of puzzles.

To get some insight, I call Paul Bloom, a man who has given a lot of thought to humanity's love of puzzles. Paul is a psychology professor at the University of Toronto and the author of an excellent book called *The Sweet Spot: The Pleasures of Suffering and the Search for Meaning,* which is all about why people do difficult things. Why do we watch horror movies and do triathlons? And why do we do crossword puzzles?

"It is a psychological puzzle: Why would I want to do puzzles?" asks Paul, himself a determined crossworder. "I'm not attracting mates, I'm not eating food, I'm not exercising, I'm not making money. I'm not doing something which is pleasurable in the obvious sense, like taking a hot bath or eating chocolate. I'm working, I'm struggling, yet I seem to be drawn to that."

"Exactly," I say. "So what's going on?"

"There are two somewhat compatible theories," Paul says. "The first is a cultural one, which is that we've learned to associate effort with a positive feeling. We've learned that good things come when we work toward them."

This definitely resonates with me. I inherited a Puritan work ethic from my dad. He's a workaholic who spends his vacations on the beach writing law books about securities fraud. I too feel compelled to put forth effort from morning till night. It doesn't have to be related to my job, but I need to be doing something *productive.* I feel guilty if I'm being too passive. Even when watching a TV show with Julie, I feel pressure to do something semi-productive, such as scroll through my phone and unsubscribe from random skincare email lists that somehow got ahold of my address.

I'm not sure this is a positive trait. It'd probably be better if I had a stronger hedonistic side. I have to work on that. Though maybe "work on" is the wrong phrase.

"But I don't think the cultural explanation is the whole story," Paul continues. "I think that there's something wired within us to take pleasure in the exercise of our abilities. Even rats exert extra effort in some cases, as if they are taking pleasure from the effort."

"But why would evolution give us that wiring?" I ask.

"It might be because it motivates us to practice our skills. That's the whole theory of play. Play is practice for a real threat. Dogs wrestle with each other to get stronger and prepare for an actual fight."

So if a knife-wielding thug asks me for a seven-letter word for "footrest," I can fend him off with an answer? Well, not exactly. Paul points out that survival and thriving are not just about physical dominance.

"Intelligence, verbal facility, and imagination are important," he says.

This theory suggests we might be wired for puzzles because they are practice for solving real-world problems. And the most important real-world problems do require the combination of hard work and flashes of insight, whether it's the chimp who figured out how to use a stick to retrieve dinner from the termite mound or the scientists who created the mRNA Covid vaccine. Evolution wants us to solve things. It's why our brains get that hit of dopamine every time we experience the aha moment.

Paul's explanations are good ones. But in the spirit of epistemic humility, I'm not prepared to say they are the end of the story. And neither, for that matter, is Paul. We discuss several other theories about the appeal of puzzles. For instance:

The Peacock Theory

Perhaps we do puzzles to signal how smart we are, sort of an intellectual equivalent of a giant, colorful peacock's tail. It's why people boast about their crossword puzzle times on Twitter ("Two minutes 25 seconds for Monday's puzzle!"), a practice I hate, because it makes my own tail feel small and drab.

Puzzles are a way of bonding with other humans.

You hear this a lot in the puzzle community. "It's not the puzzles you solve, it's the people you meet." My wife's whole job is based on this idea, that puzzles lead to team building. And there's some social science evidence for it too. Cass Sunstein, the behavioral economist and

Harvard law professor, has done research in which he tried to bridge the gap between a group of liberals and a group of conservatives. One of the few activities that brought the two sides together was doing a crossword.

Puzzles connect us with the infinite.

Some people sound almost mystical when talking about puzzles, describing how puzzles put us into a state of flow, how time disappears, how the puzzle and its solver become One.

Puzzles are an existential grasp at certainty and closure in an uncertain world.

Actor Neil Patrick Harris says that he likes puzzles because puzzles, unlike life, have a tidy resolution, which echoes Peter Gordon's sentiment. Will Shortz has said puzzles are "the Platonic ideal of a problem. We face so many problems every day in life, and we just muddle through. We don't know that we have the perfect solution. But when you solve a puzzle, you achieve perfection. You are in control."

Puzzles are good for your mental health and productivity.

In the last decade, magazines and newspapers have printed a slew of articles about the benefits of hobbies, including crosswords. They can make you more productive at your job by recharging your batteries. They can lower your blood pressure. Play is essential to our mental health.

I'm torn about this idea. On the one hand, as someone obsessed with feeling productive, this is just what I want to hear. On the other hand, I'm not convinced puzzles actually lower my blood pressure. If anything, they raise it. To me, the true benefit of puzzles is the aforementioned shift in mindset.

And maybe puzzles shouldn't be burdened with self-improvement at all. Maybe we should embrace them not as a means, but as an end. Puzzles for puzzles' sake.

Puzzles are a better way to learn.

You can find a good amount of research on this. The following quote sounds like I created it to support my pro-puzzle agenda, but it's actually from a meta-analysis of sixty-eight peer-reviewed studies by real scientists: "Escape rooms are innovative, active, collaborative and constructivist instructional approaches that can shape learning more powerfully than conventional teaching. They help learners understand the value of seeing problems from different perspectives, expose them to collaborative teamwork, promote engagement and persistence on task, strengthen social relationships, activate team spirit, and facilitate benefits of deep learning through group discussion."*

I'm guessing that all of these theories are at least partly true. There aren't enough randomized controlled trials on our love of puzzles to know for sure. Unlike a jigsaw puzzle, which has but a single solution, the puzzle about why we love puzzles probably has many.

* Panagiotis Fotaris and Theodoros Mastoras, "Escape Rooms for Learning: A Systematic Review," *Proceedings of the 13th International Conference on Game Based Learning,* edited by L. Elbaek, G. Majgaard, A. Valente, and S. Khalid (2019), 235–243, https://research.brighton.ac.uk/en/publications/escape-rooms-for-learning-a-systematic-review.

(3) *The Rubik's Cube*

et me run a number by you: 43 quintillion.

Or to be more exact, 43,252,003,274,489,856,000.

Are you picturing that in your mind? Maybe conjuring up an image of 43 quintillion bottles of beer on the wall? Or envisioning a Dr. Seuss book called *One Fish, Two Fish, 43 Quintillion Fish?*

Yeah, not so much.

Even metaphors aren't helpful: 43 quintillion is greater than the number of grains of sand on earth. It's greater than the number of seconds that have elapsed since Cleopatra's birth. But what does that look like? What does that mean? The human brain was just not built to comprehend numbers that large.

I bring up 43 quintillion because it happens to be the number of possible arrangements of the squares that make up the Rubik's Cube. Go ahead and count them if you don't believe me.

The Rubik's Cube company knew this number was too high for human comprehension. It marketed the cube as having "more than three billion combinations." As the science writer Douglas Hofstadter once quipped, that's a "pathetic and euphemistic underestimate if ever I heard one." He pointed out it's sort of like a billboard that says "Entering San Francisco—population greater than 1." Or else "McDonald's—over 2 served."

I love the number 43 quintillion for a couple of reasons.

First, it reminds me of something my high school math teacher once told me: Really big numbers are important. Our caveman brains have trouble understanding them, but we need to try. Ignoring really big numbers can lead to tragic real-life consequences. Just consider the Covid pandemic. Part of the reason we underestimated Covid's danger is that we just couldn't wrap our minds around exponential growth, how fast the virus would spread.

Comprehending really big numbers is good for our mental health too. At least for my mental health. They induce humility. The universe is 7 quadrillion minutes old, and the average human life is just a flash of that. The universe is 93 billion light-years across, and I'm just 70 inches of that. Sure, such realizations could be construed as depressing, but to me, they are an important reminder of my place in the vast scheme, a little memento mori, a nudge to make the most of my few minutes and remember the billions of people still to come.

In addition to humility, the number 43 quintillion sparks other emotions for me, such as optimism, hope, and awe. Think about this: There are 43 quintillion combinations of the Rubik's Cube—and yet, somehow, humans have figured out how to twist the sides into that single arrangement of solid red, blue, yellow, and so on. We've found that one-in-43-quintillion solution. Now *that's* creating order out of chaos! That's finding a needle in a haystack the size of the moon! (Actually, to be precise, there are twenty-seven arrangements that work, depending on the orientation of the center squares. But still.)

And not just that. Humans, especially young humans, have figured out how to accomplish this remarkable feat very quickly—namely, in 3.47 seconds, the current record held by a Chinese teenager named Yusheng Du. And also how to do it with their feet, blindfolded, underwater, and on and on.

They have found extreme pleasure in these accomplishments. To give you another big number: about 450 million Rubik's Cubes have been sold, by some estimates making it the bestselling puzzle of all time. After a lull in the 1990s and 2000s, the cube is once again everywhere, with a resurgence fueled by YouTube stars.

Back in the 1980s, I owned one of those 450 million units. But I never solved it. It's perhaps my greatest embarrassment as a puzzler. For this project, I pledge to remove that black mark from my puzzling record.

THE ORIGIN STORY

It took the first person to solve a Rubik's Cube much longer than 3.47 seconds. It took a month. As you might have guessed, that person was Ernő Rubik, the soft-spoken Hungarian inventor of the Rubik's Cube.

It was 1974, and Ernő was a professor of architecture at a university in Budapest. He was trying to come up with a fun way to teach spatial concepts.

Ernő's brainstorm came to him just before his thirtieth birthday while tinkering with objects in his room. It was no ordinary room, mind you. As Ernő wrote in his 2020 autobiography, *Cubed:*

> My room was like a child's pocket, full of marbles and treasures:
> bits of paper with scrawling notes and images, pencils, crayons,
> string, small sticks, glue, pins, springs, screws, rulers. These
> items occupied every corner, the shelves, the floor, the table,
> which doubled as a drawing board; they were hanging from the
> ceiling, pinned on the door, tucked in the window frame.
> Among them were innumerable cubes: cubes made of paper, of
> wood, in monochrome or colored, solid or broken down into
> blocks.

I'm hoping this provides comfort for all (like me) who are criticized for messy desks. You're not disorganized. You're giving yourself inspiration.

Ernő saw the beauty of the cube. He saw the appeal of something so deceptively simple, something so brightly colored and symmetrical but alterable as well. As Ernő once said, "Transformation excited me as a wonderful thing. You keep something, and at the same time, it's reborn."

After being rejected by more than a dozen toy companies—the major complaint was that the cube was too hard to solve—Ernő finally sold it to Ideal Toy Company. They came up with several names, including Inca Gold, the Gordian Knot, and the Hungarian Cube. But eventually, they settled on the sort-of-rhyming, fun-to-say Rubik's Cube.

In the early '80s, it became a bona-fide craze, the biggest puzzle obsession since jigsaws in the Great Depression. I could cite all sorts of statistics and anecdotes to illustrate how popular the Rubik's Cube was, but let me stick with one example: a Saturday morning cartoon

 series featuring a talking, flying, mystery-solving Rubik's Cube. Menudo did the theme song. The show was an absolute abomination. But it was proof that the cube had infiltrated every corner of pop culture. (Here's hoping the Rubik's Cube feature film which is, I swear, currently in development, will be better.)

My parents bought me a Rubik's Cube soon after it came out. After some hard work, I was able to solve one side. I felt pretty good. Then I watched a bunch of teenage Rubik's superstars on a show called *That's Incredible!*, which was sort of a 1980s version of *America's Got Talent.*

Instead of motivating me, it discouraged me. I would not be able to rival these savants without a tremendous amount of work, and possibly not even then. So I gave up and never went back.

THE OLD SCHOOL WIZARD

Decades later, I decide to track down one of the *That's Incredible!* teenagers who helped scare me off the cube.

I call Jeff Varasano. He's now fifty-five, looks a bit like actor Alfred Molina, and owns two pizzerias in Atlanta. He remains a Rubik's fanatic. He often entertains his pizza customers with his Rubik's skills, and he has incorporated the cube root symbol into his restaurant's logo.

"I still find it fascinating after all these years," says Jeff, who retains a touch of his Bronx accent. He tells me that he loves making order out of chaos (a recurring theme among puzzlers). "It seems so simple, just six sides, six colors. But it's infinitely complex."

Jeff was thirteen when he bought his first cube in 1980. It took him a week to solve. In that pre-YouTube age, he had to figure it out himself through trial and error, creating his own algorithms. (A Rubik's Cube algorithm is a series of moves—five, eight, twelve, whatever—that solves a particular corner or side. You turn the middle row clockwise, the top row counterclockwise, the left side clockwise, and so forth.)

One day, a classmate of Jeff's was fiddling with a Rubik's Cube during math class. "The math teacher yelled at the kid, 'Put that stupid thing away. It's not possible anyway,'" Jeff recalls. "And I said, 'No, I can do it.' So next thing you know, I get up, walk across the classroom, and I did it. Took me about two or three minutes. And the whole class broke out like, 'Holy shit!' People were screaming and cheering, and the teacher was like, 'How the hell did you do that?'"

Jeff convinced his reluctant parents to drive him to the very first Rubik's Cube competition in 1981. It was at a mall in Boston, and, to the shock of the organizers, more than a thousand people showed up.

That day Jeff came in second—though he is quick to point out that's because of an oddity in the tournament structure (he had the fastest time overall, thirty-six seconds in an early round, but lost in the finals. Jeff also believes he should be listed as the first Rubik's world-record holder but isn't because of a technicality, a fact that he says "still sticks in my craw").

Regardless, Jeff appeared on the evening news. Which led to other TV interview shows, magazine articles, his fifteen minutes of fame.

Or forty-five seconds of fame, I suppose. Jeff got a publishing deal for one of the first Rubik's how-to books: *Jeff Conquers the Cube in 45 Seconds . . . And You Can Too!* He appeared on the book cover with a helmet of hair and a Mickey Mouse T-shirt, a look he describes as "geek-factor level 1,000."

I ask if his Rubik's Cube renown led to him dating the head cheerleader. I meant it mostly as a lame joke.

"Well, yeah," he says. "I ended up dating one of the hotter girls."

Huh. I didn't see that coming. A real-life revenge of the nerd. Good for Jeff!

I ask about the difference between speedcubing now and then. Jeff has some opinions.

First of all, back then, they had much clunkier and harder-to-turn cubes. The new kids have it easy with their slick, frictionless cubes. But more important, speedcubing in the early era was about creativity and discovery, not rote memorization. Back then, you had to figure out your own strategies like a mini-scientist.

"I don't want to say that the people who are winning competitions now are cheaters because it's not their fault when they were born," Jeff says. "But we would've kind of considered them cheaters back in the day because the point to the competition wasn't who had the fastest hands. The point of the competition was who had the better *solution*."

Nowadays, says Jeff, it's all laid out. YouTube videos can teach you a thousand prepackaged algorithms.

While talking to Jeff, I can hear the clattering of plates in the background. He's in the back office of one of his Varasano's pizzerias. It seems a strange journey, from cubes to pizza, I say. Jeff begs to disagree.

Jeff's approach to making pies is the same as his approach to Rubik's Cube: discover the best algorithm. In fact, Jeff's pizza algorithm gave him a second bout of fame. Several years ago, Jeff wrote a Pizza Manifesto, which he says was the Internet's number one pizza recipe for ten years. It even landed him a segment on NPR.

It's a remarkable, absurdly detailed 22,000-word opus that leads you step-by-step to the perfect pizza. Or at least Jeff's version of the perfect pizza. It contains dozens of instructions on everything from oregano choice to dough-kneading technique.

"The flour and water should sit together for at least 20 minutes before kneading begins. It's a CRITICAL step . . . Most recipes say that the dough should double in size. This is WAY too much. In total the dough should expand by about 50% in volume."

Jeff tells me the recipe took years to perfect, the result of nine hundred failed pizzas and two exploding ovens. The keys to discovering the perfect pizza included:

a) Breaking the process down into smaller and smaller chunks.
b) Testing every combination he could. "I sampled at least fifty types of oregano and over one hundred olive oils."
c) Embracing mistakes. As with the Rubik's Cube, you can't learn unless you try and fail, repeat ad nauseam.

"Essentially, there's a universal way to model anything and to struggle through a solution for it, and then come up with rules of how to solve it," says Jeff. "It doesn't matter whether it's dance, piano, making a sandwich, or learning how to walk."

This brings up a big question I've been wrestling with for years: How many of life's messy problems could we solve like a Rubik's Cube or a pizza recipe? Are there step-by-step algorithms to happiness and success?

I desperately want there to be. I've always been a sucker for books like *1-2-3 Magic* that give you the recipe for raising kids, or articles like "10 Steps to Beating Depression."

When I worked at a magazine, one of my bosses told me about his life hack, "The Seven Minute Secret to a Happy Marriage" (one minute faster than rock-hard abs!). According to this theory, every morning you should spend two minutes giving your spouse your full and complete attention. Look deeply into their eyes, ask how they are, and really listen to the answer. Then, after work, do the same thing for three minutes. And finally, two minutes before bed.

Seven minutes a day, and—voilà!—a lifetime of matrimonial bliss. I don't actually follow this prescription to the minute. But I like the gist—more eye contact is always better.

The best argument that there are algorithms to live by can be found in a bestselling book by computer scientists Brian Christian and Tom Griffiths called . . . *Algorithms to Live By.*

They argue that everything from dating to choosing a home can benefit from algorithmic thinking. For instance, if you have one hundred apartments to choose from, how many should you see before committing? The magic number is thirty-seven, apparently. You look at the first thirty-seven to establish criteria (must have washer/dryer and no mouse problems). Then you rent the very first apartment after the thirty-seventh that meets those criteria.

The thirty-seven rule is hard to implement in real life. But I do live by some simpler algorithms. I follow a written checklist for my morning routine (brush teeth, do pushups, send note to mom). I fall asleep by going through the alphabet, thinking of something to be grateful for with each letter from A to Z (A is for the apple pancakes my son made us, and so on). I try to break life's problems into smaller and smaller chunks.

And yet, I also see the limits of trying to conquer life with a rational recipe. Many times it's a fool's errand. I'm friends with an economist named Russ Roberts, host of the *EconTalk* podcast. Unlike most in his profession, Russ has become increasingly skeptical of our ability to rationally attack all problems. He says that you can't quantify and measure everything. There's no algorithm for whether to have kids or take a new job. Algorithms are just flashlights in the fog, and maybe not even that. He believes there is a class of life dilemmas—he calls them "wild problems"—that are impervious to step-by-step solutions.

Russ has a point. I have come to accept that sometimes life is disturbingly chaotic and unpredictable. In fact, thanks to cognitive behavioral therapy, I have an algorithm for acceptance. It's on a PDF in my computer called "Practicing Radical Acceptance Step by Step." For instance:

- "Allow disappointment, sadness or grief to arise within you."
- "Do pros and cons if you find yourself resisting practicing acceptance."

And so on. Acceptance achieved.

A MOMENT FIVE DECADES IN THE MAKING

After interviewing Jeff, I decide it's time to fill that embarrassing gap in my puzzle résumé. It's time to solve a Rubik's Cube.

I call one of the best Rubik's Cube instructors in the world: a twenty-four-year-old South Carolina resident named Sydney Weaver whose journey to puzzle greatness is inspiring. In fact, it's movie-worthy, sort of *Rudy* meets *The Queen's Gambit*.

Deep in the middle of the pandemic, I reach Sydney at her home by Zoom. I was hoping she'd be in the Rubik's uniform that she sometimes wears to events: a vest and pants adorned with multicolored squares. But she's much more casual, just a brown sweater and black pants.

I spot a sword hanging on the wall of her room.

"Oh, that's merch from The Legend of Zelda," she says, when I ask about it.

She's a fan of video games but admits she feels "kind of guilty when I play them. So I'll play them in French, so at least I'm learning French."

What an excellent life hack! I make a note to have my kids turn the default language on their video games to something besides English. Then, at least they can hear Mario in the original Italian: *"Sono io— Mario!"*

I ask Sydney how she began speedcubing. At age fourteen, she received a cheap knockoff cube in her Christmas stocking. "I didn't take to it at first," she says. "But my brother said I couldn't do it. So then I was determined to do it."

And she did. She spent so much time twisting the cube, she "absolutely destroyed it." The stickers peeled off and Sydney had to replace them with Scotch-taped construction paper.

She says it gave her that feeling so many puzzlers describe: "I loved that it was something I could accomplish. So much of life is vague and open-ended. This has a clear goal. It gave me a sense of mastery."

And here's the cinematic twist: she fell in love with the cube even though it was painful for her. Sydney suffered from a form of pediatric arthritis. She was sometimes bedridden and unable to use forks and spoons. She started out turning the cube with her palms. And the more she worked on it, the less her arthritis bothered her. She says it was a form of physical therapy.

"I still struggle to this very day, to be honest. My hands will still flare, and it does make things I want to do difficult, even writing with a pencil, but the thing is, I had such a passion for the cube that I wanted to overcome it."

Sydney got faster and faster, and she started traveling to tournaments around the world, from Alaska to Australia. She won nine gold medals in her speedcubing career before retiring from competition a couple of years ago to be a teacher and lecturer. I ask her what it was like to be a woman in a male-heavy sport. "I remember my first competition. I was the only female competitor. That felt somewhat odd. Thankfully, there were female judges, so I could talk to them about being a woman in the speedcubing world."

Speedcubing has evolved a lot since that first Boston mall tournament. It's become an intense sport. And I do think "sport" is the right word:

- There are the fans: there are even speedcubing fantasy leagues where you can gamble on your favorite solvers.
- There's the equipment: hand-warmers, noise-canceling headphones, and special Rubik's lubricants to make the sides turn faster (Lubicle Silk is apparently one of the best).
- There's the specialized sports lingo: "the equator," "the buffer," "color neutrality." One algorithm is called "the Sexy." Why? Well, as one cuber told me, "Because it's sexy." Adding: "Sexy, sexy, sexy."
- There are the cubes themselves, customized like stock cars: magnets on the inside to lock the sides in faster, rounded corners for finger comfort.
- There's the proper athletic technique: speedcubers flick the sides with their fingertips instead of using their whole hands.

The secret to speedcubing isn't just finger dexterity, though that plays a part. It's about memorizing hundreds—sometimes even thousands—of algorithms to reduce the number of turns per solve.

A great speedcuber can solve a cube in less than fifty turns. That's because she knows the best algorithm for every situation. It often takes a beginner one hundred or more turns. Beginners use a one-size-fits-all algorithm you can find on YouTube. It's easier but slower. It's sort of like the difference between memorizing a thousand back-road shortcuts versus staying on the slow, traffic-heavy highway.

Sydney will be teaching me the slow, easy method today. But at the start of our lesson, I ask her to do just one speed-solve. She obliges. A flurry of fingers and, boom, a perfectly colored cube. It felt more like a magic trick than a puzzle.

Sydney emails me a file with the beginner algorithms, and over the next hour she walks me through them. She has a soothing voice, like NPR's Terry Gross. I'm impressed by her ability not to get annoyed.

"Okay, turn *B* counterclockwise," I read from the sheet. "So *B* is for bottom?"

"No, *B* is for back," says Sydney.

"Right. I mean, right as in correct. Not right like right side."

By the end of the hour, I've done it. That last yellow corner snaps into place. But truthfully, it's an anticlimax.

First, unlike Jeff, I didn't figure it out myself. I just followed Sydney's instructions, dutifully turning when she told me to. Even then, I was slow. My son Zane reminded me of this. He too took a lesson from Sydney and was finished in fifteen minutes. "We have dinner in four hours, Dad," he said. "Just so you know."

My age works against me. Most of the top-notch speedcubers are teenagers, with some as young as eight years old. I've talked to several cognitive scientists about why this is. The theories include: Young brains are more flexible. Their memories are better. And importantly, they don't have jobs. But we old folks have more wisdom, right? Sometimes anyway.

I'm even more hopeless than most adults, because spatial reasoning isn't my forte. I have a terrible sense of direction. My wife loves to remind me of the time we were in a building overlooking a park and I asked which park it was. It was Central Park, about five blocks from where I grew up.

Regardless, maybe I'll feel better if I solve a Rubik's Cube without training wheels, without Sydney's guidance and the printout of algorithms. A solo solve from memory. The following weekend, I devote an entire day to this project, starting at 9 A.M. I come up with mnemonic devices to remember the order of the turns.

Furry Rottweiler Utters RUF!
(Front, Right, Up, Right, Up, Front)

At 3:30 P.M., forty-one years after my first attempt, I solve a Rubik's Cube all by myself. As I turn that last row and behold the solid wall of yellow, I feel giddy. I may not be worthy of *That's Incredible!,* but I am now in the club.

That last move was particularly nerve racking. I had all but one middle piece on the bottom. I remembered that the algorithm said I needed to make twelve turns. But at Turn 7, the cube was a mess, a patchwork of colored squares. Could order ever be restored? It seemed impossible.

The lesson was sometimes you have to go backward to go forward.

THE BEAST

A few weeks later, I'm still working on trimming down my solve time. My personal best is two minutes and fifty-eight seconds. Not great. Sort of like bench-pressing twenty-five pounds.

My son Zane, meanwhile, has moved on to a 5 × 5 × 5 cube. Which prompts the question: Just how big do Rubik's Cubes grow? And what if I—or my son—solved the biggest one?

Google tells me that the Guinness World Record for biggest cube is a 33 × 33 × 33 behemoth, designed by a man named Grégoire Pfennig in France.* I arrange a video call with Greg. We talk after he arrives home from his day job as an engineer in Paris for BMW engine parts. He has short dirty-blond hair and wire-rimmed glasses.

Greg turns around and heaves the puzzle off the shelf behind him. It's about the size of a medicine ball. (See color insert for the image.)

"I forgot how heavy it was," he says, with just a slight French accent.

I quiz Greg on the stats:

How many moving parts? 6,153.

How long did it take to build? About 205 hours.

Was it frustrating? Well, he was on the verge of tears several times when it kept falling apart, and he got a whopping headache from the toxic chemicals in the dye.

"So you are holding the hardest Rubik's Cube in the world, right?"

* There are larger Rubik's Cubes if measured by sheer volume—there's a 3 × 3 × 3 cube in China that's about the size of a VW Beetle. But Greg holds the record for most rows.

"Depends what you mean by hard," Greg says.

The 33 × 33 × 33 is certainly time-consuming and physically demanding. It would take an estimated five hundred hours to make all the turns. But in terms of intellectual challenge? You can actually use the same algorithms you'd use for a 5 × 5 × 5 cube.

If you are talking about pure puzzle-solving difficulty, Greg has made much harder puzzles. Behind him are shelves loaded with dozens of blocky creations. I can't call them Rubik's Cubes, because they aren't cubes. They are mutants, as if a normal Rubik's Cube gave birth after having been exposed to high doses of radioactivity in the womb. One is twelve-sided. Another is star-shaped. There's one that looks like a snake and another that resembles a Christmas tree.

It turns out Greg is part of a group of 3-D printing designers pushing Rubik's Cubes into bold new territory.

"We are in the golden age of weird twisty puzzles," a puzzle collector named Tom Cutrofello told me (*Twisty Puzzles* is the official name of Rubik's-type puzzles). Tom said the trend is fueled by the confluence of 3-D printers and the Internet. "It's like the boom in craft breweries in the '90s. We're seeing this explosion of small-batch artisanal twisty puzzles being made and collected over the Internet."

And many of these twisty puzzles are far trickier than the traditional cube. So tricky, in fact, that Greg himself hasn't solved all of them. Greg has created ten Frankensteins that he himself couldn't crack, even with unlimited time. No one else has completed them either.

I tell Greg I need one of those monsters for my collection.

"Maybe try the Octahedron Starminx," Greg says.

He holds it up. The puzzle is an eight-sided baffler, with each side carved up into bizarrely shaped sections—diamonds, curved slivers, triangles.

Why is this one so hard? Partly because you have to create your own algorithms, and partly because of the Butterfly Effect. If you turn one row, it affects forty-seven parts, as opposed to nine parts in a regular cube.

"It's $500," says Greg.

I wince. That's $495 more than a normal cube. Objectively insane. But if I'm going to wrestle with the world's most difficult puzzles, I need to devote part of my research budget to getting my hands on them.

A few weeks later, a package arrives from France. At first glance, the puzzle doesn't look so intimidating: an eight-sided shape, much like a Dungeons & Dragons die, with all the colors and sides aligned. I just have to mess it up and restore it.

But after half a dozen turns, this object has totally transformed. It's no longer symmetrical. It's chaos. There are colored chunks jutting out at all angles, like a jagged crystal in Superman's Fortress of Solitude.

I feel the same sense of despair I did after watching those early speedcubers on *That's Incredible!* I'm in over my head. I need help.

As it happens, I'm scheduled to visit one of the few people who can aid me with this endeavor: Daniel Rose-Levine, an eighteen-year-old cube genius. Rubik's talent runs in his family. His mom, Lauren Rose, who is a math professor at Bard College, uses Rubik's Cubes to help demonstrate key math concepts such as set theory and commutators. Daniel often assists with the class. He started speedcubing when he was twelve, and he is lightning-fast with his hands—but also with his feet. Until recently, he held the North American record for fastest-foot-solve, a mere 16.96 seconds.

Sadly the World Cube Association removed foot-solving from the list of official events partly because it was considered unsanitary.

"Which is crazy," says Daniel, pointing out that hands are much less sanitary than feet.

Lauren and Daniel had invited me to visit them at their upstate New York home after I sat in on one of their classes. We meet on their porch, and I fish out the Octahedron Starminx from my backpack. I ask Daniel if he's up to the challenge.

"I could try it," Daniel says. "I'm starting college, so I can't do it full-time."

I tell him I have faith in him. I ask him to call me when he has three blocks left. I want to witness this watershed moment.

I check in with Daniel every week or two.

"Any progress?"

"Still working," Daniel says.

At one point, Daniel emails me that the puzzle is glitchy and hard to turn. I order some Lubicle Silk and have it sent to his house.

After a couple of months, I begin to think it's a lost cause. Which is understandable. The Starminx doesn't just have 43 quintillion combinations. It has 2-followed-by-137-zeroes combinations. Just unimaginable. Plus, the kid has to go to class.

Finally, six months after I gave him the Starminx, Daniel emails me a photo. Only three pieces left! I knew he could do it.

I arrange a Zoom call with both Daniel and Greg, so we can experience the final solve together.

"Alright, Daniel," I say. "Before the big reveal, can I ask what was it like trying to solve it?"

"Honestly? It was kind of annoying."

Daniel said the pieces kept breaking off, the stickers were peeling, and it was hard to turn.

"Annoying, but fun, right?" I ask, hopefully.

"Yes, annoying but fun," Daniel agrees, sort of.

Daniel says it took him more than fifty hours, but he finally cracked the algorithm.

"Okay, let's do it," I say.

"Here I go," Daniel says.

At which point I get concerned that Daniel's screen is frozen. He doesn't move for a full minute, just stares at the Starminx. But it's not a glitch. Daniel is just deep in thought. And then he makes several turns, smiles widely, and holds up the Starminx.

All colors match. Every piece in its proper place. I pump my fist.

Greg says, "It's a pleasure to see one of the puzzles I designed being solved, especially because I know this is one I can't solve personally."

Greg tells Daniel he should come visit him in France. "You can solve the 33 × 33 one with your feet."

We end the call. So: I didn't solve one of the hardest twisty puzzles in the world myself—but I was the enzyme that made it happen. I played a small part in puzzle history. Together, Daniel, Greg, and I have restored order to this tiny little corner of the universe.

CHAPTER

4 *Anagrams*

M any things keep me awake at night. I worry about my kids'
future. I worry about rising sea levels and declining democ-
racies. But if I'm being honest, those worries aren't the
main cause of my insomnia. No, what robs me of the most sleep is an
innocent-looking little grid of seven letters that pops up on my
iPhone every day. I speak of the delightful and infuriating *New York
Times* Spelling Bee.

To be precise, it doesn't pop up every *day*. That's the problem. For
some reason, the genial sadists at the *New York Times* puzzle section
have scheduled the find-a-word game to appear every night at 3 A.M.

Which means that when my body wakes me up around 4 A.M. for a
bathroom break, against my better judgment, against many promises
I've made to myself, I grab my iPhone and click on the Spelling Bee,
unable to fall back to sleep until I find the hidden word that uses all
seven letters.

Ah, thank God. It's "Pickled." Or "Janitor." Or "Petunia."

Only then can I close my eyes with a mixture of relief and self-
loathing.

So puzzles rule my daily schedule. The crossword at 10:01 P.M., the
Spelling Bee in the wee hours. I'm not alone. I've met many other
puzzlers who confess through gritted teeth that they are middle-of-
the-night Spelling Bee players. One Massachusetts woman wakes up,
solves the Spelling Bee, and tweets about it, all before 4 A.M.

The Spelling Bee fanatics have a name—the Hivemind. And in addition to complaining about waking up early, their other favorite pastime is griping about which words are omitted from the list of
approved words. You type in a word full of optimism, press Enter, and
the computer snaps back "Not in word list." *How can you not include
"laird"!!! The Scottish landowner!*

The Spelling Bee was created by *Times* puzzle editor Will Shortz in 2016. It was meant to be a simpler alternative to other word games. As he explained to *Times* reporter Deb Amlen: "I felt that the *Times* already had the 'tough word puzzles' audience covered with its crossword, acrostic, and cryptic. The readers we weren't reaching yet were ones who'd like something easier and more accessible."

He was inspired by a game called Polygon in *The Times* of London. But Will made two key changes: He allowed solvers to reuse letters in the same word, and he gave it the cutesy name Spelling Bee.

Here's an example:

Solvers must find words with a minimum of four letters that include the center letter. (For the above puzzle, "theme" is legal, but "gem" and "math" are not.)

And my Lord, did it take off. *The New York Times* doesn't release statistics about its puzzles, but one source told me that it's more popular online than the venerable crossword puzzle.

I don't want to throw around the word "addiction" too cavalierly. But if addiction consists of an inability to stop doing something that is harmful to my life, the Spelling Bee has qualified ever since my son Zane introduced me to it several years ago.

When I wake up for good at 8 A.M., my first task is to find enough words to reach the highest level. Article deadlines? Helping my son find a Spanish textbook? A return call to the dermatologist about the weird mole? Those can wait until I hit the top level, "Genius."

Why do I find it so infatuating? Maybe it's the constant dopamine hits, one for every word discovered, another when the computer gives me encouraging feedback like "Awesome!"

If I'm feeling generous toward myself, I'll say that I'm drawn to the Spelling Bee because it's a metaphor for constrained creativity. Here are a mere seven letters—but from them spring dozens of words. They are like Lego bricks ready to be rearranged into a boat or a tower. Or maybe they are like ingredients (butter, sugar, flour, and eggs) from which come waffles, pancakes, and a hundred other tasty carbs. Constraints lead to creativity. As Orson Welles said, "The enemy of art is the absence of limitations."

And then, of course, there's the paradoxical pleasure of getting furious about what words Spelling Bee accepts and those it rejects. The official rule of the Spelling Bee is that it accepts "common English words." But what is a common English word? Ah, that's more art than science. And the man behind that controversial call is a clean-cut twenty-five-year-old puzzle editor named Sam Ezersky. He's got one of the most powerful jobs in all of puzzledom.

I call up Sam, who says he loves his work, even though many mornings he awakens to tweets that troll him about the scandalous oversight of the day. There's even a Twitter account dedicated solely to this purpose called "Not a Spelling Bee Word."

I ask Sam how he chooses which words are allowed and which don't count.

Like so much in the puzzle world, those decisions require a human touch, he says. It's not something an algorithm can do. Sam tells me he doesn't rely on any single dictionary. He uses a combination of sources—dictionary.com, Google, Merriam-Webster, Random House.

As Sam explained in *The New York Times*, "one person's expansive vocabulary or specialized knowledge is another's obscurity or esoterica."

But the line between expansiveness and esoterica is debatable. Consider this controversial puzzle:

Sam's list of approved words included "rift," "fiat," and "train"—but not "raffia."

Raffia is a shiny, crinkly fiber from a palm tree. It's what Easter baskets are often made of. I'd never heard of it, and neither had Sam.

"I certainly learned something new that day," he says.

Raffiagate, as it is called by Spelling Bee fans, triggered a barrage of angry tweets and emails. One reader was so irate that he protested by sending a seventy-eight-yard spool of raffia to Will Shortz's house, *Godfather*-style. Sam got the message. Since then, he has included "raffia" in the approved word list of several puzzles. Activism works!

The Spelling Bee gets critiqued from both sides of the political spectrum. Sam gets flak for being too woke—he doesn't include any words that can be used as ethnic slurs, even if that word has an alternate meaning. And he gets flak for not being woke enough. Why "wingman" but not "wingwoman?"

And then there was the September 2020 puzzle that caused an epistemic crisis, at least for me.

I typed in the common verb "cope," and the Spelling Bee told me there was no such word. I typed it in again, rejected again.

Wait—Was I having a stroke? Was I in one of those psychology experiments where the researchers insist the sky is pink just to see if you have the backbone to stand up and say, No, it's not?

I wasn't having a stroke. Sam somehow had accidentally deleted "cope" from the list of approved words.

"What a shitstorm to wake up to," Sam says, laughing. "That's just a big *mea culpa* on my end . . . It was the perfect 2020 word too. The jokes just wrote themselves."

A typical tweet was "I can't cope with the fact that cope isn't on the list!"

The "cope" scandal was one of many occasions that have caused me to consider just how strange the English language is. Why do those four letters *C-O-P-E* mean something, whereas the same letters in a different order *P-O-C-E* signify nothing?

I tell Sam that one reason I like the Spelling Bee is that it makes me realize just how arbitrary the English language is.

"Oh, my goodness! I think about that all the time," says Sam.

It's not just that some letter arrangements are meaningless, while others bring up images and feelings. It's also that English is highly irregular. Verb tenses, plural nouns, spelling—the language is totally unreliable and unpredictable, like a meth addict or a Real Housewife.

"Today, there was the word *narrator* in the Spelling Bee," Sam points out. "Why does that end in *or* instead of *er* like other nouns from verbs? And why is it *rater* instead of *rator*?" Then there is the classic genre of negative words that have no positive equivalent: You can say "inept" but not "ept." Sam says, "Just yesterday, I was thinking, why is 'legalized' a common word, but not 'illegalized'?"

English "makes no sense at all. . . . Consider merely the letter string '-ough.' I might not be the first to tell you it has ten pronunciations," writes Mike Selinker in the book *Puzzlecraft:*

tough ("tuff"), cough ("cawf"), bough ("bow"), though ("tho"), thought ("thawt"), through ("threw"), hiccough ("hiccup"), hough ("hock"), lough ("lakh"—that is, when it's not pronounced "lock"), and borough ("burrah"— that is, when it's not pronounced "burrow").

English, in short, is a total mess. This has a lot to do with its sloppy origins—a mishmash of Latin, Anglo-Saxon, and words snatched from dozens of other languages.

I have mixed feelings about the chaos that is my mother tongue. On the one hand, it's terrible for those trying to learn English as a second language. Or as a first language. Think of all the time we English-speakers have wasted memorizing weird spellings and irregular verbs. Consider the thousands of miscommunications and unnecessary arguments caused by similar-sounding words and words with ambiguous meanings.

On the other hand, the insanity of the English language is precisely the quality that makes it great for word puzzles, as well as a playground for novelists and poets who like to fiddle with language. Imagine a crossword puzzle in Esperanto, with its sensible spelling and regular verbs. It'd be eye-glazingly dull.

English's abundance of strange words makes the Spelling Bee interesting—and also makes finding every single word in the grid a monumental task. In fact, the final level of the Spelling Bee is not even advertised to solvers. My son Zane recently told me that the

"Genius" level was not the Spelling Bee's top score. You achieve "Genius" when you get about 70 percent of the total possible words.

If you get every single one of the possible words, a rare feat, you are rewarded with an Easter egg: the "Queen Bee" title.

It took me several weeks and hundreds of random guesses of four-letter combinations, but one Saturday morning, after two hours of work, I finally got "Queen Bee." And then vowed to never attempt it again.

I still wake up at 4 A.M. most days to check out the Spelling Bee—but I resist the temptation to try for "Queen Bee." I consider this resolve a great victory.

ANAGRAMS, THE ARS MAGNA

The *New York Times* Spelling Bee is less than a decade old, but it's based on one of the most ancient genres of wordplay: anagrams, the rearrangement of letters in a word to form a new word.

Humans have been obsessed with anagrams practically since the birth of the alphabet. It wasn't always just for fun. Anagrams were originally seen as divine hidden messages from the gods.

Anagrams could cause wars. According to *The Puzzle Instinct* by psychologist Marcel Danesi, Alexander the Great once had a dream about a "satyr," the mythical character that is half-man, half-goat. Alexander was troubled by the dream. What did it mean? He asked his soothsayers, who wisely pointed out that, in ancient Greek, the word for "satyr" is an anagram of "Tyre is yours." (Tyre was a city Alexander's army had surrounded.) Alexander took this as a green light from the gods. He invaded Tyre and made it his. Admittedly, Alexander might have found another excuse to invade if not for anagrams. He was a big fan of invading.

Another anagram was at the center of a famous seventeenth-century trial. A British woman named Eleanor Davies claimed God had anointed her prophet, pointing out her maiden name was an anagram featuring another prophet: "Reveale, O Daniel!" She was put on trial for blasphemy, and her prosecutor argued that the name Dame Eleanor Davies was an anagram for "Never soe mad a ladie."

Notice that anagrams were a lot easier before spelling was standardized.

Humans, apparently, love searching for hidden meanings. We love to believe that there is something just under the surface, that all is not what it seems. We find patterns in the noise, the face of Jesus in a slice of French toast. Psychologists call this tendency "apophenia." And anagrams play right into that weakness. (I'll talk more about the downside of puzzles later.)

When they were not causing wars or convictions, anagrams were seen as an art form. The word "anagrams" itself is an anagram for "ars magna"—the "great art"—so there's your proof right there.

A lot of brilliant minds spent their days rearranging letters. Consider Galileo. He announced several of his discoveries—such as the existence of Saturn's rings—by hiding the information in complicated anagrammatic poems. His fellow scientists had to decode the poems to reveal Galileo's latest insight. You ever wonder why no one came to Galileo's defense during that heresy trial?

In the seventeenth century, King Louis XIII of France designated a man named Thomas Billen to be his Royal Anagrammatist and paid him 1,200 livres a year. Billen's entire job was to fashion sycophantic anagrams, rearranging the letters in royal names to create flattering descriptions.

The Victorians also liked their obsequious anagrams.

Lewis Carroll famously created this one out of Florence Nightingale:

Flit on, cheering angel

But anagrams can also be a weapon, the nerdiest form of insult humor ever invented. Consider the surrealist painter Salvador Dalí. His detractors claimed he was a sellout and called him "Avida dollars," which translates to "Eager for dollars."

And in 1936, *The New York Times* reported that

Mother-in-law
is an anagram for
Woman Hitler.

The Hitler joke—which has obviously aged poorly for several reasons—appeared in an article about the annual meeting of the National Puzzlers' League, where it was awarded the anagram of the year.

It turns out, the National Puzzlers' League still exists and is still the source of the greatest anagrams on the planet. Founded in 1883, with a current roster of about seven hundred members, the NPL is the oldest puzzle society in the world. Every month, it publishes a magazine called *The Enigma,* filled with anagram-based puzzles. *The Enigma* has a tiny circulation and low production value—it's a couple of dozen pages stapled together—but it contains brilliance. I started receiving it several months after joining the NPL (a $30 annual fee). At first, the puzzles seemed impenetrable. So I decided to get a tutorial from a fellow NPL member whom I've known for several years: Mike Reiss, a longtime writer for *The Simpsons.*

I visit Mike at his midtown Manhattan apartment. He loves New York, and refuses to move to Los Angeles, instead commuting weekly during the writing season.

Mike's apartment is home to a collection of Emmy statues, a framed platinum album of *The Simpsons Sing the Blues*—and lots and lots of puzzle books. Puzzles, he tells me, are his greatest passion.

"My mind is always going. I tried meditation a couple of times. But when I try to meditate I think I'm going to lose my mind, because I'm just sitting there going, 'I've got a million things to think about.' That's what I like about puzzles. It's like: 'Here's something for your brain to be doing.' It's a relief to have someplace to put my mind's energy."

Mike says several other *Simpsons* writers are puzzle addicts and won't start writing the episode until they've solved their fill. "My boss will say, 'Um, we're supposed to be working.' And I just think, 'Well, puzzles take precedence.' "

But Mike thinks humor and puzzles are related.

"So many of my favorite jokes are actually puzzles, and more precisely algebra problems: you have to solve for the missing element x, where x = the comedy," he says. "For instance, 'The towels in this hotel are so fluffy, I can barely close my luggage.' The joke is he's stealing towels, something never mentioned anywhere in the joke."

I think it's true: humor, puzzles, and math are all close cousins.

"Or then there's this joke, that's even more like a puzzle, where you can watch the hearer pause to solve the joke," says Mike. "A skeleton walks into a bar and says, 'I'd like a mug of beer and a mop.' "

Mike likes all kinds of word puzzles—crosswords, cryptics, riddles—but he's a compulsive anagrammer. It's almost a disease, he says. He can't see a word without rearranging the letters. For instance, when he looks at a bottle of vodka, he recalls that Stolichnaya can be shuffled to read "satanic" and "holy" (near antonyms). Sometimes he'll speak in anagrams and not realize it till later, like the time he and his wife saw a Noel Coward play, and Mike was not impressed. He said to his wife, "Noel Coward is no Oscar Wilde." He later realized "Noel Coward is" anagrams to "no Oscar Wilde."

He's had this talent/curse from childhood. "I have monocular vision—no depth perception. The whole world is flat. My mom thought that was why I'm so good at jumbling letters."

Not coincidentally, anagrams have often appeared in *The Simpsons*. In one episode, Bart rearranged the letters on a sign that said "Garden" to read "Danger." In another, he switched the sign for "cod platter" to read "cold pet rat." (Not to mention that Bart is an anagram for Brat. Reiss says he wrote a reference to that into the very first episode, but it was edited out.)

I don't suffer anagram-itis as much as Mike does, but I've caught the mild version of it since I began doing the Spelling Bee. I anagram while waiting in line, while brushing my teeth, and, unfortunately, while driving. *That's an interesting sign,* I'll say to myself. "Yield" contains "deli," "lied," "idle." Also, "die," which is what I might do if I don't pay attention to the road.

Mike has a stack of *Enigma*s, and we take one out and sit on his couch. Each issue has several types of anagram-inspired puzzles. The first type is just a straight-ahead anagram. Reshuffle the letters to discover an answer that relates to the phrase.

Here's a classic from an *Enigma* from 1898:

HEY, DOG, RUN!
which rearranges to "Greyhound."

And another from 1921:

ENSLICED EATS
which rearranges to "Delicatessen."

A more recent one:

LATTES? IN HASTE, GO NW
which rearranges to "Seattle, Washington."

BEYOND THE ANAGRAM

The anagram is just the start. Other word puzzles in *The Enigma* are even trickier. But to explain those, let's go to Colorado.

Every year, hundreds of puzzlers meet in a different beautiful city for the National Puzzlers' League convention. In summer of 2019, I attend the convention in Boulder, Colorado, home to stunning mountains and gorgeous bike trails. Neither of which I get to see, since I spend the weekend in a hotel ballroom with my head buried in puzzles.

When I arrive, the first thing I experience is clipboard envy. We've been told to bring clipboards for the sheets of puzzles that are handed out. My clipboard is fine but pretty humdrum compared with those of some puzzlers, which are tricked out with built-in compartments for pencils and erasers.

I check in at registration, using my nom de puzzle. Every member of the NPL has their own clever and/or nerdy pseudonym. Will Shortz's nom is "Willz." It's a rebus: "Will short z." He knows what he's doing.

My nom is less clever, but meaningful to me: "1-Down Saturday," a reference to my appearance in the *Times* crossword.

The night I arrive, there's a tutorial for those who want to learn about the NPL's trademark word puzzles that appear in *The Enigma*. These puzzles are called "flats," and were invented by the NPL way back in the 1800s. You can find a full explanation on the NPL website, but for a simplified summary:

A flat consists of a poem with blank spaces for the answers. The answers are two or more words that are like anagrams on steroids.

They come in various types. There are puzzles in which you remove a letter from the beginning of a word to produce another word: "Factor" becomes "actor." That puzzle goes by the gruesome name of "beheadment."

There's another type of puzzle where you remove a word's last letter: "Aspiring" becomes "aspirin." That one is called curtailment.

My tutor is Guy Jacobson, a longtime contributor and editor at *The Enigma* (who points out that my last name is a two-letter curtailment of his).

"There are dozens of types of flats," Guy says. "There's one called 'Spoonergram,' and another called 'Baltimore Transdeletion.' It's a whole thing."

The flats are hard to solve, and even harder to write. You have to look for fresh wordplay, which is an increasingly rare creature. Guy talks about the thrill when he discovers a new anagram or beheadment. "It's like discovering a new species of owl, or a cure for disease," Guy says. And he speaks with awe about one of his all-time favorites, discovered by an NPL friend:

Take the word for Spanish sausage:

Chorizo.

Add a letter to the end and get:

C Horizon (a geology word for a certain level of soil).

Add a letter to that and you get:

Chorizont.

Perhaps you don't know the word "chorizont." I sure didn't. Well, a chorizont is a person who believes that *The Odyssey* and *The Iliad* were written by two different people.*

---

* The word "chorizont" is sometimes used in a more general sense to mean someone who challenges the authorship of a work. But I prefer the original and unadulterated meaning.

What a time saver! I can't tell you how often I've been chatting with someone and had to say the clumsy phrase, "Oh, she believes *The Odyssey* and *The Iliad* were written by two different people." Now I can just use that one word, chorizont! Another great life hack!

I try a couple of flats, and they are hard. But I do crack some of them after half an hour. And when I do, I experience two emotions: joy and annoyance. Joy that I saw that "Kalamazoo" and "Lama kazoo" are related, and annoyance that it took me so long.

Guy says this exact combination of emotions is what the puzzle-maker wants to evoke in you.

"When someone solves a flat, they should feel proud of themselves, but also ashamed. The puzzlemaker wants to use a connection that's already in the solver's brain but in some corner so that when they actually stumble upon it, they go, 'Oh, that's so cool. Why didn't I see that? Shame on me.'"

After three days, it's time to leave Boulder. Which, as one attendee points out, is a homophone for "bolder," and which is what he hopes I have become in terms of solving puzzles. An appropriate ending to my trip.

Nineteen Word Puzzles from History

ANAGRAMS

Rearrange the letters in these phrases to create a relevant answer.

1) MOON STARERS
   (the answer is an occupation)

2) BAG MANAGER
   (occupation)

3) A STEW, SIR?
   (occupation)

4) MR. MOJO RISIN'
   (singer)

5) ONE COOL DANCE MUSICIAN
   (singer)

6) GENUINE CLASS
   (actor)

7) RADIUM CAME
   (scientist)

8) CASH LOST IN 'EM
   (object)

9) BUILT TO STAY FREE
   (landmark)

10) DIRTY ROOM
   (place)

11) VIOLENCE RUN FORTH
   (historical event)

NPR PUZZLES

Will Shortz hosts a popular segment on NPR's *Weekend Edition,* where he presents word puzzles written by him and his listeners. Here's one from 2004:

12) Take the third letter of a popular cartoonist. Shift that letter two spaces to the right in his name. That will give you something you might see on a city street.

   Note: The cartoonist himself called the show and pretended to be stumped.

Here is one written by Mike Reiss:

13) Think of a two-word phrase you might see on a clothing label. Add two letters to the end of the first word, and one letter to the end of the second word. The result is the name of a famous writer. Who is it?

A relatively recent addition to the word puzzle category is Equation Analysis Tests, also known as Ditloids (a word coined by William Hartston, author of *A Brief History of Puzzles,* in 1999).

   A Ditloid consists of a common phrase—usually one that begins with a numeral—that has been reduced to its initial letters. For instance "52 W in a Y" has the answer "52 Weeks in a Year." Here are a few to try:

14) 5,280 F in a M

15) 3 S in a T

16) 5 F on a H

17) 14 D in a F

18) 6 F in a F

19) 9 L of a C

Solutions to Nineteen Word Puzzles from History begin on page 303.

CHAPTER

5 *Rebuses*

A nagrams aside, there's another type of word puzzle in *The Enigma* that really caught my attention: the rebus. As you may know, the rebus is a visual word puzzle. It uses letters, illustrations, and creative typography to hide a word or phrase. Some rebuses are reasonably solvable:

$$\rightarrow \text{Secret} \leftarrow$$
$$\text{Secret}$$
$$\text{Secret}$$

The answer: "Top secret."

But other rebuses, especially those in *The Enigma,* are ridiculously hard.

Like this one:

B

The answer: "Abalone."
Because it's "a B alone."

Or:

ST

The answer: "Stingray."
Because it's "ST in gray."

Like anagrams, rebuses have a long history. Legend has it that the famously witty French writer Voltaire once responded to a dinner invitation from the king with a rebus. He wrote:

"Ga!"

which translates to:
Gé grand, A petit! ("big 'G', small 'a'!") which is a soundalike to:
j'ai grand appétit! ("I am very hungry!")

Rebuses were also popular in the nineteenth century. In fact, during my research on rebuses, I discovered a particularly tricky one from the 1870s. And therein lies a tale of my matching wits with the most famous person in all of modern puzzling: Will Shortz.

A HOUSEHOLD NAME

Will, as I mentioned earlier, is the *New York Times* puzzle editor and NPR's puzzlemaster. I'd wager that Will Shortz rivals Mark Zuckerberg in the millions of hours his creations have occupied humans—though Will's haven't endangered democracy, as far as I know.

Over the years, I've met Will in passing several times, so I emailed him to ask if I could come visit his home to talk word puzzles—rebuses, anagrams, crosswords. He agreed.

Before my visit, I brushed up on Will's biography. He constructed his first crossword when he was just eight or nine years old, at the suggestion of his mother, who was trying to distract him from interrupting her bridge club meeting. He was editor of *Games* magazine before moving over to the *Times.* He is unfailingly civil and composed. As writer Adrienne Raphel says in her crossword book, *Thinking Inside the Box:* "He carries himself with the formal politeness of a foreign affairs diplomat and the wholesomeness of a Midwestern tennis coach."

Will has been the *Times* crossword editor since 1993. He took over from the crossword community's favorite villain—a former schoolteacher named Eugene T. Maleska. The complaint was that Eugene was a snob, a fun-vacuum. He filled his crosswords with Russian mezzo-sopranos and Yemeni ports. As crossword constructor and author Stan Newman said, Maleska "took a pedant's pleasure in flummoxing other people with obscure facts."

Will Shortz reinvigorated the *Times* crossword. He put fun back into those black and white squares, adding more pop culture, more creative themes, and more wordplay.

Will is a fan of almost every type of puzzle, and a devotee of puzzle history. In fact, I stumbled across a particularly interesting nugget during my research: a letter from Will Shortz in a 2016 issue of *Word Ways* magazine, which is another obscure but magnificently geeky publication.

A SAM LOYD PUZZLE?

WILL SHORTZ
Pleasantville, New York

Below is a copy of the rebus trade card from the 1870s or early '80s that I believe is Loyd's, based on the typography and style of printing. But I have no proof it is his.

Also I have no solution to the rebus. If any *Word Ways* reader can solve it, I'd love to hear about it.

In the letter, Will said he had "no solution to the rebus." I searched for a response in subsequent issues. I couldn't find anything. It seemed the puzzle remained uncracked.

Which gave me an idea. Imagine if I solved a 150-year-old word puzzle that Will Shortz himself hadn't solved?

And on top of that, it's not just any rebus. It's a rebus most likely created by Will's childhood hero, Sam Loyd, who was basically the Will Shortz of the nineteenth century—the most famous puzzle creator of his day. He even had a mustache like Will does, though Sam's was bushier.

Sam Loyd   *Will Shortz*

Sam gained fame early in his career for writing chess puzzles, but soon branched out into all kinds of puzzles: word puzzles, math puzzles, and visual puzzles. One of his biggest hits was a puzzle he created to promote P. T. Barnum's circus, which sold millions of copies. It's called the Famous Trick Donkeys. To solve it, you cut out the three rectangles and then rearrange the pieces so that it looks like the jockeys are riding the donkeys.

Sam Loyd's Famous Trick Donkeys

(For solution see page 304.)

But Sam was different from Will in one significant way: he was a bit of a hornswaggler.

Consider Sam's 15 Puzzle scam. You've no doubt seen the 15 Puzzle—it's the one with sliding tiles that you have to rearrange in numerical order. It was a huge craze in the 1880s, much like the Rubik's Cube a hundred years later. *The New York Times,* in an 1880 editorial, called it a "pestilence" that needed to be stamped out.

Courtesy of Lilly Library, Indiana University, Bloomington, Indiana

First of all, Sam claimed he invented the puzzle, which was a lie. Most likely, it was first created by a New York postmaster.

But even worse, Sam perpetrated a brazen 15 Puzzle hoax. He offered $1,000 (about $25,000 in today's dollars) to the first person to solve a particular arrangement of the 15 Puzzle.

The catch: The contest was rigged. The task was impossible.

Mathematically, half of the initial 7 billion arrangements of the 15 Puzzle can be solved, and half cannot. Sam chose one in which the tiles were arranged in an impossible-to-solve formation. He never had to pay the prize. Despite Sam Loyd's duplicity, I printed out his unsolved rebus and put it in my backpack before leaving to visit Will.

Will lives on a leafy, quiet street in Westchester. His house is part residence, part office, and part puzzle museum. On arriving, I get a tour. Will shows me some of his proudest gems—a wooden 15 Puzzle from the 1880s. A book of Latin riddles from 1533. A copy of that first crossword puzzle from *The New York World*—the only one in private hands.

"Here's a note Bill Clinton wrote me for my fiftieth birthday," Will says, pointing to a framed piece of paper on the wall. Clinton wrote: "Even when I can't finish them, they're the only part of the *Times* that guarantees a good feeling."

Nearby, Will shows me a closet containing a huge stack of papers. It's the crossword puzzles slated to run in the coming weeks.

In one cabinet, there's a copy of his college thesis. Will created his own major at Indiana University: enigmatology, the study of puzzles. His thesis was on the history of early American word puzzles from colonial times to the nineteenth century. It's informative and also poignant.

At the end of his thesis, the young Will Shortz writes that he hopes his paper "adds a certain dignity to the pastime, a dignity which word puzzling justly deserves." More than forty years later, in part because of Will himself, puzzles have gained some dignity in the eyes of the public.

"I think the estimation of puzzles has risen," says Will. "People used to look down on puzzles. The articles about the National Puzzlers' League conventions in the 1930s, it was always about how nerdy the people were. They made fun of them. And now the articles, they don't make fun of puzzle people anymore."

Well, less anyway.

I tell Will that part of my quest is to wrestle with the hardest puzzles on earth. And my quest would be complete if I could solve a puzzle that he hadn't solved yet.

Will chuckles.

"Did you ever solve this one?" I ask, pulling out a copy of the Sam Loyd rebus.

"No," Will says.

"Well, I still haven't either, but can you imagine if I did?"

Will agrees that it would be quite a feat.

"There you have it," he says. "Okay. You're talking about the hardest puzzle. There's one that's not solved."

After an hour, Will apologizes that he has to go. He has to get to his club, where he's hosting a table tennis champion from Ghana. That last sentence is not a riddle or coded language. In addition to puzzles, Will is passionate about Ping-Pong, and he owns a table tennis club in Westchester.

He drops me off at the train station. On the ride back to Manhattan, I pledge to do nothing but work on the rebus. For forty minutes, I stare at the puzzle. I stare at it till the lines start vibrating.

What if there is no answer? What if it's a hoax, like Sam's 15 Puzzle contest?

And then . . . an insight. A scales-falling-from-the-eyes moment.

I think I just solved a puzzle Will Shortz hasn't. This is HUGE!

As soon as I get back to my office, I type an email to Will. I'm so excited that my hands are shaking.

> Hello Will,
>
> I had a bit of an AHA moment on the train back.
>
> It's about the (possibly) Sam Loyd rebus you sent into Word Ways.
>
> What if the answer is . . .
>
> "The forces overtake and surround the enemy."
>
> (The "Four C's" over "Take" and surround "The Enemy")
>
> What do you think?
>
> A.J.

I spend the next seven hours pressing the refresh button, waiting for Will to reply something like "Congratulations! You are the greatest puzzler ever. I resign my title."

I'm anxious for Will's response, but I'm also experiencing a strange high. I have communed with a mind from 150 years ago. Our brains are in sync, even if one of us is dead.

Finally, an email pops up. Polite as ever, Will starts by saying he enjoyed our conversation. Then . . .

> "Regarding the Sam Loyd rebus puzzle . . . now that you mention it, I had come up with your answer myself. I'd forgotten about it, it's been so long.
>
> I'm pretty sure this answer is correct.
>
> Take a bow!"

Oh, man. My ego deflates. I feel like I went to claim a lottery jackpot, but they changed the winning number at the last minute. I do believe Will solved the rebus before me. Unlike his hero Sam Loyd, Will is an honest, upstanding, kind man with nothing to prove, puzzle-wise. I just wish Will had either not solved it or lied and pretended he hadn't and threw me a bone.

But I remind myself: Will allowed my name to appear in a Tuesday crossword puzzle. So I can't be angry.

Plus, I'm the second living person to solve a 150-year-old puzzle.* Will Shortz and I are in a club of two. So that's something, right? As instructed, I take a bow.

---

* I found out after writing this book that I'm actually the third living person to solve the rebus. My fact-checker discovered a letter proposing a similar solution to mine that was printed in *Word Ways* several months after Will's letter. So also take a bow, Lori Wike of Salt Lake City.

Seven Rebuses from History

1) The rebus below dates back to at least 1780s England, when it gained fame as the name of a champion racehorse. According to legend, the rebus was inadvertently created by a stableboy who misunderstood the horse's name, and wrote it down in this unusual form:

POT OOOOOOOO

2) Rebuses were popular in the nineteenth century, including this rebus-style "escort card" a man might give a woman at the end of a date.

3) During the Great Depression, Old Gold cigarettes ran a rebus contest that became a nationwide craze. Contestants had to solve 270 rebuses for a $100,000 prize. A 1937 *Life* magazine article reported that two million people entered. Crafty entrepreneurs sold cheat sheets for $1.45. So many puzzlers flooded America's libraries for research that some librarians put a fifteen-minute limit on reading reference books. The winner was a U.S. Navy pilot, who split the prize with four friends. Here's a sample rebus (potential answers include Mark Antony, Knute Rockne, Charles Dickens, William Penn, Horace Greeley, and Patrick Henry).

4) Lone Star Beer put rebuses on the inside of their bottle caps starting in 2001. The caps are now collectors' items.

5) Modern-day rebuses abound on the Internet, such as the three following.

yourballcourt

6)

TRAVEL / CCCCCC

7)

M1Y L1I1F1E

Solutions to Seven Rebuses from History begin on page 304.

Jigsaws

L et me start this chapter with a confession: for most of my life, I was not much of a jigsaw puzzle fan. It was perhaps my least favorite genre of puzzle. I didn't hate them, but I saw them as more of a chore than a joy, more akin to loading the dishwasher than eating lemon meringue pie. I agreed with comedian Naomi Spungen, who said, "Why should I assemble an artwork when so many are already good to go?"

I was also kind of snobby. I saw jigsaws as obvious and lacking in nuance. I thought they were to the puzzle world what Larry the Cable Guy is to the comedy world. When my family did their annual jigsaw puzzle on New Year's Eve, I'd sit in another room like a grump, waiting for Scrabble or Boggle or the time when it'd be socially acceptable to start drinking.

Well, reader, over the course of writing this book, I have seen the light. So much so that I ended up becoming a competitive jigsaw puzzler. An embarrassingly bad competitive jigsaw puzzler, but still.

Here is the tale of my conversion.

Right from the start, I knew I had to write about jigsaws, despite my lifelong indifference. They are perhaps *the* prototypical puzzle. When you say the word "puzzle," most people's minds conjure up those knobby little interlocking pieces.

So one day, I begin, as I always do, with a Google search. I find one article that reports Bill Gates is a jigsaw puzzler. That's a good sign. He's no intellectual slouch. Other puzzle fans include Theodore Roosevelt, Queen Elizabeth II, and non-dorky actor Hugh Jackman. Jigsaws, I learn, are a huge business: Puzzlers spend more than

$700 million on them a year. During 2020, the year indoors, outlets reported that sales tripled or even quadrupled.

Then deep into my Google search, I spot an intriguing link: the World Jigsaw Puzzle Championship.

Huh. I didn't know there was such a thing as competitive jigsaw solving. To me, jigsaws were, at best, a meditative hobby, a relaxing way to let a few hours slip by. Speed-solving jigsaws sounded weird and paradoxical, like a yoga tournament or a napping derby.

But there it is—the World Jigsaw Puzzle Championship being held in just a couple of months in a small city in Spain. Nearly forty countries are represented—Brazil, Bulgaria, Malaysia, Canada, Italy, and on and on.

Yet, oddly, no Team USA. Why is my country not on the list?

On a whim, I fill out the application for the four-person team event. I figure this will be the first step in a rigorous screening process—timed trials, perhaps an interview—that I will surely fail.

A day later, an email pings back: "Congratulations. You are confirmed as Team USA in the World Jigsaw Puzzle Championship."

I am equal parts thrilled and horrified. I mean, I know it's not the Olympics or the World Cup. But still, there's pressure. It's an international competition, and I will be representing my fellow 330 million Americans.

I am vastly underqualified. I haven't finished a jigsaw puzzle since I was eight years old. My only relevant skills are my ability to fill out an online form and pay the 20-euro entry fee. Apparently, no other Americans had the initiative—or overabundance of free time—to sign up.

First step, I need three teammates. Admittedly, my search is not exhaustive.

"Are you ready to do your patriotic duty?" I ask my wife and kids.

They're skeptical, but they agree to do it, as long as they don't have to wear any kind of uniform. No problem, I assure them.

Next step, training. I decide to consult an expert. I call up Karen Kavett, a New Jersey native with a popular YouTube channel about jigsaw puzzles. She knows her stuff.

Karen tells me up front that she's not a speed-solver herself. She's much more Zen about it. She embraces the process. Instead of rushing through a jigsaw, she savors it, feeling crestfallen when she fits the last piece in.

"I get into a trancelike state when I'm doing a puzzle," she says in one of her videos. "I'll forget to eat. I never forget to eat." She explains that doing jigsaws fills her brain, leaving no room for stress or anxiety. Three hours will pass, and it feels like five minutes.

Karen, a twenty-six-year-old with long brown hair and rectangular black glasses, is speaking to me from her apartment in Los Angeles.

She says sometimes she'll try to prolong it. "I won't look at the cover art, so that it's harder for me." She says she once solved a puzzle with her feet. That took some time. I make a mental note to introduce her to Daniel, the Rubik's foot-solver.

I ask her why she's obsessed with jigsaws, and I hear a common refrain: She likes making order out of chaos. As she said in one of her videos, "When you're doing a jigsaw puzzle, there is one right answer. I find that comforting . . . Virtually every other aspect of the world is in shades of gray." She quotes an article she once read: "A jigsaw puzzle won't solve all your problems, but it's a problem you can solve."

Jigsaws are also an antidote to the pervasive screen culture, she says. They are tactile. We're in the midst of a jigsaw renaissance, partly fueled by millennials like Karen, who want something to feel, not just swipe.

Though Karen doesn't love speed-solving, she still knows all the best strategies. She gives me a crash course:

- Yes, you should usually start with the edges. But not always. It depends on how colorful the puzzle is. Some experts start by sorting the colors instead, assembling those, and then working outward to the edges.
- If you're not sure two pieces actually fit together, hold them up to the light and make sure no brightness seeps through.
- Sometimes you should work backward. Visualize what's missing and look for that piece.
- When confronted with a dreaded big sky, or any other monochromatic expanse, switch strategies. Instead of sorting by color, sort by shape. Make a pile of pieces with two outies and

two innies. Make another pile with one outie and three innies. And so on. This will make it much easier to assemble.

- Look for the "teensiest, tiniest" bits of color on the piece's nubs, and use them as clues.
- Focus on the shades of color. Even in a blue sky, there will usually be different nuances of blue. In her spare time, Karen uses an app called "I Love Hue" that teaches you to distinguish subtle color differences.

I thank Karen for her coaching, and she wishes me good luck.

TRAINING

Two days later, I embark on my first jigsaw puzzle as an adult. My son Zane will be my co-puzzler. The puzzle is of a Dr. Seuss illustration—an underwater scene of multicolored fish. But inspired by Karen, we've decided to make it more of a challenge by refusing to use the picture on the box cover as a guide.

We open the plastic bag and spill the pieces onto the table—along with a fair amount of dust. In one video, Karen recommends pouring the pieces into a colander to filter out jigsaw dust. Too late for that.

Zane and I start sifting out the borders. This is not an activity that is grabbing me. It seems like busywork. Eventually, I spot two pieces that go together. I slide the outie knob into the innie and hear that soft thud. Well, that felt good. I'd forgotten how satisfying that sensation is, the one where the pieces lock into place and create a new beast, double in size. A little aha moment. A tiny hit of dopamine. I click another. More dopamine.

I recall a scene from a TV series Julie and I are watching: *Unorthodox,* about ultrareligious Hasidic Jews. On the eve of a young woman's wedding, a marriage counselor explains to her that sex is like a jigsaw puzzle. The pieces just fit together.

I decide my twelve-year-old son doesn't need to hear this insight.

I'm concentrating far more than I anticipated. This is not mindless, at least if you're in training. The best puzzlers are always thinking of meta-strategies. *What strategy will work best in this situation? Should I focus on shape? Or on color? Or should I try to keep both in my brain at once, along with texture and orientation? Should I make a separate pile just for fish eyes, or just sort the fish eyes according to their eyelid color?* (In Seuss-land, fish do have eyelids.)

Suddenly it's two hours later, and we have to stop so Zane can get ready for bed. I really want to keep working, get more of those aha moments, but I resist. I realize, my God, I'm an easy convert, a cheap date. Perhaps my crankiness toward jigsaws was based on ignorance and a faulty memory.

I'm glad we didn't look at the cover art and are doing it blind, like our courageous jigsaw forefathers. It allows for more revelation, a mystery slowly being solved. Oh, that weird red shape—it's a fishing hook!

I understand what Karen was saying about creating order out of chaos. Working on a jigsaw is a quiet protest against the tyranny of the second law of thermodynamics. I'm all too aware that everything tends toward disorder. Stars, mountains, society. My middle-aged body is losing its order, with hair falling out and stomach sagging. My chosen industry, publishing, seems to be heading toward disorder, the victim of the Internet and short attention spans.

But here, on my dining room table, order is having a tiny victory.

Over the coming weeks, I start dreaming of jigsaws, connecting pieces in my mind. I start seeing the world through a jigsaw lens. The chapters of my book? Those are jigsaw pieces to arrange. And my life's problems? Maybe I can sort them into piles—financial, marital, parental, career—and solve them from there.

Or maybe not. Maybe, in my jigsaw honeymoon phase, I'm trying to force a jigsaw paradigm onto the world when it doesn't fit. I have lunch with one of my smartest friends, a mathematician named Spencer Greenberg, who devotes his life to thinking about problems.

"Do you think life is like a jigsaw puzzle?" I ask.

Spencer takes a pause from his Impossible Burger.

"Yes and no," he finally says. "Some people will look at a problem and say there's no solution. Some will say, there's only one solution, and it's my solution. Those are both bad approaches. In reality, with most problems, there are several solutions. None of them is perfect, but life is about choosing which is the best of the non-perfect solutions."

Nodding, I suggest that life is more like a jigsaw puzzle where the pieces are always changing shape and color. They'll never fit together just right, but you can find something that allows you to make out the general gist of the big picture.

But enough philosophizing. Back to training. The tournament is looming. That night, Zane and I open up another jigsaw.

EL TORNEO

Four weeks later, we're far from prepared, but the time has come. My family and I board an overnight flight to Madrid, then hop on a two-hour train ride north. We arrive, bleary-eyed, in the small city of Valladolid. It's a beautiful town. A central plaza lined with cafes selling churros and melted chocolate. Ornate churches seemingly on every corner. It's one of about six cities claiming to be the burial place of Christopher Columbus.

The next morning at nine, we show up at the Millennium Dome, a bubble-shaped structure with an indoor space the size of a minor-league baseball stadium.

There's no doubt we're in the right place. The floor is packed with jigsaw enthusiasts—hundreds of them. I see shoulders, wrists, and calves adorned with jigsaw tattoos. I see jigsaw earrings and jigsaw-patterned clothes. One Spanish team is wearing T-shirts with jigsaw pieces arranged in the shape of a menacing human skull.

"The bad boys of the tournament," I say to my sons. "Keep an eye on them."

As in every puzzle subculture, participants are legally required to make laborious puns. The Canadian team, which apparently likes combining puzzles and booze, has nicknamed themselves "Team Jig-Sauvignon Blanc."

My family is wearing jigsaw T-shirts too. Yes, I know. I promised my kids they wouldn't have to. But I couldn't resist designing and ordering customized shirts for my first world championship. After much cajoling, my sons and wife have reluctantly put them on. The shirts feature an American flag in the shape of a jigsaw piece, along with the motto "E pluribus unum pictura." It translates to "Out of many, one picture." Right. I'll see myself out.

As geeky as this whole thing is, I'm not feeling embarrassed. I'm feeling almost giddy, partly from Spanish coffee and lack of sleep, but partly because I'm a sucker for people who are passionate about something, regardless of how silly that passion might seem to others.

The night before, I'd attended a little get-to-know-you mixer with the other jigsaw competitors. There were fifty of us, from all over the globe, united by the love of uniting cardboard pieces. I met a man from the Singapore team who works in human resources for the Singapore government.

"Your job sounds like a puzzle," I said.

"I prefer solving jigsaw puzzles to solving people puzzles. The pieces don't talk back."

A tall Belgian man gave me some advice. The tournament lasts eight hours, which is hard on the back. Too much crouching. "A lot of people take Advil before," he said. He added—with just a tinge of bitterness—that shorter teams had an advantage, like jockeys in horse racing. Closer to the action.

I learned there have been other regional jigsaw tournaments over the years, but this is the first world championship. Maybe that explains the lack of other U.S. teams. Not everyone knew.

Today, though, there's no time for chitchat. We are shown to our spot, one of eighty-six tables (some countries have more than one team), each with a name card adorned with a flag. We are seated between Bulgaria and Turkey. The Turkish team consists of four women wearing hijabs and skirts with a multicolored jigsaw pattern.

"I can't believe it, but I've got butterflies," says Julie.

I agree. I'm surprisingly nervous.

Julie starts doing stretches like she's running a 5K. One of the Turkish puzzlers has her head down and hands cupped in prayer. I say my own secular prayer to myself: please don't let us finish last.

The crowd settles down as a man with a blue blazer and microphone walks onto the stage. He announces the rules:

Each table has a stack of four unpublished puzzles from Ravensburger, the well-known manufacturer. The puzzles range from one thousand to two thousand pieces.

We have eight hours to finish them in any order.

"Cinco, cuatro, tres, dos, uno . . ."

And we're off!

We grab one of the boxes on our table—the African safari scene. Immediately, we're at a disadvantage. Other teams have brought letter openers and knives to rip off the plastic wrapping on the box. Team USA is reduced to using our fingernails.

And it's not our only equipment failure. I spot teams that have brought a variety of trays and fiberboards to organize their piles. We've got nothing. I curse my lack of preparation.

We start sorting the edges and colors. It's become clear the monkey will be a problem—it's the same color as the tree.

"Monkeys used to be my favorite animal," says Julie. "Don't make me hate you, monkeys!"

I love that Julie, once skeptical, has fully committed. She's trash-talking the puzzle. She has also sworn not to take a bathroom break for the entire eight hours. This is a first in the twenty years we've been together.

I wipe my brow. The dome is starting to get hot. I glance over at the announcers sitting at a table up front, commenting into their head mics for a livestream. I can't understand most of what they say, but I do hear them repeat the word "brutal," which I guess is the same in English and Spanish.

We're making headway on the zebras, but the elephant is troublesome. "I wish I'd brought scissors and a hammer," Zane says.

At least it's a strategy with a long history. While researching this book, I ran across a scene of Ann-Margret in *The Cincinnati Kid* trimming jigsaw pieces with her nail file so she could ram them into place.*

As Karen has suggested, I'm paying attention to the hues. The elephant and the rhino—both gray, but slightly different. This is a good life lesson, I tell my sons. Life is full of subtleties, different shades of gray. Nothing is black and white.

No response. I tell myself it's because they're focused.

At the two-hour mark, a mini-crisis. On the carpet between our table and the Bulgarian table, I spot a yellow-and-green piece.

"Is that your piece?" I ask them.

"Not ours," says a Bulgarian man with a tone that implies "Do we look like we'd make a rookie mistake like that?"

I pick it up. Imagine the nightmare I just dodged—a missing piece at the end.

I glance at the Bulgarians' puzzle. They're close to finishing, only missing the lake and the sky. On the other hand, we are not close to finishing. In fact, we are well behind every other team that I can see.

Several proctors in yellow vests are patrolling the floor.

One of them—a guy with raven-black hair—has taken a special interest in our team. He approaches our table and breaks into a chant:

"USA! USA! USA!"

"Gracias," I say.

"USA! USA! USA!"

Maybe he's genuinely urging us on. But with our puzzle so full of gaping holes, I'm suspicious he's mocking us, which is irksome. These days, America's reputation is already in the dumpster. I don't want to add to the damage.

The proctor looks at the placard on the table, which has the American flag and my legal name "Arnold Jacobs."

"Arnold Schwarzenegger!" he says in a Spanish accent, raising his arms in a Mr. Universe pose and flexing his biceps.

"Sí," I say. I do indeed have the same first name as a famous person.

I keep my head down, working on the grass, indicating that I don't

---

* There's a lovely subgenre of stories about people who solve puzzles by breaking them. Alexander the Great unraveled the Gordian Knot by slicing the rope with his sword. A Chinese legend features an empress who disentangles a jade ring puzzle by smashing it with a hammer.

have time to discuss my opinions of *Terminator 2: Judgment Day*. The proctor wanders off.

At around the four-hour mark, we hear some sort of hubbub. There's a scrum of people around a table on the far side of the dome. They are chattering, holding their iPhones aloft to get video.

"What's happening?" I ask a group of Canadians near our table.

"It's the Russians. They are close to finishing."

"Finishing a puzzle?"

"No, finishing."

As in all four puzzles. It's been barely four hours.

I'd heard about the Russians last night. They'd skipped the mixer—they are famously single-minded, no time for socializing—but the other competitors spoke about them in reverent tones. One called them the Usain Bolts of jigsaw puzzling. Another compared their dominance to the Soviet Union's Olympic ice hockey team in the '80s.

"We should do a urine test to make sure they're not doping," added one woman. We laughed. But maybe?

The hive around the Russian table buzzes louder. Moments later, a loud cheer.

I see four women—three blondes and one brunette—emerge from the little mob. They're in their twenties, and they are wearing striped T-shirts with the colors of the Russian flag: white, blue, and red.

They walk to the stage to be interviewed for the livestream by the man in the blazer.

"*Campeonas del mundo!*" he says. They are beaming.

"That's insane," my son Jasper says. "How'd they do that?"

"Just keep working," I say.

Every five or six minutes, we hear another burst of applause from the spectators.

The Brazilians finish. Then Japan. Then Mexico.

Each round of applause is a knee to my ribs. Finally, at six hours and two minutes, we do it. We finish. Our first puzzle, that is. My sons don't even fight about who gets to put in the last piece, which makes me proud. Julie whoops it up and applauds. Other tables join in, before realizing we're only one-fourth of the way through.

We grab our next puzzle: a series of red objects—roses, sneakers, scooters. We've barely finished the border and—*tres, dos, uno!*—

"hands away from the table!" We look at each other and shrug and laugh. Julie hightails it to the bathroom.

Later, the results are posted on a TV screen. I jostle my way to be able to see it, and there we are. Way down at the bottom. But not the very bottom. We beat one of the hometown Spanish teams.

My prayers have been answered. We did not finish last.

I don't mind being second to last. I don't even mind that we were beaten by the man from Uganda who later told me he is color-blind, but he loves puzzles so much he still chose it as his hobby. A color-blind jigsaw puzzle champion! Now *that's* inspiring. Like Jim Abbott, the one-handed baseball pitcher who threw a no-hitter.

It's humiliating, yes. But we are in the mix, here with the best of the world, participating, not spectating. During the awards ceremony, the Russian team accepts their 4,000-euro prize along with a jigsaw-shaped trophy.

I approach the champions to congratulate them and ask for an interview. Irina—one of the blond women—is the spokesperson, since she speaks better English than the others.

"Where in Russia are you from?" I ask.

"Siberia," says Irina.

Makes sense, I think to myself. What else is there to do in Siberia? I stop myself from saying it out loud. I'm sure they've heard the same lame observation a thousand times.

"What do you do when you aren't doing jigsaw puzzles?"

Irina says she's an accountant. Another teammate works in a nail salon, and she has painted the team logo on all their nails. (The nails, of course, aren't too long, otherwise they'd interfere with puzzling.)

"What's your secret?"

"I can't tell you. It's a secret."

Fair enough. But Irina eventually relents and tells me one key to success: division of labor.

One of them specializes in sorting the colors.

Another specializes in the edges.

Yet another is master of the monochromatic sections—the skies, the oceans—and solves them by shape.

Another reason for their success is far from revolutionary: practice. They practice for four hours several times a week, skipping drinks with friends.

"What are you going to do with the prize money? Champagne?"

"No," says Irina. "We need the money to travel to other tournaments." There's one coming up in Belgium.

"Wait a moment, please," Irina says. She goes off to a duffel bag and returns with a gift. A little stuffed animal. Their team mascot: Ivan, the bear.

"We want you to have this," she says.

I may hate Vladimir Putin with his corrupt election meddling and his anti-gay policies, but this? This is a lovely moment of humanity. Jigsaw diplomacy.

As absurd as a jigsaw puzzle tournament might seem, and as badly as we performed, I enjoyed this experience for many reasons.

I got to spend time with my kids, who took a break from Nintendo Switch. I got to see people demonstrating total mastery. Watching people performing at peak skill is inspiring, even if this skill isn't one prized by the Olympic Committee or ESPN. (I later watched a video of the Russian team solving. Their hands flew around the table so quickly, I had to check to make sure the video wasn't on double speed.) And, finally, I felt part of a community that transcends national borders. Consider the Turkish women. They were cold to us before and during the competition, but moments after it ended, they smiled, congratulated us, and gave us jigsaw-shaped cookies in the colors of the Turkish flag.

Geopolitics is a messy business. The pieces don't fit smoothly. But every little bit of face-to-face interaction helps.

A BRIEF HISTORY OF JIGSAWS

The next day, I track down the organizer of the World Jigsaw Puzzle Championship. His name is Alfonso Alvarez-Ossorio, a software developer who lives in Valladolid and looks a bit like actor Colin Firth. I ask him if he has a minute to chat. Alfonso confesses that he's so exhausted from running the tournament, he can barely speak his native Spanish, much less be coherent in English.

"But I will try," he says.

Alfonso is the eighth of nine brothers who grew up here in Valladolid. He started an all-Spanish tournament in 2009, and it's been going so well, he decided to open the borders this year.

"I like to joke that puzzles are genetic in my family," he says. His grandparents hand-carved puzzles as a passion, and amassed a collection of several hundred.

Alfonso and brother number seven, Fernando, took the family hobby to a new level. They've traveled the planet and scoured the Internet, building up a collection of nearly four thousand puzzles, one of the biggest in the world.

"I will show you," says Alfonso. "Come."

Alfonso leads me to a large white tent next to the Millennium Dome where he and his brother have created an exhibit about the history of jigsaws.

"Let's begin at the beginning," Alfonso says.

By which he means the very first jigsaw puzzles ever. Who started this insanity? Most historians believe the first puzzles were created by a British mapmaker named John Spilsbury. Sometime around 1760, Spilsbury glued a paper map onto a wooden board and carved up the countries. Probably the most benign case in history of a Brit carving up a map. Spilsbury sold his "dissected maps" to British nobility as a geography aid.

Alfonso points to a large photograph of Spilsbury's original puzzle from the British Museum. The puzzle is sepia-toned, and it is missing the pieces for Scotland and the Netherlands. (Incidentally, in case the British Museum is interested, there is a United Kingdom–based company called the Jigsaw Doctor that makes missing pieces for frustrated puzzlers.)

Geography-themed puzzles remained popular for centuries. Alfonso shows me a black-and-white photo of World War I soldiers smoking pipes and assembling a puzzle. The caption reads: "The English air force pilots are preparing for combat with puzzles . . . These pilots disassembled and reassembled maps to familiarize themselves with the combat zone." More proof for my thesis that puzzles can save the world!

But jigsaw makers went beyond geography soon after Spilsbury's invention. Early designs featured religious tales, fables, and royalty. Most early puzzles were not yet of the interlocking innie-outie shape we're used to. They were more often wavy or geometric.

In the last couple of centuries, the world has seen several jigsaw puzzle crazes. As Anne D. Williams writes in *The Jigsaw Puzzle: Piecing Together a History,* one mania arrived during World War II, when people were apparently desperate to escape reality. Jigsaws sold big on the home fronts, but also to British and American submariners.

An even bigger craze came earlier, during the Great Depression. Film stars such as Bette Davis appeared in photos doing jigsaws. Laurel and Hardy made a slapstick comedy about jigsaws. Companies like Once-A-Week Dime Jig Saw released their puzzles at newsstands, where they were quickly snapped up.

A satirical magazine in the twenties devoted an entire issue to the craze, including a cartoon of a mom ignoring her weeping child as she fits together a puzzle. As you might remember, this is a recurring theme: puzzles as a menace to society, a jagged-shaped version of reefer. Depression-era preachers condemned puzzles, with one saying, "Nero fiddled while Rome was burning. We will go down in history as the nation who worked jig-saw puzzles while our country was falling to ruins."

The preachers were wrong. Jigsaws did not destroy society. In fact, there's a chance they improved society. You can find several studies about the mental benefits of doing jigsaws. It improves working memory. It puts the brain into the alpha state, where we can make connections on a deeper level. Is this true? Maybe. I'm wary of unreplicated social science studies, but I guess I trust them more than the angry preacher.

No doubt the Depression puzzle fad was partly due to high unemployment and a population craving distraction. But the Depression jigsaw boom was also spurred by a technological breakthrough. For the first time, puzzles were being mass-produced. Instead of hand carving wood with a pedal-powered saw, manufacturers were using a method of "punching" cardboard.

It's an efficient process. Designers slice a photo or illustration into shapes—making sure no two shapes are identical. A thousand different shapes for a thousand-piece puzzle, to avoid the wrath of frustrated puzzlers. Metalworkers then turn the design into a razor-sharp steel contraption, like a giant cookie cutter. The cutter thuds down on the cardboard with more than a thousand tons of force. And voilà: instant puzzle.

The most recent puzzle craze, of course, is the one spurred by the 2020 quarantine. *The Onion* ran the headline "Violently Bored Americans Begin Looting Puzzle Stores."

Which didn't happen, as far as I know. But the gist was true. Facebook feeds filled up with families piecing together jigsaws of Renoirs or *The Little Mermaid.* Celebrities got in on it, with Ellen DeGeneres posting a photo of her table covered with a four-thousand-piece puzzle. Factories and retailers struggled to keep up with demand. "It almost feels like a war footing," one told *The New York Times.*

The quarantine boom coincided with an explosion of niche puzzles by independent makers. You can find millennial-themed puzzles (yes, there's avocado toast) and feminist puzzles that spell out "Nevertheless, she persisted."

For better or worse, jigsaws are fascinating windows into the mindsets of their eras. As historian Williams writes, during World War II, patriotic puzzles were popular. You could solve images depicting the American flag and guns and bombs. Other early puzzles featured horrifically racist images, including blackface minstrels or stereotypical Asian people in coolie hats.

There was also a brief trend of pornographic puzzles, such as a 1965 series of jigsaw centerfolds put out by *Playboy* magazine. Which I guess is a notch up from Internet porn. At least it teaches the importance of delayed gratification.

Alfonso ends the tour with some unusual modern jigsaws—one is 3-D, another is a "fractal" puzzle with pieces that look like an intricate coral reef. As I'm saying goodbye to Alfonso, he asks me if I will be president of the USA Jigsaw Puzzle Association and recruit others to be in next year's tournament. I agree, confident that I can find a team that will do better than eighty-fifth place.

THE CHIEF TORMENTOR

In Spain, I got to see some of the world's fastest jigsaw solvers. But the puzzles in the competition were of just average difficulty. In my quest to solve the most painfully difficult version of every type of puzzle, I embarked on a search for the Hardest Jigsaw Ever.

As always, it's a contested title. I mean, what makes a puzzle difficult?

Maybe it's size. There's a continuing arms race to produce the Biggest Jigsaw Puzzle Ever. A few years ago, you could buy a 40,000-piece puzzle of Disney characters. That was replaced by a 42,000-piece puzzle of astrology signs, which was then replaced by a 48,000-piece monster featuring great cities.

For this project, I decided to commit, so I bought that 48,000-piece puzzle. It arrived in a box the size of a small refrigerator. Solved, it's about as long as three Ping-Pong tables. I told my wife we'd have to move to the suburbs to make room for the puzzle.

Every night for two weeks, we knelt on the living room floor and got to work, starting with Santorini, the Greek island. We began with the windmills and the blue church domes. We finished a couple of weeks later with the whitewashed cottages and sandy hills. Now we had just twenty-three other scenic cities to go!

And then, three days into Tokyo, I went online to check the latest puzzle news, and I saw a crushing article: Kodak had just come out with a new world's biggest puzzle. A 51,300-piecer of international landmarks, such as the Taj Mahal and the Colosseum.

Ugh. Even if we finished ours, we would still not have completed the biggest jigsaw ever. My motivation faded. We Scotch-taped Santorini to a big sheet of cardboard and stashed it in the closet, where it sits today, a mocking reminder of overambitiousness. Four hundred dollars, gone. Damn.

Then again, maybe size doesn't matter. You could argue that the jumbo puzzles don't challenge your frontal cortex. They're just tedious. Perhaps it's the content, not the size, that makes for the hardest puzzle. Here too we find a decades-long competition.

In 1965, Springbok Editions, a puzzle company, debuted its so-called World's Most Difficult Puzzle: a 340-piece version of one of Jackson Pollock's most splattery paintings. (See color insert for image.)

In the '70s came a wave of monochromatic puzzles. No image at all. Just the same frustrating color on every piece. You could buy puzzles with names such as "Little Red Riding Hood's Hood" (entirely red) and "Snow White Without the Seven Dwarfs" (totally white). During the Covid crisis, a startup sold a self-described "clearly impossible" jigsaw puzzle in which the pieces are transparent plastic.

But my favorite difficult jigsaw puzzles are created in an unassuming one-story building in the small town of Norwich, Vermont. On an August day, mid-Covid, I drive up to the headquarters of Stave Puzzles.

I'm there to interview founder Steve Richardson, who lists his job as "Chief Tormentor."

"To be paid to drive people crazy? It's a dream come true," he tells me.

Steve is eighty-two and gray-haired, but he has the energy and hustle of a twenty-four-year-old. I'm interviewing him in the Stave visitor room. In front of us is a table with several puzzles—one based on a painting of a penguin, another of a lion.

Stave Puzzles can boast a lot of superlatives. First, they are probably the most expensive jigsaws in the world. Like absurdly expensive. As in a minimum of $400 per puzzle, right on up to $10,000. Bill Gates is a client because he can be. Barbara and George H. W. Bush were also fans.

The high price tag gets you a unique hand-carved puzzle. The pieces are made of wood (the type of wood is a secret), each one sliced by a worker who sits in front of what looks like a giant sewing machine. No two puzzles are carved the same way. The carvers let their muses guide them.

Another superlative: these are likely the hardest jigsaws on earth. Steve delights in listing the ways he inflicts agony:

- There's no picture of the solution provided. Just a dark blue box.
- The pieces can be bizarre—some are in the shape of objects like a dog or rainbow or astronaut, others are 3-D. There can be pieces from unrelated puzzles to throw you off. Or pieces that fit in multiple ways. Pieces that look like edge pieces but aren't. And so on.

- When assembled, the puzzles are rarely rectangular, but instead come in odd shapes, sometimes asymmetrical, other times with empty spaces in the middle.

Steve laughs as he recounts the reactions from customers. Early on, a customer sent a message with just one word: "Arrrggghhhhh!" Many customers call the company's president, Paula Tardie, pleading for hints, for which she charges a bag of peanut butter M&M'S (though she doesn't collect).

Sometimes Steve goes too far. A few years ago, he released an April Fool's Day puzzle where some of the pieces were too big to properly fit. There was no solution. "Man, people were pissed," he says. "I had to refund everyone who bought it."

A more heartbreaking mishap occurred when Stave made a customized puzzle for a man who wanted to propose to his girlfriend. When assembled, it said, "I love you, will you marry me." She said no.

Steve grew up in Massachusetts and has been a puzzle lover since he was a kid. When he was eleven, he tried to carve up a wooden puzzle. "Blood was running down my hand," he told one interviewer. "My mother unplugged my cute little saw, threw it in the trash, and said, 'Your puzzle cutting career is over.' "

In 1974, Steve and a friend started the company after he read that another high-end wood-carved jigsaw puzzlemaker had gone out of business. Steve thought he could fill the void.

They called the company Stave, a portmanteau of Steve and Dave, his cofounder whom he later bought out. Steve designed a signature piece, the Stave jester, which can be found in almost every puzzle. (Other woodcut jigsaw companies have their own trademark shapes. For instance, Long Island–based Par Puzzles, founded in 1932, opted to have their signature piece be an ancient design from the Near East: the swastika. As you might have guessed, this didn't age well. They switched their signature piece to a seahorse, hoping no authoritarian regime co-opts the seahorse.)

"I'm obsessed with puzzles," Steve says. "Everything is a puzzle. I just solved the puzzle of my golf swing. I invented a whole new swing. I broke it down, and said, 'There's gotta be another way.' " It's a weird swing, he says, where you start with the club just above your knees. "My friends tried to bust my balls because it looks so strange, but then I kicked their asses."

"What's your hardest puzzle of all time?" I ask.

Steve thinks for a bit. "It might be Olivia. That's a bitchy design and a bitch to solve."

Olivia is an octopus-themed puzzle. The trick is that the pieces can be assembled in ten thousand different ways—but only one of those ways is correct and allows Olivia to fit inside the coral reef. (See color insert for image.)

I tell him I'd like to try it.

"Well, you have to earn it," he says.

They won't sell Olivia to just anyone. It's too frustrating. You have to work up to it. "We want to lure people into the depths of misery," Steve tells me.

Steve and Paula graciously offer to loan me a selection, including the bitchy Olivia.

I start with one of the easier puzzles, one with a circus theme. Zane and I work on it together. It is both exasperating and hilarious. I've never found jigsaws funny, but when Zane and I fit the pieces together in an unexpected way, I actually laugh out loud.

My wife, Julie, is not as amused. She joins us for twenty minutes before saying she prefers the meditative joy of regular jigsaws. "I have enough frustration in my life."

Before starting Olivia, I wait for our niece, Ally Schoenberg, who is staying at our apartment for the weekend. She's the best jigsaw solver in our family. We work on it for several hours, fitting together the octopus and the mermaid and the sea anemone. Solved! Except not at all. It's one of the 9,999 incorrect solutions. Olivia the octopus is intact, but she doesn't fit inside the coral reef.

Ally and I work on it the next day for eight hours. I think back to how Karen, the YouTuber, said she likes to savor puzzles and is sad when they are finished. She would love this. At one point, after a particularly close call, Ally, normally an even-keeled woman, shouts, "I HATE THIS PUZZLE!!!" and storms out. She returns a few minutes later.

Eventually, we solve it—sort of. Massive hints were required in the form of a PDF file from Paula. It turned out to be a physical as well as a mental challenge: we had to use all of our forearm strength to lock those last two pieces together. Which might mean ours is an alternative, Ann-Margret–style solution. But who cares? It fits.

There's a feeling of relief. But also of gratitude. Gratitude that I'm lucky enough to be in a position where I can enjoy mental pain. That's a crazy luxury. It's like marathons—our ancestors didn't find pleasure in running twenty-six miles on a weekend, then going out to brunch. They were too busy fleeing predators and rival tribes. Same with these puzzles. Our brains were evolved to solve problems like "How do I eat?" but we get to use them for Olivia. I am a lucky bastard.

Three Jigsaws from History

1) The Ellis Island jigsaw

This might be the highest-stakes jigsaw puzzle in history. It was given to immigrants at Ellis Island in the early 1900s as a test that would allegedly weed out what they referred to as "the feeble-minded." It is currently housed at the Smithsonian. My great-grandparents likely had to assemble this puzzle when they arrived by steamship in New York.

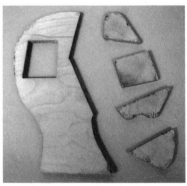 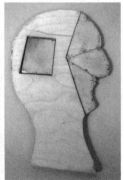

2) The Eternity puzzle

Another contender for the title of Hardest Jigsaw Ever: the Eternity puzzle from 1999. Its story is a delightful little tale of hubris and revenge of the geeks, which I will now briefly summarize:

There was once a British aristocrat named Lord Christopher Monckton, 3rd Viscount Monckton of Brenchley, who had an unexpected side hustle: he designed puzzles. In 1999, Monckton came out with Eternity, an allegedly impossible jigsaw puzzle. Eternity consisted of 209 aquamarine pieces in a variety of geometric shapes that sort of resembled Southwestern states (Utah, New Mexico, and so forth). The goal was to fit the pieces together perfectly to form a big twelve-sided shape.

Monckton calculated that there were so many potential arrangements (about 10 to the five-hundredth power, which is more than the number of atoms in the universe) that it would be impossible for any human to solve. In fact, impossible for any computer to solve—it was just that big.

Monckton offered a £1 million prize if anyone cracked his puzzle within four years. Enter Oliver Riordan and Alex Selby, two young, skinny British mathematicians. Riordan and Selby studied the puzzle and found two loopholes—miscalculations in Monckton's plan. First, you didn't have to solve the whole puzzle at once. You could solve it in sections. Second, there was more than one solution. The pair programmed two personal computers, which churned away for six months before spitting out the correct answer.

They got their £1 million prize, which they spent on appropriately rational things such as grad school tuition. Monckton said that he had to sell his sixty-seven-room home in Scotland to afford the prize. He later said he was just joking.

Regardless, I love this story. It's a victory of optimism over pessimism. A victory for the people over the aristocracy. A victory for flexible thinking and multiple solutions over a narrow-minded single solution.

I would have a little more sympathy for Monckton, but I looked him up, and it turns out he has since devoted his life to denying the science of climate change and advocating that climate scientists be thrown in jail.

So all in all, a happy ending.

3) The Missing Piece

It's the jigsaw puzzler's prototypical nightmare: you get to the end of a puzzle, and there's one piece missing. This is what happened to a German man named Peter Schubert in 2021. Only in Peter's case, the puzzle was 54,000 pieces, the largest in the world.

I know! He got to 53,999 and then was confronted with that tiny empty hole. Heartbreaking. But keep reading.

Peter, a fifty-two-year-old divorced sawmill worker, has been doing huge puzzles for nearly two decades. He calls himself the Puzzle King, and says he finds them beautiful and that they help distract him from daily life. In September of 2020, he bought the "Travel Around Art!" puzzle, the biggest commercially available jigsaw. It featured a series of paintings such as Van Gogh's *Starry Night* and Grant Wood's *American Gothic*.

Peter says he trained "like an athlete" in hopes of breaking the record for assembling the biggest jigsaw. No one else had finished the puzzle at the time. He worked on the puzzle for five hours a day on weekdays, and up to fourteen hours a day on weekends. "I cut down my sleep to four hours," he says. After 137 days, he finished the puzzle. Except for that one infernal piece in the Renoir painting *Young Girls at the Piano*.

"I was despairing," he tells me, through a translator. "I moved the furniture around for two days looking for it. I checked the bag in the vacuum cleaner. I thought about it all the time, even at work. I broke out into sweats."

It never turned up. He made his own replacement piece by Frankensteining together three pieces from another puzzle, but it wasn't the same. He finally called the jigsaw company (it's a French manufacturer called Grafika) and told them his tale of woe. They sent him the missing piece. On March 19, 2021, he took all the assembled sections of the puzzle to the town hall (it was too big to fully assemble at his house), put them together, and placed in that final piece.

"It was like Christmas," he says. "I felt like giving everyone a big hug."

He later was recognized by the German Record Institute for his feat.

It's a happy ending, and I'm glad for Peter. But part of me wishes he never filled in that space. That the giant jigsaw remained forever a monument to imperfection and incompleteness. It would be the ultimate exposure therapy for those with mild OCD like myself, a lesson in radical acceptance of the world's flaws. I decide not to tell Peter this.

To see an image of Peter and the puzzle, turn to the color insert.

(7) *Mazes*

On a fall weekend before the quarantine, I go to the Labyrinth Society Annual Gathering to learn about mazes. This turns out to be a big mistake. A wrong turn, appropriately enough.

I'm informed of my error soon after arriving at the retreat in rural Maryland. One of the conference organizers, a tall man from Tasmania, tells me in a gentle but stern tone that the gathering of the Labyrinth Society is NOT the place to study mazes.

Labyrinths? Yes. Mazes? No.

They are two very different things.

And one is better than the other.

"God created the labyrinth to help people deal with the trauma of mazes," he tells me, as we stand in a field near a stone labyrinth. He is not smiling.

I'd always thought of the two words as synonyms, but devoted labyrinth fans say they are oceans apart.

Mazes are puzzles. You have choices. Do I turn left? Right? Go straight? The point is to get lost before finding the exit.

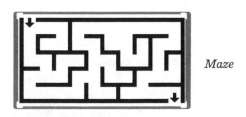

Maze

Labyrinths, on the other hand, are not puzzles. Labyrinths offer zero choices. You follow a single winding path from start to finish. Their purpose isn't to entertain, it's to enlighten. According to labyrinth fans, walking a labyrinth can be a profound experience, a meditative and healing experience. Sometimes even a life-altering experience, akin to St. Paul's road to Damascus or Steve Jobs's acid trip.

Labyrinth

Many hardcore labyrinth fans see mazes as a source of anxiety, confusion, and stress. "I don't want to make any decisions," one man told me during lunch break. "I make enough decisions in my real life. One path in, one path out, that's what I like."

Much to my surprise, I learn that labyrinths have had a considerable resurgence in the last few decades. The modern labyrinth craze was ignited by a 1996 book called *Walking a Sacred Path* by Lauren Artress, an Episcopal minister. She wrote about her experiences walking the labyrinth made of stones embedded in the floor of the Chartres Cathedral in France, describing it as a powerful way to pray.

Since then, labyrinths have been embraced by various spiritual seekers—Christians, Buddhist-influenced mindfulness fans, New Agers, and users of psychedelics. Thousands of labyrinths, both temporary and permanent, have popped up in private homes, hospitals, retirement communities, rehab centers, and church parking lots. Some are made of rocks artfully arranged in grass. Others are painted on pavement. Still others are printed on portable tarps. (Unlike mazes, labyrinths rarely have high walls; they are usually knee-high or lower.)

But all labyrinths share one trait: "The labyrinth is not a puzzle to solve," a woman tells me. "The puzzle is you. And you solve it by walking the labyrinth."

Since I'm writing a book on puzzles, what should I do? Maybe I should take the next train home and never speak of this again. Or maybe I need to relax and explore the idea of the anti-puzzle. The joys of freedom FROM choice. The novel idea of not subjecting myself voluntarily to confusion and hardship. And maybe work on that "puzzle of you" thing.

So I spend the day exploring labyrinths with about a hundred other gatherers from all over the world. I attend speeches about the history of labyrinths, from patterns drawn on pottery in ancient Syria, to medieval Swedish stone arrangements.

I listen to testimonials of people who talk about energy vortexes and chakras. (This New Age lingo is partly why some conservative Christians disapprove of labyrinths, seeing them as too pagan.) I read pamphlets about how labyrinths have supposedly cured people's arthritis and nearsightedness and I hear about how labyrinths can enhance life's rituals, including marriage (the couple walks in separately, and leaves together) and divorce (the opposite, of course).

And, of course, I walk a labyrinth.

The organizers have set up several on the hotel grounds, and the one I choose sits in the field behind the hotel. The labyrinth consists of dozens of square stones arranged in a spiral and embedded in the patchy brown-green grass. It's about the size of a tennis court.

I've joined a dozen other walkers for a workshop being led by Mark Healy—the Tasmanian who warned me of mazes' psychic toll. Mark is a young-looking blond man of sixty-two and father of seven. He's wearing a black T-shirt that says, "I lost my mind in a labyrinth but gained my heart."

In a speech the previous night, Mark talked about how labyrinths saved his sanity. In 1999, he was the owner of an organic food business that went bankrupt. He spent six months building a labyrinth to help him through the ordeal. "It purged me of shame and grief," he said.

This labyrinth has two entrances side by side.

"If you are feeling masculine energy," Mark tells us, "then go right and come out left. If you are feeling feminine energy, go left and come out right."

Hold on. I thought the whole point is I wouldn't have to make choices! Regardless, I'm not feeling either gender's energy particularly strongly. I decide to go with the male route.

I step onto the path and walk slowly, like I'm in a funeral procession. I'm hoping for a mind-blowing experience. A blast of trumpets, a Technicolor hallucination of a world beyond. This is not happening.

But I'm going to do my darndest to get the most that I can out of this labyrinth. I focus on the sound of the grass crunching under my sneakers, the breeze on my cheek, the brisk air filling the alveoli in my lungs, the slight dizziness when I do a 180-degree turn, which makes me wobble drunkenly and almost bump into another walker.

I focus on not focusing so much.

Three minutes later, I step out of the labyrinth. Mark is waiting at the end with a beatific smile and his hands in the namaste position.

"You lost your virginity!" Mark congratulates me.

I smile. I can't say I am reborn. But I do feel my pulse has slowed. I'm relaxed, serene, like I've just had a nice glass of white wine. Which is not nothing.

It's certainly a contrast to wrestling with a puzzle. And in some ways, a welcome one. I think of Barack Obama's dream of opening a T-shirt shop. He once said he was so sick of hard decisions that he fantasized about opening a T-shirt shop on the beach that sold only one item: a plain white T-shirt, size medium. Freedom *from* choice. Several years ago, I wrote a book in which I followed all the rules of the Bible, and even though I'm not religious, I saw the appeal of a highly structured life. The freedom to choose has many benefits, but in certain circumstances, so do strict limitations. Should I work on the Sabbath? No. I don't have to think about it or weigh the pros and cons. The answer is clear.

Puzzles follow a narrative: you struggle, you struggle some more, then you break through to the joy of the solution. It's the same narrative we like in our books and movies. Conflict, then resolution. But sometimes I agree with Mark: Why should we have to endure that painful conflict phase if we don't have to? Maybe we're unhealthily masochistic. It's why I have an odd habit that drives my wife crazy: sometimes I watch the first half of a romantic comedy, then turn it off. I just want to see the part where the couple is falling in love and the montages of ice-cream eating and roller skating. But as soon as Act 2 starts, with those stressful misunderstandings and complications, I'm out.

Don't get me wrong. I still love puzzles, even with the anxiety they provoke. Partly because of the anxiety. But I can see the appeal of the labyrinth.

Before I leave the labyrinth gathering, I buy a book in which each page contains a simple black-and-white labyrinth. You're supposed to trace the labyrinths with your index finger and get that mental peace without leaving your sofa. Perhaps, when I'm banging my head against a frustrating puzzle, tracing these simple, choice-free paths will be a meditative gift.

THE MICHELANGELO OF MAZES

After so much maze skepticism, I wanted to hear a pro-maze perspective. So I set up a Zoom call with a British man named Adrian Fisher.

Adrian is the most prolific maze designer "in the history of humankind," as he puts it, modestly. He and his company have designed more than seven hundred mazes to date. He's created mazes that can be found in forty-two countries on six continents. He's designed them for amusement parks, museums, and private homes. He's made them out of hedges, mirrors, corn, colored bricks, and spraying water. He has set nine world records, including for the biggest permanent maze, called "The Maze of the Butterfly Lovers," in China, with more than five miles of hedge-lined paths.* The polar opposite of Mark Healy, Adrian is convinced that mazes are a great source of pleasure. Sometimes very physical pleasure.

"I was in a corn maze in southern England and there was a couple there with a baby," Adrian tells me. "They came up to me and said, 'Did you design this maze?' I said yes. They said, 'This little baby was conceived in this maze two years ago.'"

"Weren't they afraid of getting caught?" I ask.

"I suppose that was the fun of it."

Adrian is speaking to me from his home office in Dorset, England. He's got bushy gray eyebrows, and he is wearing a navy blazer. His office is packed with piles of books on gardening and masonry.

Adrian's conversational style is, appropriately enough, filled with unexpected byways and occasional dead ends. He talks about waterskiing barefoot in Hong Kong and longbows in medieval warfare.

"As you may have detected," he says, "my life consists of telling stories. Some of them are true."

Eventually, we do discuss mazes, his first love.

"I'm an artist," Adrian says. "And my chosen medium is mazes."

---

* Another maze in China (this one in the shape of an elk) recently broke the Butterfly Maze's record for largest maze.

How did he embark on this curious career path?

A puzzle fan since childhood, Adrian created a hedge maze in his father's garden when he was twenty-four. He decided it was his life's calling. His first commissioned maze opened in 1981 at a historic British manor near Oxford.

Some of his more notable mazes? He helped design a Beatles-themed maze in Liverpool with a yellow submarine at its center. "The Queen opened that one," he says.

There's the maze in the passenger terminal at Singapore's Changi Airport. "Doesn't that cause people to miss flights?" I ask.

"Yes, I've read that has happened several times." He doesn't seem particularly guilt-stricken.

And there's the maze on the side of a fifty-five-story skyscraper in Dubai. "It's not to be attempted unless you happen to be Spider-Man," Adrian says.

He's incorporated rotating floors, walls that change colors, and waterfalls that part when you walk through them.

The beauty of a maze, says Adrian, is that when you solve it, "you walk out one inch taller." It imbues a sense of danger, but not too much danger, followed by joyous accomplishment.

"When I'm designing a maze, it's like I'm playing a chess game with you. But I have to make all my moves in advance. And I have to lose."

He says mazes are best when they're a social activity. "You have to share the decisions, figure out how to work together."

He loves the symbolism of mazes. "Mazes can work on so many levels. They contrast the rigidity of man's designs with the exuberance of nature—and the folly of man trying to control nature." And he adores the mystery. "Mazes are like bikinis of life. They have to hide the important bits, but still reveal enough to keep things interesting," he says. I suspect I'm not the first one he's used that line on.

MAZES START HERE

Adrian is also a writer, and has authored no fewer than fifteen books on mazes. Some are collections of his pencil mazes, a genre that was faddish in the 1970s and '80s. Others focus on the history of mazes.

As I dug into Adrian's history books, as well as those by other authors, they reinforced my contention that history is almost always far weirder than we imagine.

Consider the tale of the most famous maze of all time: the ancient Greek labyrinth, home to the fearsome Minotaur (just to complicate things, it's usually called a labyrinth, but it might have been a maze, since people got lost in it).

I knew the bare bones of the Minotaur myth but not the full story. And the full story isn't just weird. It's depraved. As in *Human Centipede–*level depraved. Ancient societies were far more disturbing than the sanitized versions we are taught.

With that warning, here goes:

The Greek god Poseiden got angry at King Minos of Crete for failing to sacrifice a white bull to him. So Poseidon, using flawless misogynistic logic, decided to punish King Minos's wife. He put a curse on the queen that made her fall madly in love with the white bull.

The queen tried to seduce the bull, but the bull wasn't interested. Not his species. Desperate, the queen hired Daedalus, Greece's greatest inventor, to help with her cause. Daedalus's task: build a realistic-looking cow out of wood and cowhide. And make sure that the wooden cow has a secret compartment that could fit a naked person.

Daedalus did his job. The queen climbed into the compartment sans toga, and the cow was wheeled over to the bull. This time, the bull took the bait and mated with the wooden cow, perhaps figuring that if someone went to that much trouble, it was the least he could do.

The bull impregnated the queen, and she gave birth to a monster: a creature with the head of a bull and the body of a man. The Minotaur.

Horrified by his wife's bastard child, the king ordered Daedalus to build a maze. And in this maze, the king imprisoned the Minotaur, where it grew into a fearsome beast which, every year or so, ate fourteen virgins captured in Athens. (Not addressed in the myth: why a herbivorous bull would require human flesh to survive.) This bloody ritual continued until the hero Theseus slew the Minotaur and escaped the maze with the help of a ball of yarn.

The tale has an interesting maze-related coda: Daedalus later ran afoul of the king and was imprisoned in his own maze. But clever

Daedalus and his son, Icarus, escaped by making wings of wax and feathers and flying away. That's some impressive, out-of-the-box puzzle solving by Daedalus (despite the well-known mixed results of that flight).

So there you have it: cannibalism, bestiality, and high-end carpentry. Not the story line taught to my kids during their sixth-grade Greek Festival, where they recited myths in togas made of bedsheets.

Despite centuries of digging, archaeologists have not found the ruins of King Minos's original labyrinth. Likely, it didn't exist in the form described by the legend. The closest parallel is the ruins of a palace from the Minoan civilization on Crete. The palace's many connecting rooms might have inspired the myth.

After the mazes of Greek myth, the most famous mazes are probably the great hedge mazes of Europe. Starting in the Middle Ages, it became fashionable for nobles to construct giant leafy puzzles on their palace grounds. Some still survive, including the Hampton Court Maze, built circa 1700.

The Hampton Court Maze has six-foot-tall hedges made of yew. It's a pretty simple maze, just five turns, but still, a questionable legend says that a man once got lost in it overnight and froze to death. What is certain is that the Hampton Court Maze has made an impressive contribution to science. It inspired nineteenth-century psychologist Edmund Sanford to put rats in mazes.

The Hampton Court Maze attracts thousands of tourists a year, in part because most mazes of yore no longer exist. Some were chopped

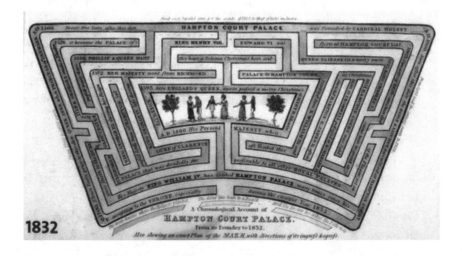

down during the rule of Puritan Oliver Cromwell, who detested them as trivial pursuits. Others just languished.

Perhaps the most popular type of maze nowadays is made of a different plant: cornstalks.

The corn maze is of surprisingly recent origin. In the early 1990s, a former Disney producer was flying over cornfields in the Midwest when he had an epiphany. Let's turn these boring farms into something fun. Agri-tainment!

He hired Adrian Fisher (of course) to design the first corn maze, which opened in 1993 in Pennsylvania. And here we get an unexpected cameo from the late Stephen Sondheim. Turns out, the Disney producer was friendly with Sondheim, and the legendary lyricist told him, "You have to call it the Amazing Maize Maze." Which he did.

Maize mazes are now an established autumnal ritual. Late every summer, hundreds of cornfields in America get converted, a boon to struggling farmers and puzzle fans alike.

THE HARDEST MAZE

A few months later, I did an Internet search for "Hardest Maze in America." There's no governing body that officially ranks mazes by level of difficulty, but one result seems intriguing: the Great Vermont Corn Maze. As one article puts it, "It's not the Mediocre Vermont Corn Maze."

I phone the number on the website and speak to the owner, Mike Boudreau.

"I'd love to come up," I say.

"That'd be great," Mike says.

"I'm thinking of bringing my son to do it with me," I say.

"How old is your son?" Mike asks.

"Thirteen."

Mike pauses. I sense some concern.

"It's just that ninety percent of teenagers hate the maze. They give up after an hour or so. It's too hard for them."

I like what I'm hearing. This maze sounds nice and frustrating.

Mike explains that it usually takes at least three hours to finish the maze, sometimes as much as five or six. "Most people find themselves back at the start after two hours."

This is getting better and better.

Mike says he's had plenty of customers burst into tears out of frustration. He's seen dozens of bickering couples. "Let me put it this way. It's NOT recommended for a first date." One father got so exasperated, he abandoned his family in the maze, went to the parking lot, and drove off without them.

Crying? Screaming? Splintered families? I'm sold! It's like Mark Healy's warning came true.

"Hopefully I'll make you hate me as much as everyone else does," Mike says.

On a late-summer day, I rent a car and drive up to rural Vermont, not far from the Stave headquarters, oddly enough. As recommended, my teenage son is not with me. I meet Mike, who is wearing mirrored sunglasses and a khaki jacket. He walks me to the start of the maze, a clearing with an eight-foot statue of a relatively demure Minotaur (the monster is shirtless but is wearing a pair of blue jeans).

I ask Mike how he got started. He says he married a farmer's daughter, and, in 1999, in a quest to help get new income for the family farm, he set up a relatively simple maze and opened it to the public.

Every year since then the maze has grown bigger and more elaborate. This year it's approximately twenty-four acres. Over the years, Mike has added tunnels, bridges, statues, a platform with a motorboat. And themes! One year had a dinosaur theme, with a T. rex carved into the rows of the maze that was only visible from a bird's-eye view.

The year I visit—2020—the theme is more sentimental: a big thank-you note to the essential workers who kept us alive during Covid. If you look at it from above, you can see the words "Thank you," along with the symbol for medical workers, the staff of Hermes surrounded by twisting snakes.

Because of the pandemic, Mike's maze is allowing in fewer than half as many solvers as normal.

"I'm going f-ing broke, but I thought I'd do something to thank people."

Another couple comes to the entrance. They've been here before and don't need to hear Mike's intro spiel. They set out on the journey.

"See you tomorrow!" Mike says.

Mike tells me that Covid is just one of the challenges of maintaining his maze. He reels off a list of problems he faces every year:

- Cheaters who use video drones to try to hack the maze.
- Hungry bears. "They'll come at night and eat up two whole squares. They just keep eating till they throw up."
- Weeds. Climate change has made them sprout more quickly.
- Women who wear high heels. Not only is it painful for the wearer, but they leave little holes throughout the maze. Hiking boots are recommended.
- Petty thieves who steal ears of corn. "The thing is, this is feed corn," says Mike. This type of corn is meant for pigs, not humans. "I've been told it's a laxative. So when I see people walking out with their pockets stuffed with corn, I'm like, 'You got me! You got one over on me, buddy!' "

Mike is old-school. He designs the mazes himself by hand. He and his family plot the paths out with a tape measure and clear the rows with hoes and a rototiller.

"This is not a McMaze," he tells me. Some corn mazes are made using prefab computer programs that are like giant stencils. Instead, Mike sees himself as an artisan, akin to a Brooklyn pickle maker.

It's time for me to set out on this homemade wonder. There are three paths at the entrance, marked "eeney," "meeney," and "miney." I choose meeney. I enter, and I walk between the cornstalks towering over my head. I try to use the clouds to orient myself as I make a left, then a right, then a right.

Much like my nightly crossword experience, navigating the maze is a surprisingly emotional experience. Over the next four hours, I cycle through the following feelings:

Optimism.

Frustration.

Extreme frustration.

Resentment—I feel manipulated, like a lab rat.

Bitterness—when I get to a dead end, I laugh out loud.

Joy—I'm making progress!

Discomfort—I'm thirsty, and my shoulders are sore from my
    backpack.

Smugness—I pass a dad carrying his kid in a BabyBjörn. At least I
    don't have a twenty-pound whining weight pulling me down.

Guilt—I inadvertently cheat by taking one of the emergency
    exits. Yes, this maze has emergency exits. Mike guides me back
    to where I made the wrong turn.

There is a science to solving a maze. Mathematicians have developed several algorithms, and before my trip, I'd printed out a list from the Internet.

I'd planned to start with the easiest tactic: the Wall Follower algorithm. So named because you put your right hand on the wall, and make every right turn you can. The solver may double back a few times, but eventually you'll reach the exit.

Or not. The maze designer can mess with the Wall Follower strategy by creating islands in the maze unattached to walls. Which Mike has done. Don't even bother with that trick, he tells me.

I try another couple of mathematical strategies, including Trémaux's algorithm: if you walk a passage, mark it with an X at the start and end, then avoid all passages with two Xs (I arrange twigs on the ground to make the Xs).

But if I'm being honest, my most reliable strategy is the Random Mouse algorithm. As Wikipedia describes it: "This is a trivial method that can be implemented by a very unintelligent robot or perhaps a mouse. It is simply to proceed following the current passage until a junction is reached, and then to make a random decision about the next direction to follow. Although such a method would always eventually find the right solution, this algorithm can be extremely slow."

It is indeed slow. Four hours and twenty-two minutes. And that's with an embarrassing number of hints from Mike, whom I called on my cell.

I finally finish. I reach a clearing with a red bell labeled "Bell of Success." I kick it until it clangs. And then I get the real reward: the use of the Porta Potty of Relief (not its actual name).

Before I drive home, I reenter the maze and say goodbye to Mike. He's standing on a wooden bridge, and I climb the stairs to join him.

"I kind of feel like a god up here, controlling people's fates."

He tries to be a compassionate god, smiling and bantering and giving copious hints. Less like Poseidon, more like George Burns in *Oh God! Book II*.

I ask Mike what life lessons he's learned from twenty years of observing mortals.

"A lot," he says. "I feel like I've gotten a PhD in sociology."

First, the folly of inflexible thinking. "Some people learn from their mistakes. Other people—especially young men—you just watch them and are like, 'Why do you keep returning to that wall? You can't go through the wall!' They just won't let go of it because they think they are right."

Second, the dangers of trying to take the shortcuts.

"When people hear the bell, they're like lemmings. They all just start heading toward the sound of the bell. But you'll never find the exit just by going in the direction of the exit."

The easy straight path is rarely the correct one. This is a circuitous maze.

A few years ago, Mike tried to emphasize this lesson by adding a second bell in the middle of the maze—the Bell of Frustration. He hoped this would dissuade people from just following the clangs.

The point is, don't always be looking for a shortcut. Realize that sometimes, as with solving a Rubik's Cube, you have to retreat further away from your goal before you get on the correct path.

I say goodbye to Mike and drive home. As suggested by my GPS app, I take an appropriately circuitous route of obscure back streets to get onto the George Washington Bridge.

In the days that follow, I give some more thought to the idea that mazes are metaphors for life. It's an old theme. There's a famous (at least to mazers) 1747 poem by an anonymous British writer:

> *What is this mighty labyrinth—the earth,*
> *But a wild maze the moment of our birth?*
> *. . . Crooked and vague each step of life we tread,*
> *Unseen the danger, we escape the dread!*
> *But with delight we through the labyrinth range,*
> *Confused we turn, and view each artful change.*

The poem goes on until a few lines later the Maze of Life inevitably ends:

> *Grim death unbinds the napkin from our eyes*
> *. . . And Death will shew us Life was but a jest.*

So you die and the big reveal is: life was all a big joke! Even for a secular skeptic like me, that's a little bleak. I hope life isn't just a cruel cosmic joke. I hope it's not an elaborate bait-and-switch prank, like when parents tell their kids that Christmas is canceled and then post YouTube videos of them crying. If life is a joke, I hope it's a gentle and goofy joke, like a Steven Wright one-liner (for example, "All those who believe in psychokinesis, raise my hand").

But regardless of what lies at the end, the poem gives us some solid advice for the present: delight as we range through life's corridors, embrace the confusion and the inevitability of change. Enjoy that arrow between the question mark and the exclamation point.

Three Pencil Mazes from History

Solutions to these three mazes can be found at thepuzzlerbook.com.

1. Lewis Carroll, the author of *Alice in Wonderland,* drew this maze for his family in the 1850s. You must start at one of the three entrances on the left and find your way to the diamond in the center. Incidentally, the famed puzzle writer Martin Gardner said that pencil mazes should not be solved with a pencil, but instead with a toothpick. He said "morons" could be taught to do it with a pencil. But I say, go ahead and use a pencil if you want. I won't judge.

2. Here is a pencil maze by the prolific Adrian Fisher.

3. Detroit-based artist Michelle Boggess-Nunley owns the world's record for largest hand-drawn maze: two feet by more than five hundred feet. It was her quarantine project. The maze, which helped raise

money for charity, took more than three months and three hundred Sharpies.

I don't have room to print that maze, but here's another one of Michelle's works called "Path to Giza." Warning: one classic hack for solving pencil mazes is to start at the end and work backward. It's often easier, because the maze makers frequently draw their mazes from the entrance to the exit, and inadvertently frontload the choices. Michelle says she avoids that, so no need to try that strategy here. (More of her mazes and books can be found at boggessart.com. A bigger version of this maze can be found at thepuzzlerbook.com).

Math and Logic Puzzles

My father was the one to introduce me to math puzzles. He didn't focus on the traditional kind. His were weirder than that, more homegrown. My dad's greatest joy comes from baffling unsuspecting people—strangers, friends, family, whomever—and he often accomplishes this with math-based hijinks.

One time, when I was about eight years old, I asked my dad how fast race cars went. This was before Google, so my father was my version of a search engine.

"The fastest ones get up to about 50 million," my dad said.

Even to my unschooled mind, 50 million miles per hour seemed off.

"That doesn't sound right," I said.

"Yes it is," he said. "50 million fathoms per fortnight."

I just stared at him.

"Oh, you wanted *miles per hour?*" my dad said. "I thought you meant in fathoms per fortnight."

As you might know, a fathom equals six feet, and a fortnight is two weeks. My dad had decided that fathoms per fortnight would be his default way to measure speed, on the probably correct theory that no one else on earth had ever used that metric. I thanked him for this helpful information.

When not calculating fathoms per fortnight, he spent time obsessing over the mathematics of February 29.

For no other reason than that it amused him and perplexed strangers, he'd boast at cocktail parties that he was born on February 29. And not just him. His wife, daughter, and son (me) were also born on February 29.

This despite the fact that none of us was born on February 29.

"What do you think the odds are that all four of us would be born on Leap Day?" he'd ask.

The stranger would usually shrug, uncertain what to say.

"It's 4.5 trillion to 1," my dad would say.

He didn't tell dad jokes so much as Dada jokes—surreal and beyond logic.

So, as you can see, I was exposed to recreational math early on, leaving me with a mixed legacy—a love of numbers, a healthy skepticism about numbers, and paranoia.

Unfortunately, I was decent at math puzzles, but never a superstar. (I'm still annoyed at myself for flubbing a sixth-grade math test that asked for the total number of legs in a yard with twenty-three cows and fourteen chickens. I just multiplied the total number of chickens and cows by four. How was I supposed to know chickens only have two legs? I grew up in New York City, not on a farm in West Virginia! I didn't have a PhD in avian anatomy. Okay. Yes. I should have known that chickens have two legs. I should also be mature enough not to revisit this mistake every week of my life for the ensuing several decades, but neither is the case.)

For this puzzle project, I've bought a dozen books with math and logic brainteasers. Reading these books often induces a mild panic. How would I know how many spheres can simultaneously touch a center sphere? I can't even figure out where to start. What's the entry point?

To remedy this problem, I decide to consult one of the world's experts on math puzzles, hoping to learn some of her methods. Tanya Khovanova greets me on a video call. But before I'm allowed to ask her anything, she has a question for *me*.

"I have two coins," she says, in a Russian accent. "Together they add up to 15 cents. One of them is not a nickel. What are the two coins?"

My palms begin to sweat. I did not expect a pop quiz.

Maybe she's talking about foreign coins? Maybe rubles are involved, I say?

"Not foreign coins," she says. "American currency."

I employ one of the puzzle-solving strategies that I do know: Look closely at all of the words and see if you have fallen for any hidden assumptions.

Two coins.

Add up to 15.

One of them is not a nickel.

That last phrase is kind of ambiguous. She didn't say "neither of them are nickels." So . . . what if one is not a nickel, but the other one is?

"A dime and a nickel?" I say, tentatively. "Because the other one is a nickel?"

"Okay. You passed the test. So you can continue," she says, smiling.

This is a relief. Because Tanya is a fascinating character. She is a Russian émigré who is now a lecturer at MIT. She writes a popular blog about the world's twistiest math and logic puzzles (it's called, simply, *Tanya Khovanova's Math Blog*). And she has cracked pretty much every great math puzzle ever created. We're talking coin puzzles, matchstick-arranging puzzles, river-crossing puzzles, math equation puzzles.

Tanya is on a mission. "I am very upset at the world," she says. "There is so much faulty thinking, and puzzles can help us think better."

Consider probability, she says. We are terrible at thinking probabilistically, and puzzles about odds can help us learn. They could teach us, for instance, the folly of playing the lottery. "The situation is unethical. I think that lottery organizers should spend part of the money they make on lotteries to educate people not to play the lottery."

Tanya has been fascinated with math since her childhood in Moscow.

"The first thing that I remember, it wasn't a puzzle, it was an idea. I remember that I was five years old and we were on a vacation in a village, and I was trying to go to sleep and I was thinking after each number there is the next number, and then there is the next number. At some point, I realized that there should be an infinity of numbers. And I had this feeling like I'm touching infinity, I'm touching the universe, just a euphoric feeling."

Being a female Jewish math genius in 1970s Soviet Russia was not easy. She faced sexism and anti-Semitism. Tanya says the test for the prestigious Moscow State University—the Soviet equivalent of MIT— was rigged against Jews. Jewish students were given a separate and more difficult test. The problems were called "coffin problems," which translates to "killer problems." Tanya studied with other Jewish students and managed to pass the unfair test.

In 1990, Tanya left Russia. She moved to the United States and married a longtime American friend. She worked for a defense contractor near Boston but hated it because "I thought it destroyed my karma." She started teaching as a volunteer at MIT before they hired her as a full-time lecturer.

Her philosophy: puzzles should be used more often in teaching math. First of all, they entertain us while educating us how to think rigorously. And second, puzzles can lead to genuine advances in mathematics—topics such as conditional probability and topology were originally explored in puzzle form.

MATH PUZZLES 1.0

The very first math puzzles—at least according to some scholars—date back to Egypt's Rhind Papyrus, about 1500 B.C.E. They're closer to problems than puzzles, since they don't require much ingenuity. But the unnamed author did try to spice them up with some whimsical details, such as in Problem 79.

> **Problem 79.** *There are seven houses.*
> *In each house there are seven cats.*
> *Each cat kills seven mice.*
> *Each mouse has eaten seven grains of barley.*
> *Each grain would have produced seven hekat (a unit of*
>   *measurement).*
> *What is the sum of all the enumerated things?*

(For solution see page 305.)

Arguably the first book with actual twisty and turny math puzzles came several centuries later. The ninth century Holy Roman Emperor Charlemagne was a puzzle addict, and he hired a British scholar named Alcuin of York to be his official puzzlemaker. Alcuin's book *Problems to Sharpen the Young* introduced, among other things, the first known river-crossing problem. Here it is:

> *A man has to transport a wolf, a goat, and a bunch of cabbages across a*
> *river. His boat could take only two of these at a time. How can he do this*

without leaving the wolf alone with the goat (as he might eat it), or the goat alone with the cabbages (as it might eat them)?

(For solution see page 305.)

By the way, this problem launched a thousand river-crossing variations. Depending on the era and place, river crossings have replaced the goat, cabbage, and wolf with jackals, geese, and bags of beans. Some versions feature lecherous men and innocent women, while others are disturbingly colonial, with missionaries and cannibals.

For river-crossing problems, you need to realize that you must take a counterintuitive step backward before continuing forward. You must think outside the box.

WAY OUTSIDE THE BOX

Tanya reminds me that "thinking outside the box" wasn't always a cliché. The origin of the phrase is an actual puzzle: Connect all the dots in this diagram using just four straight lines:

• • •

• • •

• • •

The answer:

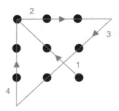

Nowadays the phrase is overused and is often a punchline, as in the cartoon of the cat thinking outside its litter box. But it's still an important concept: to find a solution, you often have to break expectations.

"My students have taught me as much as I have taught them about this," she says.

"How do you mean?" I ask.

She tells me to think about this puzzle: "You have a basket containing five apples. You have five hungry friends. You give each of your friends one apple. After the distribution, each of your friends has one apple, yet there is an apple remaining in the basket. How can that be?"

The traditional answer is: you give four friends an apple, and then hand the fifth friend the basket with the apple still in it. So each friend has an apple, and there's still one in the basket.

"For that answer, you have to think out of the box," says Tanya. "But my students have come up with answers that are even farther out of the box."

Their suggestions include:

One friend already has an apple.
You kill one of your friends.
You are narcissistic and you are your own friend.
The friend who didn't get an apple stops being your friend.
An extra apple falls from the tree to the basket.
And Tanya's favorite: The basket is your friend. We should not
    discount people's emotional connection with inanimate objects.

"The lesson my students taught me is that I'm good at thinking outside the box. But I realized, I'm inside my own bigger box. And maybe we all are."

HOW TO SOLVE PROBLEMS

But how do you get yourself to think outside the box? How do you approach a math problem? I know how to start a jigsaw puzzle (the edges, usually) and a crossword (look for plurals and fill in the Ses). But how do you approach a math problem?

After talking to Tanya and another great math puzzle expert, Dartmouth professor Peter Winkler, I've come up with a list of tools for math and logic problems. Here are three of my favorites.

1) Reverse it.

When confronted with a problem, try reversing it. Turn it upside down.
Sometimes quite literally, turn it upside down.
Such as this problem:

What number belongs in the blank in this sequence:

16 06 68 88 __ 98

(It's 87. Turn the page upside down to see why.)

There are other puzzles that require you to reverse your thinking in a slightly less literal way. Like this one (wording adapted from *Of Course!* by Zack Guido):

> A man is imprisoned in a ten-foot by ten-foot by ten-foot room. The walls are made of concrete, the floor is made of dirt, and the only openings are a locked door and a skylight. The man has a small shovel and starts to dig a hole in the floor. He knows that it is impossible to tunnel out of the prison cell, but he continues to dig anyway. What is the man's plan?

Pause here if you want to figure it out yourself.

The solution is: The man wasn't just digging a hole. He was also doing the opposite: building a little mountain of dirt. And his plan was to climb the mountain and get to the skylight.

I love reversing my thinking. Earlier this week, I was cleaning up the trail of clothes left by the males in our family (including me) that littered our apartment. I picked up an armload of clothes, then went to the hamper in my bedroom and dumped the clothes, then went back out. But wait. What if I . . . took the hamper with me. If I bring the hamper to the clothes. I'd save myself several trips. As Will Shortz once suggested, I took a bow.

2) Figure out the *real goal.*

One of my favorite brainteasers comes from Martin Gardner, who wrote a famous monthly column about math puzzles in *Scientific American* for three decades, starting in 1957. He died in 2010, but he still has tons of devotees, hundreds of whom attend a biannual event, the Gathering 4 Gardner, where they talk puzzles, paradoxes, and the genius of Martin.

Martin posed this puzzle in his book *Entertaining Mathematical Puzzles:*

> Two boys on bicycles, 20 miles apart, began racing directly toward each other. The instant they started, a fly on the handlebar of one bicycle started flying straight toward the other cyclist. As soon as it reached the other handlebar, it turned and started back. The fly flew back and forth in this way, from handlebar to handlebar, until the two bicycles met.
>
> If each bicycle had a constant speed of 10 miles an hour, and the fly flew at a constant speed of 15 miles an hour, how far did the fly fly?
>
> Pause here if you want to try it yourself, spoilers ahead.

So how to solve this? Most people's first instinct—including mine—is to trace the back-and-forth path of the fly and try to add up the distance.

With this method, you'd try to calculate the distance from Biker 1's handlebars to Biker 2's handlebars. Then the fly would make a U-turn, so you'd calculate the next distance, from Biker 2 to Biker 1. And so on until the bikes met.

This turns out to be a highly complex computation involving the speed of the bikers, the speed of the insect, and time and distance. The operation is called "summing an infinite series."

This calculation is impossible to do in your head. Well, practically impossible. Legend has it that the brilliant Hungarian mathematician John von Neumann was once asked this brainteaser at a party, and, to the amazement of the quizzer, gave the correct answer by summing the infinite series in his head, no calculator needed.

20 miles

At the start, the fly is on Bike 1.

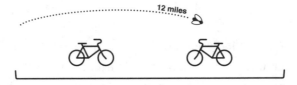

12 miles

After 48 minutes, the fly reaches Bike 2. It has flown 12 miles.
It then turns around.

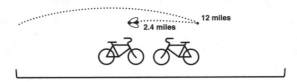

12 miles
2.4 miles

At 57.6 minutes, after a 2.4-mile flight, the fly lands back on Bike 1. The fly has flown a total of 14.4 miles. Then it turns around again, and so on.

Von Neumann was too smart for his own good. If he had paused for a moment, he might have realized there's a much easier way to solve this problem.

Which brings me back to the strategy: What is the real goal?

You want to phrase the problem in the simplest possible way. Strip the problem to its basics, and you'll realize you are looking for one thing: the distance the fly can fly in an allotted amount of time.

You can ignore the fly's back and forth switch of directions. You can ignore the handlebars. They're irrelevant. You just need to know how far the insect can go in the time it takes the bikes to meet.

Which turns out to be a pretty easy calculation:

If each bike was going at 10 miles per hour, and they were 20 miles apart, then it would take the bikes one hour to reach each other.

So the fly was buzzing around for one hour. What is the distance the fly can cover in one hour? Well, it's going 15 miles per hour. So the answer is fifteen miles.

We often complicate problems when there's an easier method right in front of us. I think this is true in more than just math puzzles.

I'm not sure if this is exactly analogous, but it's staring me in the mirror, so let me tell you about one example. Recently, I was faced with the puzzle of how to cut my own hair. During quarantine, I couldn't go to the barber, and Julie claimed she wasn't qualified. I had to do it myself using YouTube tutorials.

My first attempt to cut my own hair had mixed results. The front turned out okay, but the harder-to-reach back of my head was a disaster, filled with uneven patches.

So I paused. I rephrased the problem. The goal is not to cut my hair flawlessly. The goal is to look respectable on Zoom. And on Zoom, no one ever sees the back of my head.

So the simplest solution: Just cut the front of my hair and leave the back alone to grow wild and free. Puzzle solved! Though for the first time in my life, I have a mullet.

3) Make it small.

If you google "What is the hardest logic puzzle ever?" you'll get a stumper about a green-eyed guru and a bunch of islanders with blue and brown eyes. Well, you'll get that and several other riddles. There are a handful of contenders for "hardest logic puzzle," but the islanders puzzle is my favorite. (The Three Gods Puzzle by Raymond Smullyan is another contender, and definitely worth a google if you're a glutton for this stuff.)

I first learned of the green-eyed guru puzzle not on the Internet but from my cousin Douglas during a family reunion a few months ago. The puzzle wasn't so good for my relationship with my relatives. I spent much of the reunion muttering to myself and drawing pencil diagrams instead of catching up with Aunt Kate's stories of her grand-kids. But I couldn't resist.

Here it is (this wording is courtesy of Randall Munroe, creator of xkcd comics):

> A group of people with assorted eye colors live on an island. They are all perfect logicians. No one knows the color of their own eyes. Every night at midnight, a ferry stops at the island. Any islanders who have figured out the color of their own eyes then leave the island, and the rest stay. Everyone can see everyone else at all times and keeps a count of the number of people they see with each eye color (excluding themselves). They cannot otherwise communicate.
>
> On this island there are 100 blue-eyed people, 100 brown-eyed people, and the Guru, who happens to have green eyes. So any given blue-eyed person can see 100 people with brown eyes and 99 people with blue eyes (and one with green), but that does not tell him his own eye color; as far as he knows the totals could be 101 brown and 99 blue. Or 100 brown, 99 blue, and he could have red eyes.
>
> The Guru is allowed to speak once (let's say at noon), on one day in all their endless years on the island. Standing before the islanders, the Guru says the following:
>
> "I can see someone who has blue eyes."
>
> Who leaves the island, and on what night?

My first reaction: What?

How could anyone leave the island based on such scant informa-tion? It'd be like figuring out the GDP based on one woman's pur-chase of a grapefruit.

But it turns out to be solvable. (If you want to try it yourself, pause here—spoilers ahead.)

The puzzle has been around for decades, though it's not clear who came up with it first. It's part of an odd but long-standing puzzle genre: non-talking people who have to figure out something about themselves. Sometimes these puzzles are about people wearing col-ored hats. Sometimes they're about kids with muddy faces.

But it's always the same idea: You need to figure out what *other* people know about you. It's actually related to an important concept in game theory called "common knowledge," and it has implications for everything from business strategy to voting patterns.

When my cousin told me this puzzle, I was at a loss. I didn't know where to start. And then, inadvertently, I cheated. I overheard Douglas whispering to another one of my cousins: "Yeah, you have to scale it down."

I pretended I didn't hear so as to seem smarter than I was, but that phrase was the breakthrough.

What if I reduced the puzzle to the simplest version? What if the island had just two people: the green-eyed Guru and one blue-eyed islander—let's call her Sapphire.

In that situation, what night would Sapphire leave? Well, Sapphire would see there's no one else on the island, so when the Guru says, "I see someone with blue eyes," that had to be Sapphire. She realizes she has blue eyes! She leaves on the ferry the first night.

Okay, that was easy. Now imagine if the island has just three people: The green-eyed Guru and two blue-eyed people, Sapphire and Cyan. The green-eyed Guru would say, "I see someone with blue eyes." Sapphire would look at Cyan and see that Cyan has blue eyes. So Sapphire figures the Guru could be referring to Cyan's blue eyes. Sapphire has no info about her own eye color. Could be blue, could be brown.

Now switch to Cyan's point of view. She has the exact same chain of reasoning about Sapphire.

So neither of them leaves the island that first night.

Sapphire and Cyan wake up the next morning—and see that they are both still on the island.

Aha! They now have new information.

Sapphire can now deduce that her own eyes are blue. Why? Well, she simply has to look at the situation from Cyan's point of view. If Sapphire's eyes were brown, Cyan would have known the Guru was seeing Cyan's blue eyes. Cyan would have known her own eyes were blue, and she would have left the island.

And vice versa for Sapphire's point of view. On the second day, Sapphire also knows that her own eyes are blue; otherwise, Cyan would have caught the ferry.

On that second night the ferry comes, and both Sapphire and

Cyan get on board. The answer to this version of the riddle is: both islanders leave on the second night.

Now, scale it up to a situation where there's the Guru and three blue-eyed islanders, Sapphire, Cyan, and Beryl. I'm not going to go through it here, but the result is analogous: all three leave on the third night.

They all have reached conclusions by observing how the other women acted. Now here's the crazy part: if you keep scaling it up to 100 blue-eyed islanders, the same reasoning holds.

All 100 blue-eyed islanders leave on the one hundredth night.

The lesson is: Break the problem down. Miniaturize it. Tackle parts instead of the whole. I use this problem-solving strategy often in my real life. Take the puzzle of how I can get my lazy butt to walk the treadmill for a few minutes a day. If I say to myself, "You have to walk on the treadmill for an hour today," I will delay this task forever. So I break it down. I put the big picture out of my mind. First, I tackle the subgoal of putting on my sneakers. I can do that. Then the subgoal of turning the treadmill on. I can do that. And step onto the rubber belt for just five minutes. I can do that. And eventually, I'm walking and realize this isn't so bad. I can do this. I stay on for the full hour.

But I love the blue-eyed problem for another reason. It's a crash course in perspective-taking, in seeing the world from someone else's point of view. Which to me is an absolutely crucial skill, especially in these times of heightened tribalism.

Nine Math and Logic Puzzles from History

1) Matchsticks have been a puzzle staple since the 1800s. Here is one from *The Moscow Puzzles* by Boris A. Kordemsky (1956), the most popular puzzle book in the history of the Soviet Union.

Correct the equation by shifting just one match.

2) Kinship-themed puzzles have also been around for centuries. Here's a classic:

> Two girls were born to the same mother, on the same day, at the same time, in the same month and year, and yet they're not twins. How can this be?

3) And here's another kinship puzzle from Lewis Carroll:

> The Governor of Kgovjni wants to give a very small dinner party, and invites his father's brother-in-law, his brother's father-in-law, his father-in-law's brother, and his brother-in-law's father. Find the [minimum] number of guests.

4) Kobon Fujimura was the most famous puzzlemaker in Japan in the decades before his death in 1983. This is one of my favorites from his book *The Tokyo Puzzles:*

THE MISSING YEN

Three men stayed at an inn. Their bill was 30,000 yen and each guest put up 10,000 yen. The money, along with the bill, was taken to the cashier by the maid.

In the meantime the inn, as a token of goodwill, had reduced the amount of the bill by 5,000 yen. From the balance of 5,000 yen the maid took 2,000 and returned only 3,000 to the men. They split this three ways, so each man received a refund of 1,000 yen. Since each paid 10,000 yen and received 1,000 yen he spent 9,000 yen.

Each man paid 9,000 yen, so that the total spent by all three was 27,000 yen. The maid took 2,000 yen. These two amounts add up to 29,000 yen. What happened to the remaining 1,000 yen?

5) One type of logic puzzle—often called Fermi problems—provides excellent training for solving some real-life problems. A Fermi problem is one like this: "How many piano tuners are there in New York City?" You have to estimate the size of something about which you are totally ignorant.

If you just take a wild guess without reflecting, you'll probably be off by orders of magnitude. Instead, as David Epstein explains in the psychology book *Range: Why Generalists Triumph in a Specialized World,* the best method is to break the problem down into parts you can reasonably estimate.

As Epstein writes: "How many households are in New York? What portion might have pianos? How often are pianos tuned? How long might it take to tune a piano? How many homes can one tuner reach in a day? How many days a year does a tuner work?"

You won't guess it exactly, but you'll be much more likely to be in the ballpark. As Epstein writes, "None of the individual estimates has to be particularly accurate in order to get a reasonable overall answer."

Epstein calls it an important tool in his "conceptual Swiss Army knife." I too find it helpful when reading statistics from dubious media sources, or listening to wild cocktail party speculation. For starters, try this sample Fermi problem:

How many rolls of toilet paper would it take to cover the state of Texas?

6) A staple of escape rooms nowadays, liquid measuring problems date back at least four hundred years. One of the earliest is from a 1633 book by Henry van Etten with the search engine–optimized title: *Mathematical Recreations; or, a Collection of Sundrie Problemes Extracted out of Ancient and Modern Philosophers, as Secrets in Nature, and Experiments in Arithmetick, Geometry, Cosmography, Horologography, Astronomy, Navigation, Musick, Opticks, Architecture, Statick, Mechanicks, Chemistry, Waterworks, Fireworks &c. Not Vulgarly Made Manifest Until This Time, Fit for Scholars, Students, and Gentlemen, that Desire to Know the Philosophical Cause of Many Admirable Conclusions:*

How do you split a vessel which is full of 8 pints of wine into two equal parts using only two other vessels containing 5 pints and 3 pints?

(Thanks to William Hartston's *A Brief History of Puzzles* for unearthing this one.)

7) Cake-cutting (or pie-cutting or pizza-cutting) problems are a genre that can get surprisingly complex, sometimes necessitating higher math. Here's a classic that doesn't require calculus:

You have a birthday cake and have to cut it into 8 equal pieces by making only 3 cuts.

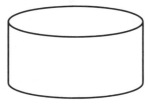

8) Some of my favorite puzzles ever were created by my then-four-year-old son, Lucas, who would play "Which one doesn't belong," but only give me a choice of two objects. "Which one doesn't belong: a baseball or a lamp?" If I said baseball, Lucas would tell me it was a lamp. And vice versa. I admired his surrealist take.

A few years later, my son's sixth-grade math teacher, Inanna Donnelley, gave her students which-one-doesn't-belong puzzles that were just as innovative. In these puzzles, there are multiple correct solutions. For instance, in the example below, 8, 10, 12 doesn't belong because it's the only set of numbers that doesn't fit into a Pythagorean equation.

But you can also make an argument for any of the other sets. Many in the puzzle world consider a problem with multiple solutions to be broken. But I embrace the idea as an exercise in creativity.

3, 4, 5	6.9, $\sqrt{84.64}$, 11.5
8, 10, 12	5, 12, 13

9) Logician and puzzle legend Raymond Smullyan created a genre called "Knights and Knaves Puzzles" in his 1978 book, *What Is the Name of This Book?* These puzzles take place on an island where there are two types of people: knights, who always tell the truth, and knaves, who always lie.

Here is one of the least confusing examples—and yet it's still confusing:

On the island of knights and knaves, you meet two people on the road. The first one says, "We are both knaves."
What are they?

Solutions to Nine Math and Logic Puzzles from History begin on page 305.

(9)   *Ciphers and Secret Codes*

I have infiltrated the CIA headquarters in Langley, Virginia, on a top-secret mission.

Okay, "infiltrate" might be an exaggeration. I spent several weeks getting permission from the CIA media relations department. I underwent a thorough background check. I am accompanied by several CIA officers at all times. Also, I'm being followed by a TV crew for a segment that will air when my book comes out.

So I'm not quite Jason Bourne. But still, I have made it inside the CIA headquarters, and I am, in fact, on a mission. My fellow sleuths—whom I've never met in person—have instructed me to observe everything. Look for anything suspicious. Be vigilant about the play of shadows, unusual magnetic activity, and patterns in the floor tiles. My mission is to discover clues to help solve a decades-old mystery. I'm on a quest to decode Kryptos.

For those who don't know, Kryptos is one of the most famous unsolved puzzles in the world. In 1988, the CIA commissioned a Maryland-based artist named Jim Sanborn to create a sculpture for its expanding headquarters. The agency wanted to install some art that would be relevant to its mission of cracking secrets. Sanborn's sculpture, Kryptos (Greek for "hidden"), was unveiled in 1990, located in a courtyard abutting the CIA cafeteria.

Kryptos is a wavy wall of copper about twenty feet long and twelve feet high. Into the copper, Sanborn has carved about eighteen hundred seemingly random letters and four question marks. It's a code, a secret message. No one knows the solution except Sanborn and possibly the former director of the CIA (Sanborn has hinted he didn't tell the director everything). Thirty years later, the code has not been fully cracked—even by the CIA itself. There Kryptos remains, right in the CIA's backyard, silently taunting the agents.

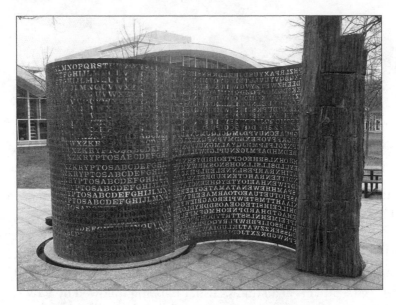

Granted, it has been partially cracked. In the '90s, government codebreakers from the NSA and CIA, as well as amateur puzzlers, independently solved three of the four sections. When decoded, the first section of the sculpture contains a mysterious sentence from Sanborn about "subtle shading and the nuance of illusion." The second section contains what seem to be GPS coordinates and hints that something is buried. The third section is a paraphrase of archaeologist Howard Carter describing his experience in 1922 of peering through an opening to discover King Tut's tomb.

But the fourth section—called K4 by fans—remains opaque. It's just ninety-seven letters, but they are perhaps the most exasperating ninety-seven letters ever written:

OBKR
UOXOGHULBSOLIFBBWFLRVQQPRNGKSSO
TWTQSJQSSEKZZWATJKLUDIAWINFBNYP
VTTMZFPKWGDKZXTJCDIGKUHUAUEKCAR

Over the last ten years, most recently in 2020, Sanborn has given tantalizing hints to K4. He has revealed that K4 contains the words "Northeast," "Berlin," and "Clock." But as this book goes to press, K4 remains unbroken.

"It's funny to look back now," says CIA historian Randy Burkett. "When [the CIA was] going to announce Kryptos to the world, there was an internal memo that said, 'Maybe we should give our own employees a head start on how to solve this puzzle.' They thought a two-day head start would be good enough. And thirty years later we still don't have the whole thing."

When I started researching this book, I joined an online community of thousands of Kryptos obsessives. Several times a week, I get messages about the latest theories. Maybe the code is related to Egyptian hieroglyphics? Or Dante's *Inferno*? Or the Native American Ghost Dance? Or the strings on a guitar? Or the World War II Enigma machine? The theories are endless and endlessly creative.

There's also speculation about what comes after K4. Sanborn has said that even after all the sculpture's codes are solved, there will still be a further mystery. Perhaps a buried treasure? A combination to a safe? No one knows.

Sanborn is clever, but what I really love about the Kryptos phenomenon is the tenacity of the solvers. They're still going at it thirty years later. It's a diverse group—computer scientists, artists, doctors, professional cryptographers—all united by this quest. What grit! Well, some might call it an unhealthy obsession. But I prefer to see it as grit.

I once heard an interview with a professional mathematician who said that most days he'll work on a problem and make absolutely no progress. And he has to be okay with that, or he'd go insane.

I have moderate grit, but I'm in awe of this next-level grit. I need positive reinforcements along the path. I need to accomplish something every day, even if it's just writing a sentence fragment. These folks—they're the puzzling mindset at its best.

Despite its warm and fuzzy reputation, the CIA is not welcoming of your average tourist. Most solvers must try to decode Kryptos from photos and drawings and secondhand accounts of those who have seen it. But because I'm writing a book, I've been granted permission to visit. Perhaps being in its presence will yield new hints. Before my field trip, I post a message to the Kryptos community asking what they want me to look for. I get a barrage of requests, including:

Bring a compass and see if it behaves oddly.
Look for any shadows that are cast on the sculpture.
Look for odd-colored patches of grass.
Look for weird markings on the bottom of the statue.
Peer inside any nearby holes.*

On a summer Saturday, armed with my list, I pass through security and enter the CIA's main office building. Turns out it's a bit of a hike to get to Kryptos. The Langley compound is huge—and surprisingly serene. There are lawns, elms, and a koi pond. If not for the helicopter from the war in Afghanistan displayed near the parking lot, it might be mistaken for a high-end college campus.

Along with my escorts, I walk through the corridors, past the red telephone booth that was a gift from "your friends in Britain," past the paintings of famous moments in CIA history (for instance, the hostage rescue in Iran that inspired the movie *Argo*), past the Dunkin' Donuts in the cafeteria. It's the weekend, so the offices are virtually empty.

We finally arrive at some glass doors that lead to a courtyard with red patio tables and chairs. And there it is, in all its frustrating glory: Kryptos.

It's smaller than I expected. In my mind, I had somehow built it up to rival Stonehenge. But it's also prettier than I expected. The sculpture's undulating shape is almost relaxing, and the copper's oxidized green tinge makes it stately.

"Can I touch it?" I ask.

My tour guide—the historian Randy Burkett, friendly but strait-laced, in a black suit—nods yes. I run my hand over the carved-out letters. The copper is cold, despite the warmth of the day. Maybe it will relinquish its secrets to my touch, like when Spock puts his hands over someone's face. Sadly, there is no rush of images to my brain.

---

* Kryptos is actually a multipart sculpture. In addition to the main copper wall, Sanborn sprinkled smaller elements throughout the CIA grounds—including a pond and several granite slabs containing copper plates with Morse code on them.

"Got any clues?" I ask Randy.

"No clues here," says Randy. He's not a math or code guy. "I'm in the human intelligence business."

I continue my snooping. Maybe the whirlpool next to the sculpture holds the secret? Does the sound of the swooshing of the water have a pattern? Is apophenia rearing its head again?

MY KRYPTOS GURU

Before coming to the CIA, I did my research. My guide has been Elonka Dunin, who runs the most popular Kryptos website. Elonka is a professional game developer and management consultant, but outside of her day job, her true passion is ciphers and codes. She's written multiple books and articles on cryptography and is the inspiration for a character in a novel by *The Da Vinci Code* author Dan Brown (the character's name is Nola Kaye, a scrambled form of Elonka). A few years ago, she moved from Tennessee to the D.C. area for several reasons, but one of them was to be closer to Kryptos.

Elonka had an interest in codes from childhood, but this interest blossomed into a bigger part of her life after she solved a challenge at a hacker convention in 2000. Turned out she had a knack for it. She got even more motivated after 9/11.

"I was as enraged as everyone else by what had happened," says Elonka, whose cousin worked at the Pentagon but just happened to be out of the office that day. "I was wondering if maybe I could help with the war on terrorism, sort of like in England during World War II with Bletchley Park."

Elonka contacted the FBI and offered her services. She was invited to give a lecture on codes that terrorists might be using. This talk turned out to be popular and eventually got her an invitation to lecture at the CIA so she could see Kryptos in person. She says she hasn't cracked any terrorist codes, though of course she'd have to say that even if she had.

Through her website, Elonka gets emails, some intriguing, some less so. "I get a lot of emails that say, 'I've cracked part four.' I'm like, 'Great. Tell me what it is.' One person said, 'Well, if you take this letter, and that letter, it's my home address. It's proof that the government's watching me.'"

"What if it's all just a prank and there is no possible solution?" I ask Elonka. "Or what if Sanborn made an error and the code can't be solved?"

"I think it's real," she says, but it will require a new way of thinking. "The people with the big computers have tried to crack this for decades. It hasn't been cracked, so I think it's going to be someone who comes up with an idea out of left field and looks at it with a completely different perspective. Could be someone who is a gardener, or a chef, or maybe a kid."

SECRETS THROUGH THE AGES

Codes and ciphers hold an interesting niche in the puzzle world.* On the one hand, they make for entertaining puzzles. On the other hand, they play a role in shaping the world's fate.

Ciphers have been used in wartime communication at least since ancient Greece. In World War II, the Allies won in part because they cracked the Nazi cipher. And now, of course, secret codes are more relevant to our lives than ever. Your credit card, your bank account, cryptocurrency, passwords—all rely on codes and ciphers.

That's not to mention their role in millions of romances. Lovers have been writing to each other in secret codes for millennia. In Victorian times, British paramours would send each other encrypted messages via the classified ads in the newspapers (for an example see page 139). When Julie and I first started secretly dating at work, I'd send her coded messages to avoid the prying eyes of the IT depart-

---

* Technically, codes and ciphers are slightly different. According to *The Code Book* by Simon Singh, "a *code* is defined as substitution at the level of words or phrases, whereas a *cipher* is defined as substitution at the level of letters." If you say "The pigeon is in the nest" to mean "The spy has infiltrated the party," that's a code. A cipher is what Sanborn used in Kryptos. But most people use the terms interchangeably, as I do in this chapter.

ment. The subject line "Third quarter results" was my romantic code for "I love you."

The cryptology community loves ciphers, no matter the original purpose. There are websites devoted to cracking the mysterious notes left by the Zodiac serial killer from the 1960s and books about the tattoo symbolism used by Russian prisoners. There is a cottage industry around trying to decode the Voynich manuscript, a fifteenth-century treatise filled with odd symbols. Decoders work on diaries of historical figures, including the teenage diary of children's author Beatrix Potter. When decoded, Potter's diary contained such scandalous observations as her critique of the Michelangelo portrait at London's National Gallery. "I say fearlessly that the Michelangelo is hideous and badly drawn. No one will read this."

Should we feel guilty about decoding personal diaries? I'm not sure.

"Frankly, I don't care about the content," says Klaus Schmeh, another cryptology fan with a well-regarded blog called *Cipherbrain*. "It's about the joy of deciphering."

Over the millennia, humans have hidden information in an astounding variety of ways. The most famous code is probably the Caesar cipher, called that because legend has it that Caesar invented it. But my guess is he took credit from the real inventor, maybe a summer intern in the Roman army or something.

Chances are you've seen the Caesar cipher, perhaps on a restaurant's puzzle place mat for kids. The idea is to shift each letter of your message a fixed number of positions in the alphabet. For example, you could shift each letter three places to the right: A becomes D, B becomes E, C becomes F, and so on. The word HELLO becomes KHOOR. Since the letters are shifted three places, this version is called Caesar 3. Shift them four places, and it's called Caesar 4.

The Caesar is pretty easy to crack. But if you want to give it a confounding twist, you can use the Vigenère cipher. The Vigenère cipher uses several Caesar ciphers within the same message, along with a keyword that tells you which Caesar goes where. Kryptos uses the Vigenère cipher in its first and second messages (the keywords include "palimpsest" and "abscissa.") If this sounds confusing, that's kind of the point.

The third section of Kryptos uses a totally different but equally perplexing type of cipher: a transposition cipher. Transposition ciphers rely on a secret arrangement of the letters. For instance, here's a message written with a transposition cipher known as the zigzag cipher (or rail fence cipher).

TPTEBELEDPRPEADVADUTRPESSNHLADANSSAEE

The solution—or "plaintext," as it's called—is revealed only after you arrange the letters in a predetermined way and read them in a zigzag direction.

T				P				T				E				B				E				L				E				D				P
	R		P		E		A		D		V		A		D		U		T		R		P		E		S		S		N		H		L	
		A				D				A				N				S				S				A				E				E		

The message here is:

"Trapped at Dave and Buster's. Please send help."

So what method did Sanborn use in K4? It could be anything. Wikipedia lists 120 different ciphers—Bacon's cipher, the straddling checkerboard—and that's far from a comprehensive catalog.

THE ATTACK

With so many potential ruses, how do you even start to decode a code? You attack it. That's the violent metaphor of choice among cryptologists. Attack the code! Find the weak point! Exploit! There are tons of attack methods (if you want to read further, I recommend Elonka's book *Codebreaking: A Practical Guide,* which she co-wrote with the aforementioned Klaus Schmeh).

Elonka tells me the most important attack is "frequency analysis." This means noticing how often certain letters or symbols appear in the cipher. English has certain letters that are very common (E, S, R, for instance) and other letters that are used more rarely (X, J, Z). Suppose you are trying to crack a code where animals stand for letters. You might notice there are a ton of turtles, so you can make the guess that the turtle might represent an E, S, or R. It's probably not Z. You can take it a step further. Some letters appear frequently in combination (S followed by H, for instance) while others almost never appear (Q followed by F, for instance).

Little by little, you chip away. You look for repeating patterns. This holds for easy codes and complex ones alike. The Nazis' Enigma cipher in World War II was cracked using several methods, but one breakthrough came when the codebreakers noticed that many Nazi messages started with the same encrypted term at the top: the German word for "to." This led them to the phrase "Nothing to report."

Speaking of the Allied project to crack the Enigma code, it was a milestone in the development of the computer. Alan Turing—one of the great heroes of all time—invented an early version of a computer to run through thousands of possible combinations of the German cipher system. The collaboration between Alan Turing's computer and human observation was what enabled the Allies to break the Enigma messages.

The computer/human partnership continues to be powerful. In 2020, a new software program helped decode a note that the Zodiac serial killer sent to the police in the late 1960s. The program ran through 650,000 variations of the symbols. A cryptology enthusiast noticed one variation contained the phrases "hope you are" and "trying to catch me," and, working with two other enthusiasts, figured out the solution. The same software was used on Kryptos, but it revealed nothing.

INTERROGATING THE MAN HIMSELF

Before my Langley visit, Elonka gave me Jim Sanborn's email address, and he agreed to an interview. I call him on a summer day midquarantine. I was worried he'd be cranky, as some on the board warned, but he actually seemed open to talking—at least to a point.

I ask Sanborn what he thinks about Kryptos thirty years on. Sanborn has mixed feelings about his most famous work. On the one hand, he gets annoyed at the thousands of people pestering him for clues or hints. Some of them politely, some not so much. "I got threatening mail, threatening phone calls, weird packages left at my front porch that I had to open almost robotically." (Sanborn added that people have become better behaved over time.)

On the other hand, he's grateful that Kryptos continues to fascinate. "Frankly, the greatest satisfaction I get is that I have created an artwork which keeps on giving," he says. I ask if he hopes K4 will ever be cracked.

"Oh, I couldn't care less if it's cracked. I mean, I really don't want, I would rather it, you know, outlive me."

"Why have you given out clues, then?" I ask.

"To allow it to keep simmering."

It's true. When it's cracked, it's over. No more threatening emails, but also no more message boards devoted to Sanborn's conniving mind.

I ask Sanborn what it was like to create Kryptos. It wasn't easy, he says. He had to get lessons in cryptology from a retiring CIA agent. And as for the sculpting itself, "I went through fifteen different assistants, nine hundred jigsaw blades, and twelve Bosch jigsaws over two and a half years," Sanborn says.

I mention that the Kryptos solution so far contains a handful of misspellings, such as "iqlusion" instead of "illusion." Were those intentional, or just mistakes? Sanborn says some were included to make the code harder, but at least one was just a mistake. "There was nobody I could ask to proofread Kryptos."

I bring up the idea that there's a mystery to solve even after K4 has been cracked, and that one of his passages hints at something buried.

"What's in the treasure?" I ask.

He just laughs.

"Is it the poisoned cigar they sent Castro?"

"Yeah, that would be a good one. Why not?"

After I finish my interview, I transcribe it and send it off to Elonka. I apologize to her for not getting Sanborn to spill all the beans. Elonka sends me back the transcript with notes in the margin. She marks two passages as "important," two others as "very important," and one "HUGELY important."

I'm ecstatic. I feel like I've just gotten a good grade in elementary school.

The "hugely important" passage, by the way, is about how Sanborn studied different types of codes, including "codes that are woven into blankets in some countries in Africa." Maybe the blankets hint will be the key to cracking K4. Or maybe it's nothing.

I post the highlights of my interview with Jim on the Kryptos board. Some solvers, like Elonka, are encouraging. Others aren't so impressed. "He's so full of shit," one emails me. "Every story sounds like B.S. to me." It's fair to say that the Kryptos community has a love-hate relationship with Jim.

After my visit to the CIA, I once again post my observations on the Kryptos message board. They are deeply arcane, but that's the point. I write about the whirlpool abutting the sculpture, my compass going crazy when placed on a nearby magnetic stone, and the position of the bolts that run through the middle of Kryptos.

I get a bunch of emails back. The community is overall thankful, but they have more questions:

Did the whirlpool swirl clockwise, or were the waves random?

Do you think there could be a speaker or microphone hidden inside the drain, the metal box, or the hole in the granite?

I don't have the answers. I did my best, but I obviously didn't observe closely enough.

I decide to contact Sanborn one final time. It should be noted that Sanborn is not just a talented artist, he's also an astute businessman. A few years ago, Sanborn got annoyed that he was wasting so much time responding to emailed guesses, so he instituted a new rule. You can send him a guess, and he will send you a short response telling you if you're right or wrong. For that, you pay him $50.

I'm jealous. Fifty bucks for a sentence or two. That's an enviable rate for a writer. Others in the Kryptos community aren't fans of the $50 charge. On the message board, some K4 solvers call this rule "tacky" and accuse Sanborn of a scam.

I send in $50 via PayPal and submit my guess, which is just that—a guess. My method was more impressionistic than scientific: I tried to enter the mind of Jim Sanborn and come up with something in his voice. My guess is:

"Took you long enough. Two steps Northeast of the coordinates. Face seven pm on Berlin clock. Walk twelve steps. Dig. Enjoy!"

I see it as a lottery ticket, a 1 in a 4 billion chance these are the right letters.

A few days later, I get my answer. Jim thanked me for the money, but "unfortunately it's not the decrypt." Not the wisest $50 I've spent in my life, but it felt oddly satisfying to take my shot.

Four Ciphers and Secret Codes from History

1) Victorian love ciphers

In the late 1800s, British paramours sent each other coded messages via classified ads in the newspapers. They are compelling and voyeuristic reads. Some are like heartbreaking short stories, such as this deciphered one from 1869:

Papa has arrived. Knows all. I refused your name. Fearful scene. Proposed. Accepted. Should we ever meet, Remember, utter strangers. Don't write, unsafe. Pity and forget me. Farewell forever.—Greenwich.

Or this one from 1856:

I have the most beautiful horse in England, but not the most beautiful lady. Your silence pains me deeply. I cannot forget you.—M

You can read many more in the book *The Agony Column Codes & Ciphers* by Jean Palmer. Here's an 1886 message for you to decipher:

A.B. to M.N.—Tn dvcr trw rhtn yltcfrp drtln yln srsd t s uy dn trw t uy.

2) Newspaper cryptograms

Ben Bass is the official cryptogrammist for *The New York Times*. His cryptograms, which appear twice weekly in the printed version of the paper, began during the early months of the pandemic. With no concerts or Broadway shows to cover, the *Times*'s arts section needed to fill pages. Puzzles came to the rescue. Will Shortz asked Ben—a lawyer who has written cryptograms for *The Enigma*—if he could hire him to create ciphers for the *Times.* "I felt like a winning lottery ticket landed in my lap," Ben says. "I would have paid *them!*" (Ben tweets puzzle-related thoughts at @BenBassBeyond.)

a) PAPYIP CY OKB JZAG YOPOB DKJYB ZPUB QPZ TB OGWBH JZ JZB VJD JX P IBGTJPVH.

b) VNWU CYMFB'I YFTNQ "JA BMW'L WAAB WM ABPQZLNMW" NI Z IAYC-BACAZLNWK ZTKPDAWL.

c) RWKW JYUWP PQEZQ JFQTP RWKW JYUWP PQEZQ JFQTP, KAORZ IYVE PQEZQ JFQTP FQEW. VRQZ QKW ZRW YIIP?

d) UXJMUX PKGCNVUQJV'G LJJTA XUUVJU MXINYX NVIRFSXS QCNG NVGQMFIQNJV: "QKGQX EMXZFXVQRA."

3) Edgar Allan Poe's ciphers

Edgar Allan Poe was a lover of ciphers, and he included one in the plot of his short story *The Gold-Bug.* But he went further than that. He challenged his readers to stump him. In an 1840 article in *Alexander's Weekly Messenger,* a Pennsylvania newspaper, Poe boasted he could unlock any substitution cipher. Over the following months, Poe claimed to have solved one hundred reader-submitted ciphers—and he was hilariously cocky about it, saying, for instance, one gave him "no trouble whatever."

When Poe announced he was ending the challenge, he printed two additional ciphers from a reader. Poe claimed he had solved them—but never printed the solutions. It took cipher fans more than 150 years to crack, which they finally did in 1992 and 2000 (the results were pastoral passages about nature, "sultry" afternoons, and "delicious breezes," which I can't imagine the macabre Poe could have liked).

Here's an example of a reader's cipher that Poe solved for his newspaper column. Poe pointed out several mistakes made by the man who sent in the cipher—who identified himself only as "H." I've corrected as many mistakes as I could find.

850;?9

o   9?   9   2ad: as   385   n8338d—   ?†   sod—

3   —86a5:   —8x8537   95:   37od: o—   h—

8shn   3a

s9d?8d—   ?†   —og37   —8x8537

95: sod—3   o—   9   ?o—

67o8xah—   95o?9n   ?†   5o537   —8x8537   95:

sod—

3   o—   378   n9338d—   858?†   ?†   38537   —8x8537

95:   sod—

3   —h!!ad3—   nos8   ?†   sahd37   sos37   —8x8537

95:   —og37   o—   9   sdho3   ?†   sahd37   95:

8o;737   o—   9   !a28dshn

o?!n8?853   ?†   27an8   o5:o6938—   9   2o—8   ?95

4) The NASA code

The Mars *Perseverance* rover launched in July 2020 with several puzzles and ciphers on board. See if you can find the three-word message encoded on this aluminum plate:

Solutions to Four Ciphers and Secret Codes from History begin on page 307.

(10) *Visual Puzzles*

In the spring of 2020, *The Baltimore Sun* printed what might be the greatest correction in newspaper history:

The images in the "Spot the difference" feature in the Sunday, April 26, editions were mistakenly the same image and not in fact different. *The Baltimore Sun* regrets the error.

It turns out that the first illustration of the boy inexplicably over-joyed to be brushing his teeth is identical to the second illustration of the boy inexplicably overjoyed to be brushing his teeth.

When I first saw this correction on puzzle Twitter, I had a mix of emotions.

I felt terrible for the editor, who was no doubt ribbed by colleagues for months after. I pitied the exasperated would-be solvers. Imagine the hundreds of hours of mental energy that were spent looking for nonexistent differences. As one reader tweeted, this non-puzzle puzzle drove her "half-insane." It had to be the greatest waste of human labor since the search for the Holy Grail or your average Senate filibuster.

But I was also strangely thrilled by it. So much so that I printed it out and taped it to my wall. I'm not sure why. Maybe it's because it's so Kafkaesque. Maybe it's because, at least in my darker moments, I wonder if it might be a perfect metaphor for life. What if I spend the next thirty years searching for the meaning of existence only to discover on my deathbed that the universe is a juvenile prank? "Oops! Sorry! Forgot to mention, there is no meaning at all. It's all just the arbitrary motion of quarks!"

On the upside, not all visual puzzles send me into a spiral of nihilism. I'm actually a big fan of the genre. And, after looking at hundreds of visual puzzles, I've come up with my own not-so-scientific classification system. It seems to me that most visual puzzles fall into one of two buckets:

1) Hide-and-seek
2) Optical illusions

I like them both—partly because they are just plain fun. But partly because I think they both contain important lessons. Namely, don't trust your first impression. Eyewitness testimony is not always reliable. Our senses are imperfect and biased and can deceive us.

HIDE-AND-SEEK

Let's start with the first type of visual quiz, the hide-and-seek puzzle. It comes in many versions—"Spot the Difference," "What's Wrong with This Picture?," "Where's Waldo?" But the goal is always the same: discover the hidden or camouflaged object.

One of the founders of this genre—Waldo's artistic great-grandfather—was a sixteenth-century Flemish painter named Pieter Bruegel the Elder.

Bruegel specialized in elaborate crowd scenes with all sorts of hard-to-spot Easter eggs. My favorite Bruegel painting is called *Netherlandish Proverbs,* in which Bruegel has hidden 112 literal depictions of proverbs. Can you spot the image of a man in a river "swimming against the tide"? Or the knight with a knife clenched in his mouth, representing "armed to the teeth"?

Bruegel's Netherlandish Proverbs

Those idioms have rough equivalents in modern English. But many old Dutch sayings are unique to their time. The Dutch seemed particularly obsessed with scatological expressions. Bruegel's painting includes depictions of:

"Horse droppings are not figs" (meaning: don't be fooled by appearances).

"A man who eats fire will poop out sparks" (don't be surprised when a dangerous venture goes awry).

"They both poop from the same hole" (they are close friends).

"He poops on the world" (he despises everything).

You get the idea. I'm not an expert, but I'd wager *Netherlandish Proverbs* holds the record for most poop jokes in a Renaissance painting.

Bruegel was just one of many artists to create visual hunts. Another Renaissance painter, Carlo Crivelli, always hid a pickled cucumber in his paintings, with pickles floating above Jesus or lying at the feet of the Virgin Mary. The source of his pickle obsession is unknown, though I'm sure Freudian scholars have a few theories.

This genre continued to flourish for centuries. The nineteenth-century engravers Currier and Ives hid animals in their etchings. The 1872 image below contains an obscured horse, lamb, wild boar, and several human faces:

THE PUZZLED FOX.

As a kid, I spent many happy hours searching Al Hirschfeld's illustrations in *The New York Times*. He was famous for hiding his daughter's name, "Nina," in the folds of clothing or eyebrows of his celebrity drawings. The Meryl Streep image below has three hidden Ninas:

© The Al Hirschfeld Foundation.
AlHirschfeldFoundation.org

And then there's Waldo. In 1987, Waldo's black glasses and red-and-white-striped shirt appeared in their first picture book, hidden among crowds at the carnival and beach. The book was an immediate hit. Waldo—or Wally, as he's known in the United Kingdom—has spawned dozens of sequels, an animated show, a world record of 4,626 people dressed as Waldo in one place at an amusement park in Japan, and many parodies (such as the one pictured on this page).

Waldo's creator is British artist Martin Handford. Before Waldo, Handford did another hide-and-seek painting. It's the cover art for a 1981 album by the band the Vapors—and this painting isn't so kid-friendly: it's a crowd scene with a hidden assassin on the roof.

Waldo finds himself

I wanted to interview Handford about his art and Waldo's homicidal predecessor. But it turns out he is quite reclusive. As far as I can tell, he hasn't done an interview in decades. I briefly considered going to England to try to track him down, thinking it might be fun in a meta sort of way to search for Waldo's creator. *Where's Martin?* But I decided to respect his privacy.

I'm not particularly skilled at hunt-and-find visual puzzles, especially now. I've reached the age when, much to my kids' embarrassment, I need to hold the restaurant menu at arm's length while shining my smartphone flashlight on the words, which means hope for improvement is minimal.

Yet even though I'm no expert, I do enjoy them. They stretch a different mental muscle than crosswords or Sudoku, but still provide a solid aha moment, that good old dopamine rush. Maybe it's an evolutionary thing—our ancestors were wired to seek the berries hiding among the thickets.

"I call it the treasure hunt instinct," says my friend Noah Charney, an art historian who has written books about hidden symbols in paintings. "We have this desire to know things that are hidden or secret. If you put 'secret' or 'lost' in the title of a book, it will sell." (And Noah did just that: one of his books is called *The Museum of Lost Art*.)

But I think hide-and-seek puzzles might have an even bigger benefit than teaching us not to trust our first impressions. They encourage us to look more closely at the world. To admire the details. To notice. My previous book was all about gratitude, and I became a big fan of noticing. I wrote about my quest to notice while waiting in line at a coffee shop. "While waiting, I force myself to stash my smartphone in my pocket and actually notice my surroundings. The act of noticing, after all, is a crucial part of gratitude; you can't be grateful if your attention is scattered. Glowing indigo lamps the shape of doughnuts hang from the ceiling. That indigo light is lovely, I think to myself. You don't see enough indigo lamps."

Maybe when walking down the street, we should picture what's in front of us as a two-page spread in *Where's Waldo* and just relish the hundreds of glorious details. Who knows what we'll find?

APOPHENIA

For all the benefits of visual puzzles, there's a danger. A big one. It's the aforementioned apophenia, the tendency to see hidden things that are not there, to find a nonexistent pattern in the noise.

Visual puzzles are a perfect breeding ground for apophenia. Consider *The Da Vinci Code*. While I was writing this chapter, my kids and I watched the *The Da Vinci Code* movie, which features the best and nerdiest quote from any action movie ever. Tom Hanks says: "I have to get to a library, fast!" (He ended up using a phone instead, but still, library devotees everywhere should appreciate the sentiment.)

But the main reason I wanted to watch it was the visual puzzle element. The movie's (and book's) plot, as you might remember, centers on hidden symbols in paintings. There's a scene where the eccentric scholar character points out a series of hidden symbols in Da Vinci's *Last Supper*.

So is it true? Did Da Vinci really hide these messages?

"Most of what's in *The Da Vinci Code* is bullshit," says Noah, my art historian friend.

St. John is St. John, not a sneakily disguised Mary Magdalene, for instance. "John the Evangelist is traditionally shown beardless, so there's nothing mysterious going on here."

That said, Da Vinci might have hidden some less blasphemous nuggets in his paintings. He was, after all, a lover of riddles and backward writing.

"The arrangement of the bread rolls on the table actually does appear to be based on a musical score," Noah says. "And if you google this, you can even hear the music played, and it actually sounds like music appropriate to the era. So that one I do believe."

I wish the other *Da Vinci Code* secrets were true. Who doesn't love a cache of mysterious messages hidden for centuries? But Da Vinci conspiracy theorists are just overzealous searchers finding patterns in the noise, like medieval people who saw the man in the moon and thought he was real. That's the lure of apophenia.

I've battled apophenia for years. When I was ten years old, I spent a Saturday working on a "what's-wrong-with-this-picture" puzzle on the back of a cereal box. It was Smurf-themed cereal, now discontinued. You were supposed to find five things in the Smurf picture that didn't make sense, such as a telephone receiver that was a banana.

Well, I found ten things. For instance, the phone wasn't plugged into an outlet (this was long before 5G). I fired off a letter to the Smurf cereal maker asking if I could get any prize for going above and beyond, perhaps an annual supply.

I received back a note from the company. I don't remember the exact wording, but the message was:

Please stop bothering us, you little twerp, and just buy more of our product.

Which was a fair point.

Another encounter with apophenia came via a gorgeous picture book called *Masquerade,* which I mentioned in the introduction. I loved that book. It was published when I was eleven years old, and I spent many hours discovering nonexistent clues to the buried treasure.

For those who weren't similarly obsessed, *Masquerade* was a 1979 book by the British artist Kit Williams. It's a series of detailed and fantastical images—a man with rabbit ears and a violin, the Sun dancing with the Moon, and so forth. The paintings contained clues to the location of a real-life treasure buried somewhere in England: a golden rabbit about the size of a paperback book, insured for £100,000.

Well, it drove the world insane—or at least a certain portion of the world.

"Masqueraders dug up acres of countryside, traveled hundreds of thousands of miles, wrote tens of thousands of letters to Williams, and occasionally got stuck halfway up cliffs or were apprehended by police while trespassing on historic properties," as an article in the literary journal *Hazlitt* puts it.

I never went to England, but I did have my theories. That seagull means it must be on the coast!

At the time, Kit Williams told reporters that all the unexpected attention from *Masquerade* wrecked his life. People would knock on his door at 3 A.M. He got bags of letters and terrifying packages, such as a disembodied, blood-covered plastic hand.

But when I tracked down Kit and chatted with him on the phone, he seemed more bemused and mystified than angry. "People flew from all over, spent their life savings. It was a bit embarrassing. . . . One man wrote me seven thousand words a day. That's more than I ever wrote in my life!"

After two years of ransacked gardens, the rabbit was found. It was dug up in a park in the county of Bedfordshire near a monument of

Catherine of Aragon, underneath the tip of the shadow it casts at noon on the equinox.

The discovery itself was a little messy, since the man who found it apparently had gained inside information about the general location from an ex-girlfriend of Kit's.

But regardless, the great *Masquerade* hunt was over.

Or was it?

A British journalist devoted an entire book to the phenomenon called *The Quest for the Golden Hare,* and he writes:

"Tens of thousands of letters from Masqueraders have convinced me that the human mind has an equal capacity for pattern-matching and self-deception. While some addicts were busy cooking the riddle, others were more single-mindedly continuing their own pursuit of the hare quite regardless of the news that it had been found. Their own theories had come to seem so convincing that no exterior evidence could refute them."

What a scary insight into how we think! We are not always swayed by evidence. We spot a pattern, fall in love with it, and refuse to change. QAnon followers are basically obsessed Masqueraders but chasing a nonexistent cabal of cannibals instead of a golden rabbit.

Surely, I could write an entire book about armchair treasure hunts, but let me just tell you about one more, since I kind of got enmeshed in it.

This hunt was started by a 1982 book called *The Secret,* not to be confused with the woo-woo self-help megahit *The Secret,* which promises to make every five-foot-five-inch accountant an NBA superstar if he just visualizes it hard enough.

No, this *Secret* was created by a writer named Byron Preiss who buried twelve treasures around the United States and Canada—little boxes containing precious or semiprecious gems. He hid clues to the treasures in twelve paintings and twelve cryptic poems.

So far, three treasures have been found: one in Cleveland, one in Chicago, and, most recently, one in 2019 in Boston. That leaves nine for treasure hunters to obsess over.

And obsess they do—on websites, podcasts, YouTube channels, episodes of a reality show. Preiss died in a car accident many years ago, but thousands of fans still try to get inside his mind.

And things can get pretty heated.

There are hoaxes (people pretending to find a treasure) and trolls who are banned from forums. One *Secret* hunter agreed to email with me, so long as I didn't use his name, explaining: "While 99% of armchair treasure hunters are perfectly normal people, there are a few who are literally insane yet computer-literate enough to post on forums, harass people, etc."

I found this to be true. For instance, here's a message on Reddit: "It's a shame the people best equipped to find this treasure are clowns like you who can't pull your head out of your ass far enough to see the goddamn map in the goddamn painting."

After reading several such messages, I think 99 percent might be a bit optimistic.

One of the big names in the *Secret* quest goes by the handle "the Oregonian." He has a website where he dissects clues and gives his theories. I email him mid-quarantine and tell him that I'd like to find the New York–based treasure for my book. He responds that he can help. He believes he knows exactly where it is. He includes an eleven-page attachment dissecting the painting and the poem.

He explains that the painting—which is of a white-robed, long-haired figure floating above the ocean—has a hidden *74* in the ocean waves. This is probably the longitude of New York City.

The face on the hovering figure looks like the Statue of Liberty's, so that's another clue that it is buried within sight of the statue.

The poem has a line about New Yorkers speaking of an "Indies native." This likely refers to Alexander Hamilton, who was born in the West Indies. That, says the Oregonian, is a hint to a Hamilton-related location (the Oregonian asked me not to reveal said location in my book).

And on and on.

The final answer: the treasure is buried under a tree on a side street with some abandoned storefronts (again, he asked me not to reveal which borough).

The Oregonian admits that this sounds preposterous: "To anyone who hasn't spent some time studying *The Secret*, this solution is going to sound convoluted and ridiculous. And that's kind of the point. It IS convoluted and ridiculous. The brain of Byron Preiss worked in fairly mysterious ways."

So if the Oregonian knows where it is, why hasn't he dug it up?

Well, he doesn't want to go to jail. The tree is under the jurisdiction of the Parks Department. A few years ago, he got permission from the department to dig, but only if he hired an internationally certified arborist and used a power tool called an air spade—which he's never gotten around to doing. I said I might be willing to arrange the rental of the air spade. We contacted the Parks Department. They changed their mind—no digging allowed.

And yet . . . a few months later, the Oregonian emailed me that maybe he'd found a loophole? On the Parks Department's website, he spotted a note to New Yorkers who care about trees that it's important to loosen "the top few inches of soil with a hand cultivator to undo compaction."

"So . . . *maybe* you could bring a hand tool and dig a little ways?" the Oregonian wrote. He also suggested I bring marigolds and plant them to avoid suspicion. He'd do it himself, but he lives far away.

So on a Sunday, off I went on my secret horticultural mission with a shopping bag containing marigolds and a trowel. It took me nearly an entire day. I can report that one tree in New York now boasts a couple of lovely marigolds at its base, but I can also report that the *Secret* treasure is not buried under that tree—or at least it's more than four inches deep, which is as far as I felt comfortable digging.

OPTICAL ILLUSIONS

At this point in the chapter, you might have forgotten there's another type of visual puzzle: the optical illusion, an image that is not what it seems. With optical illusions, the puzzler has to try to figure out what's going on. How are your eyes being tricked?

Warning: in discussing optical illusions, I'm going to brazenly contradict myself, specifically my warnings about the dangers of over-interpreting, of finding deep meaning where none exists. Because I believe that optical illusions contain a hidden message about life. I don't think they are merely silly visual tricks but instead are profound metaphors for humanity's flawed thinking. They teach us not to trust our senses, that we are bad at accurately interpreting the world.

Apophenia be damned!

Consider two of my favorite optical illusions.

 You've probably seen this image before.

I've seen it many times. In fact, it's possible I've spent more time looking at this image than any other on earth. As a kid, I suffered from mild OCD and I had many strange rituals. Before going to sleep each night, I had a checklist of important projects to take care of:

1) Adjust the window shade four times.
2) Pick up the Quaker figurine I made in first grade and spin its hat 360 degrees.
3) Look at the silhouetted vase-and-faces image Scotch-taped to my bedroom wall.

I'd stare at that image on my wall for a minute each night, switching between perspectives. First I'd force myself to see the vase. Then the faces. Then the vase. Repeat eight times. It felt good, like I was accomplishing something, doing mental push-ups.

The face/vase illusion was created by Danish psychologist Edgar John Rubin, and it's an example of foreground/background illusions. The perspective-switch illusion comes in many varieties: Rabbit or duck? A wizened old lady or attractive young glamour girl? The letters *FedEx* or a white arrow?

But the message is always the same: What you see depends on how you approach the image. It's about your preconceptions. If you come to the image looking for a vase, you'll probably see the vase. If you're thinking about faces—maybe you just spent your afternoon working on a family photo album—you'll probably see the faces.

Our mental frames change the way we interpret the world. And that's why I think these optical illusions are such powerful metaphors for life. I've come to believe in the importance of frames and reframing. As with the vase and the face, there are often different ways to interpret the same situation.

If I'm feeling jittery before a speech, how do I interpret that? Fear or excitement? It's up to me. If I get patted down by the TSA at the airport, I could see that as an invasion of my bodily privacy. But what if I reframe it as a free massage? Okay, that one doesn't always work.

But there are a lot of studies that show the power of the frame you adopt. I just read one in which strangers play the prisoner's dilemma game with different results depending on how it was framed. People will act much more generously if you call it "the community game" than if you call it "the Wall Street game."

Below, you'll see my second favorite optical illusion:

Which black circle is bigger?

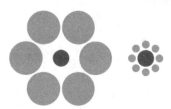

The answer to the puzzle is that both circles are the same size. The black circle on the left just appears to be smaller because the surrounding circles are so big and imposing.

The illusion was created by psychologist Hermann Ebbinghaus to show just how important context is. Our perceptions are not pure. They change depending on what we compare the object with. It's the visual representation of the phrase "It's all relative."

This is another one of my obsessions. It's one I try to impart to my kids, but with mixed success. If you have a problem, don't ignore it, but do try to put it into perspective. Maybe it is, in fact, huge. But maybe, if you take the thirty-thousand-foot view, it doesn't look as big.

I write a column for a magazine called *Mental Floss* with this thesis. It's called "The Bad Old Days." The idea is that, while we face tremendous challenges now, things were often not better in the past. In fact, they were usually much, much worse. Nostalgia for "the Good Old Days" is misplaced.

The column is basically an extended version of "When I was a kid, I had to walk eight miles uphill to school," but for all of history. I just finished a column about household chores. Yes, doing chores nowadays is a pain in the butt, I tell my sons. But imagine having to do laundry in Victorian England, which involved at least eight painstaking steps, as described by Bill Bryson in his book *At Home:* soak the laundry in smelly lye for several hours, pound it, scrub it, boil it, rinse it, wring it out, haul it outside, and bleach it. It was surprisingly violent work. You had to beat the dirt out of your clothes with wooden bats called "beetles."

Your experience is the black circle in the middle. You have the power to choose what other circles to compare it with.

Eleven Visual Puzzles from History

HIDDEN LOGOS

In the 1980s, there was a rumor that the old Procter & Gamble logo of a moon with stars contained hidden Satanic symbolism (the moon's beard hid a *666,* for instance). Of course, this was hogwash. But there are at least one hundred instances of corporations hiding much less controversial secrets in their logos. See if you can find the hidden images in these logos.

1)

2)

3)

4)

5)

6) The Missing Square puzzle

This puzzle is credited to magician Paul Curry, who created it in 1953. The white section in Triangle A has seven squares. The white section in Triangle B has eight squares. How can this be?

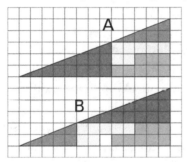

7) The Soviet camping puzzle

Here's a great visual puzzle given to Soviet students in the 1980s. The questions (translated) are below. A bigger version of this image can be found at thepuzzlerbook.com.

a) How many tourists are staying at this camp?
b) When did they arrive: Today or a few days ago?
c) How did they get here?
d) How far away is the closest town?
e) Where does the wind blow: From the north or from the south?
f) What time of day is it?
g) Where did Alex go?
h) Who was on duty yesterday? (Give their name)
i) What day is today?

BONGARD PROBLEMS

The four puzzles that follow are not your average spot-the-difference puzzles. They are called Bongard problems, and *Gödel, Escher, Bach* author Douglas Hofstadter wrote that "the skill of solving Bongard problems lies very close to the core of 'pure' intelligence, if there is such a thing."

The Bongard problems were invented by Russian computer scientist Mikhail Moiseevich Bongard in the 1960s. The idea is that the six diagrams on the left have a common factor, attribute, or pattern lacking in the six diagrams on the right. You have to figure out what that difference is.

One method to figuring this out is similar to the scientific method—you come up with a hypothesis and look for confirming and disconfirming evidence. The problems have been used in the development of artificial intelligence.

Here's a relatively trivial example. What is the difference between the left and right sides?

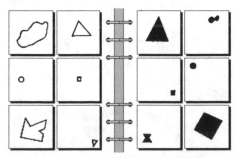

Answer: The shapes on the left are outlines, and those on the right are solid black.

Here are some more challenging Bongard puzzles.

8)

9)

10)

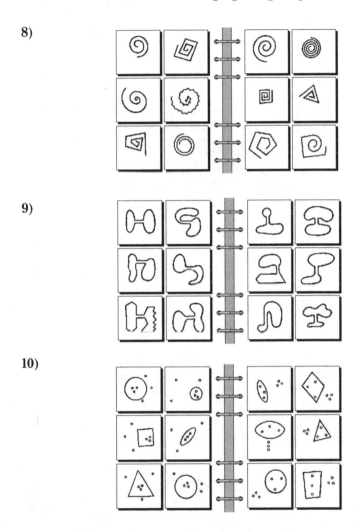

11) California-based scientist Elisabeth Bik spends her days playing a high-stakes version of spot-the-difference or spot-the-similarity. Bik is a crusader against scientific fraud. Apparently, some biologists insert duplicated or doctored images into their studies to make their data look more convincing. Bik's efforts have resulted in more than five hundred retractions. She shares them as puzzles on Twitter at @MicrobiomDigest. Here's one that is relatively easy: The

image purports to show four distinct cell colonies. But actually, there are only two distinct colonies. The other images are duplicates. Can you find the pairs that match?

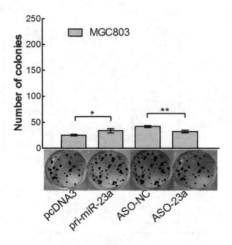

Solutions to Eleven Visual Puzzles from History begin on page 309.

Twisty puzzle designer Grégoire Pfennig with his record-breaking 33 × 33 × 33 cube PHOTO BY DANIELE ROVERSI

Thanks to 3-D printing, we are in the golden age of twisty puzzles, with a stunning variety of Rubik's-like stumpers. Above, a collection from Brett Kuehner (thatguywiththepuzzles.com). PHOTO BY BRETT KUEHNER

Early jigsaw puzzles often featured Biblical scenes or monarchs. Above is a nineteenth-century puzzle of British royalty. COURTESY OF THE BODLEIAN LIBRARIES, OXFORD UNIVERSITY

Modern jigsaws are usually not hand-carved. They are created using something resembling an elaborate cookie cutter. Jigsaw makers sometimes use the same die-cut pattern for different puzzles. Artist Tim Klein takes advantage of this fact to mash them together and create stunning original images. Here is his piece called "Iron Horse." COURTESY OF TIM KLEIN, PUZZLEMONTAGE.COM

German puzzler Peter Schubert spent months assembling a 54,000-piece jigsaw of great paintings throughout history—only to find out at the end that he was missing a piece. Luckily, after several weeks, he retrieved the missing piece from the manufacturer and finished his magnum opus (right). At left, a stack of sections Peter assembled before connecting the entire jigsaw at a community center (his home was too small to fit the puzzle in its entirety). PHOTOS BY DANIEL BAUER

Springbok puzzle company published this Jackson Pollock jigsaw in 1965, proclaiming it the World's Most Difficult Puzzle. COURTESY OF THE STRONG, ROCHESTER, NEW YORK

No offense to Jackson Pollock, but this is probably the most difficult puzzle: the $2,700 Olivia puzzle from Stave. There are 10,000 ways the pieces fit together, but only one is the correct solution with Olivia the octopus fitting entirely inside the reef. This is one of the 9,999 incorrect arrangements. COURTESY OF STAVE PUZZLES

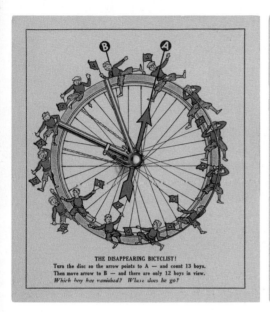

THE DISAPPEARING BICYCLIST!
Turn the disc so the arrow points to A — and count 13 boys.
Then move arrow to B — and there are only 12 boys in view.
Which boy has vanished? Where does he go?

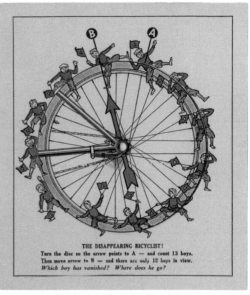

THE DISAPPEARING BICYCLIST!
Turn the disc so the arrow points to A — and count 13 boys.
Then move arrow to B — and there are only 12 boys in view.
Which boy has vanished? Where does he go?

You remember Sam Loyd, the brilliant but untrustworthy nineteenth-century puzzlemaster? One of Loyd's most famous illusions, which sold more than ten million copies, was called "Get Off the Earth." It was an illustration of the globe, with thirteen men dressed in stereotypically Chinese clothing. The drawing was on a disk that rotated a little bit. If you rotated it one way, one of the men disappeared. The image is racist, so I'm not going to print it here. But Loyd did create less offensive versions, including this bicycle-themed one.

Turn the disc so the arrow points to A—and count 13 boys.

Then move the arrow to B—and there are only 12 boys in view.

Which boy has vanished? Where did he go? (See answer on page 318.)

An early predecessor of Waldo: "The Netherlandish Proverbs" by Flemish painter Pieter Bruegel the Elder. Bruegel has hidden 112 literal depictions of proverbs, including "swimming against the tide." COURTESY OF CREATIVE COMMONS

Medieval and Renaissance art is replete with hidden symbols. The strangest, in my opinion, is the pelican, which is a symbol for Jesus. Some medieval bird scientists believed quite wrongly that pelicans were vengeful birds who ate their young. But they also believed pelicans would feel remorse three days later, and would tear open their own body and revive the baby pelican by feeding it their own blood. At the time, the pelican's alleged behavior was seen as a metaphor for Jesus's resurrection three days after his death. I'm pretty sure this is the weirdest bird-related belief I've ever encountered, not counting the idea that storks are somehow involved in human reproduction. Here's an example from the stained-glass window of an Italian church. COURTESY OF WOLFGANG MORODER

Artist Kit Williams's 1979 book *Masquerade* featured beautiful artwork with arcane clues to a buried treasure. It drove Britain mad. COURTESY OF KIT WILLIAMS

In 1986, artist Mike Wilks published perhaps the most elaborate visual hunt in history. His book, *The Ultimate Alphabet,* contains twenty-six paintings, one for every letter, each containing hundreds of objects that start with that letter. In total, there are 7,777 objects—with 1,234 alone for the letter S, pictured above. COURTESY OF MIKE WILKS AND POMEGRANATE COMMUNICATIONS, INC.

Japanese puzzle boxes are coveted items, with collectors paying as much as $40,000 for the elaborate wooden stumpers. Above is a gorgeous puzzle box called "Lotus" from designer Kagen Sound. COURTESY OF KAGEN SOUND

The Coffee Cup Puzzle Box from one of the pioneers in puzzle boxes, Akio Kamei. The top of the coffee is locked. Your job is to use the sugar cubes and spoon and ingenuity to open it up. COURTESY OF STEVE CANFIELD

Akio Kamei at work. IMAGE COURTESY OF KYODO NEWS/GETTY IMAGES

In YouTube videos watched by millions, magician Chris Ramsay opens puzzle boxes, including this one that cost $30,000. COURTESY OF CHRIS RAMSAY

Wei Zhang (pictured) and Peter Rasmussen
have a vast collection of Chinese puzzles,
including this puzzle jug from the Qing
dynasty, where the puzzle is how to drink or
pour without spilling; a hairpin nine-rings
puzzle, also from the Qing dynasty; and a
nineteenth-century set of tangram
dishes. COURTESY OF WEI ZHANG, PETER
RASMUSSEN, AND CLASSICAL CHINESE PUZZLE
FOUNDATION; TANGRAM AND NINE RINGS PHOTOS BY
NIANA LIU; JUG PHOTO BY GERMAN HERRERA

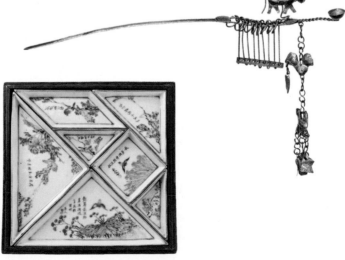

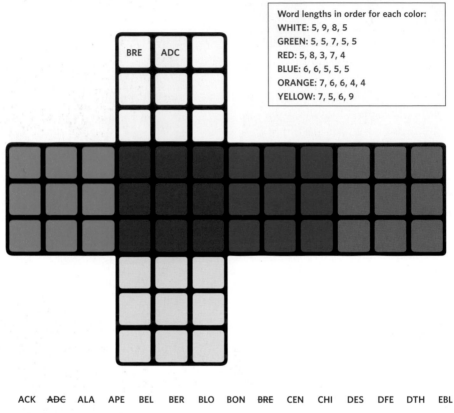

Word lengths in order for each color:
WHITE: 5, 9, 8, 5
GREEN: 5, 5, 7, 5, 5
RED: 5, 8, 3, 7, 4
BLUE: 6, 6, 5, 5, 5
ORANGE: 7, 6, 6, 4, 4
YELLOW: 7, 5, 6, 9

ACK	~~ADC~~	ALA	APE	BEL	BER	BLO	BON	~~BRE~~	CEN	CHI	DES	DFE	DTH	EBL
EHE	ELZ	ERW	EST	ETG	HAM	HAN	HAR	HOC	HOE	IAN	INE	INO	ITH	IZA
LAG	LEP	LIE	LIU	MAR	MCO	MER	NAC	NAM	NET	NGT	NTE	OLA	OON	OTH
OTT	RDW	RES	RNS	RRI	RYP	SPE	SSO	STO	SUB	SUE	SUR	TEE	TEY	TLA
TRH	UMB	UNT	VER	YJU										

Above is the color version of Greg Pliska's original puzzle Rubik's 3 × 3 × 3. The black-and-white version can be found on page 258. © GREG PLISKA

Sudoku and KenKen

Take a look at the Japanese logic puzzle below. What do you see? A colorless grid with a handful of numerals? Do you find it sterile, unemotional, about as transporting as a W-9 tax form? I know I did.

Tetsuya Miyamoto, the inventor of KenKen and creator of this puzzle, begs to differ. He sees a work of art.

"It's beautiful," he tells me one day on a video call from his Tokyo apartment. "It tells a story. It speaks to your heart." Miyamoto has created ten thousand handmade logic puzzles like this one. He believes each one is a unique gem, as gorgeous in its own way as the Renaissance paintings in the previous chapter.

Yes, computers can be programmed to spit out logic puzzle grids. In fact, most Sudokus and KenKens you find in newspapers are partly or totally machine created. But to Miyamoto, those are soulless shadows of the real thing. "Beethoven and Picasso cannot be replaced by a machine," he says.

Hmm. Might this be a bit of an overstatement? Is there really such a difference between a handcrafted and computer-made logic puzzle? I don't know for sure, but Miyamoto is far from the only true believer. I've talked to many Sudoku and KenKen fans who rave about the artistry of master logic puzzle creators. They talk about following gorgeous breadcrumb trails, and surprising twists, and the feeling of communing with the puzzler's mind.

Part of my quest in this chapter will be to see if they're right, and it's not just wishful thinking that humans are better than machines. I desperately want it to be true. I've watched the rise of artificial intelligence with a mixture of awe and terror. How long before computers can write quirky nonfiction books? How long before they can give my kids better fatherly wisdom?

After I talk to Miyamoto, he emails me a supersized 9-by-9 grid. "This is a very special KenKen," he writes. The hardest and most elegant ever created, his masterpiece, his Ninth Symphony.

MAGIC SQUARES

Before I attempt Miyamoto's opus, I dive into the surprisingly deep history of Japanese logic puzzles. The great-grandparent of these puzzles can be traced back at least to 190 B.C.E. in China. It's called the Magic Square, and according to the ancient myth, it was first found on the shell of a mystical turtle. Here's one of the first Magic Squares ever created:

16	3	2	13
5	10	11	8
9	6	7	12
4	15	14	1

As you can see, the "magic" part is that if you add up the digits in any row, they total the same number—in this case, 34. The columns going down do the same.

The Magic Square was thought to have supernatural powers. In ancient China, Magic Squares were carried around as good luck charms. Middle Easterners in the eleventh century believed they increased fertility. Centuries later, Ernest Shackleton's sailors in

Antarctica staved off the cold and boredom by creating Magic Squares. Ben Franklin was a fan of the form. When not founding the first American post office or inventing swim fins (look it up!), Franklin created, as he put it, the "most magically magical of any magic square ever made by a magician." It appeared in *The Gentleman's Magazine* in 1768.

200	217	232	249	8	25	40	57	72	89	104	121	136	153	168	185
58	39	26	7	250	231	218	199	186	167	154	135	122	103	90	71
198	219	230	251	6	27	38	59	70	91	102	123	134	155	166	187
60	37	28	5	252	229	220	197	188	165	156	133	184	101	92	69
201	216	233	248	9	24	41	56	73	88	105	120	137	152	169	184
55	42	23	10	247	234	215	202	183	170	151	138	119	106	87	74
203	214	235	246	11	22	43	54	75	86	107	118	139	150	171	182
53	44	21	12	245	236	213	204	181	172	149	140	117	108	85	76
205	212	237	244	13	20	45	52	77	84	109	116	141	148	173	180
51	46	19	14	243	238	211	206	179	174	147	142	115	110	83	78
207	210	239	242	15	18	47	50	79	82	111	114	143	146	175	178
49	48	17	16	241	240	209	208	177	176	145	144	113	112	81	80
196	221	228	253	4	29	36	61	68	93	100	125	132	157	164	189
62	35	30	3	254	227	222	195	190	163	158	131	126	99	94	67
194	223	226	255	2	31	34	63	66	95	98	127	130	159	162	191
64	33	32	1	256	225	224	193	192	161	160	129	128	97	96	65

If you add up the digits in each row or column of Franklin's square, the total is 2,056. But his square has many other secret properties, including one involving the corners and the center squares. I've put Franklin's list of the other secrets on page 310.

Two millennia after the invention of the Magic Square, the very first version of Sudoku appeared. It was born in America, not Japan, tucked into the back of a 1979 puzzle magazine. It didn't make much of a splash. This is partly because it had the most boring name ever: "Number Place." It's like if chess were called "Grid Pieces," or tennis were named "Sphere That Moves."

The creator was a retired architect named Howard Garns, who Wikipedia notes "gained fame only after his death."

In 1984 a Japanese puzzle publisher named Maki Kaji spotted the hidden gem, refined it a bit (he made it more symmetrical, for instance), and, most important, renamed it: Sudoku. Which is actually a play on words in Japanese. Sudoku means "bachelor number" or "single number," since every box contains a single number.

With the power of the new sexy (or sexless) name, Sudoku exploded. It currently appears in thousands of newspapers daily. There are Sudoku competitions and dozens of YouTube tutorial channels. Fans say it's "deeper than chess." There's even a famous Sudoku cheating scandal, in which a competitor is thought to have gotten the answers through a hidden earpiece.

The appeal is, in part, that the rules are exceedingly simple. As it says on the official Sudoku website:

- Every square has to contain a single number.
- Only the numbers from 1 through 9 can be used.
- Each 3 × 3 box can only contain each number from 1 to 9 once.
- Each vertical column and each horizontal row can only contain each number from 1 to 9 once.

The puzzler's job is to fill in the squares with the appropriate numbers.

THE GODFATHER OF SUDOKU

Early on in my book research, before I talked to Miyamoto, I got to meet Maki Kaji—the "godfather of Sudoku," as he is called—at an event at the National Museum of Mathematics in New York City. (Sadly, Kaji died of cancer about a year later, in August of 2021.)

On a fall day, I arrive at the basement room and join about twenty other puzzle fans. There he is, the godfather himself, in white sneakers and a white goatee.

"Sudoku is NOT a brain *workout*," Kaji says, with a heavy accent. He shakes his head. "It's a brain *spa*."

Kaji is pushing the narrative that Sudoku should be relaxing, meditative, fun, not a grind. Or to use another metaphor written on the handouts at the event: Sudoku is not "calculating numbers, it's dancing with numbers."

Kaji's other passion is mountain climbing, and he says he likes his Sudokus the same way he likes his mountains: gentle and conquerable, not dangerously steep and intimidating.

On the whiteboard, Kaji writes his wonderful encapsulation of puzzles, the one I cited in Chapter 2: a question mark, an arrow, and an exclamation point. He explains that they represent the three stages of solving Sudoku: bafflement, wrestling, solution!

$$? \rightarrow !$$

Kaji points to the arrow. "This should be happy time! This should not be—" and here Kaji grimaces and flails his arms, which I think is supposed to represent anxiety and freaking out. The crowd nods in approval.

Kaji says that part of Sudoku's appeal is that it's not a math puzzle. You don't have to be a master of quadratic equations. In fact, you could replace the nine numbers with anything: nine letters, nine colors, nine Supreme Court justices, not counting when the Senate refuses to let presidents fill seats because there's only a year left in the term.

And he agrees with Miyamoto: the best Sudokus are handcrafted.

EXTREME SUDOKU

Kaji may be a fan of gentle Sudokus, but it turns out not everyone wants a spa. Some puzzlers crave the equivalent of numerical Cross-Fit. Which is why you can find Sudokus boasting they are "diabolical" or "murderous."

In fact, over the last fifteen years, there's been an unofficial competition to create the hardest Sudoku that is still solvable. A Finnish mathematician created one called AI Escargot, which is available via Google in case you have a spare three months. Another is called the Easter Monster.

What makes them so hard? Well, for your average Sudoku, you only have to think one or two moves in advance. You notice that a row has all numbers except 7. So 7 goes in this box! Done.

With the torturous Sudokus, you have to think five or seven or ten moves ahead. It's like grandmaster-level chess. These puzzles still have only one solution, and a brilliant solver can still crack the code purely with logic and will never have to resort to guessing. But they require ridiculously advanced strategies.

ACROBATICS AND ADVIL

Will Shortz once explained the popularity of puzzles like Sudoku and crosswords by saying, "I think there is something about human nature that we want to fill up spaces. It gives a feeling of satisfaction that you don't get often in life."

I too enjoy filling spaces, but I prefer filling up crossword spaces. This is partly because I appreciate the fact that crossword creators sweated over their creations. With Sudoku, it annoys me that a computer can generate a grid in three nanoseconds, but it takes me half an hour to grind through it. Unfair!

The idea that logic puzzles can be handcrafted makes me more open to Sudoku and its cousins. But before I can appreciate the beauty, I need to get better at these puzzles.

I interview several Sudoku champions, and I watch dozens of Sudoku YouTube tutorials, and finally I start getting in the groove. I feel the dopamine rush as I scribble the digits. I wrestle with that familiar sign of puzzle addiction: "I'll just do one more puzzle, then go to sleep. Or just one more after that."

One huge help: I learned the strategies. There are simple strategies—look for 1s across, then 1s down, then 1s in the boxes.

But Sudoku aficionados have created about fifty more advanced strategies, with colorful names like "the X-wing" and "the Naked Single." They are sometimes called "acrobatic" strategies, and they involve variations on the process of elimination. The existence of 8 in this row betrays that we're missing 4s and 7s, for instance.

Experts flex these strategies in Sudoku competitions. Which are remarkable to watch. In the finals, the competitors work on poster-sized Sudokus mounted on easels, and they fill in the grids faster than I sign my signature.

When doing Sudoku, I feel like a hunter, cornering the numbers. Trapping them. Gotcha! You can't escape, 7, you little bastard. I know where you are going. Or maybe solving them feels more like unwrapping a gift. Or even doing a scratch-off. The numbers just yield themselves. At points, I experience the much-coveted flow, with the minutes zipping by. Though not always. While doing a Sudoku labeled torturous, I do, in fact, get a headache and have to take Advil.

THE SUCCESSFUL FAILURE

Sudoku's success has spawned a dizzying number of logic puzzle spin-offs. How many? Hard to calculate, but there are at least two hundred grid-based games, with names like Moon-or-Sun or Two Not Touch. Some involve connecting colored dots, others involve making Xs in noncontiguous squares. But they all are based on similar logical principles.

The most popular Sudoku spin-off is KenKen, played by five million puzzlers a day on the Internet and printed in two hundred publications. As with Sudoku, you can't have two of the same number in the same row or column. But there's an additional catch: the grid is also carved into sections, or "cages," and each cage contains a little math problem. For instance, a cage labeled 8 might require $7 + 1$, or 4×2. (Confused? I would be too. See appendix for more rules.)

"KenKen players kind of look down on Sudoku," says Chris Flaherty. "They see Sudoku as too simplistic."

Flaherty is the co-director of an excellent short documentary about KenKen called *Miyamoto and the Machine*. It profiles Tetsuya Miyamoto, the sixty-two-year-old inventor of KenKen introduced at the start of this chapter, and it explores the idea of puzzle artistry. The thesis is that computers don't have the creative spark. As one KenKen fan told me: "When you do a computer-generated logic puzzle in the newspaper, they're fine. But when someone has actually created one by hand, it can tell stories. It doesn't sound like it should happen with numbers. But it's elegant, it can make you smile. There is a clear breadcrumb trail that they've laid out for you to follow. Maybe the only way to break it is to do all the odd numbers, then the evens. Maybe all the twos need to be filled in last."

Before he invented KenKen in 2004, Miyamoto was a self-professed serial failure. The son of a taxi driver, he dropped out of high school and initially failed his exam to get into college. He failed at several jobs and romantic relationships.

And for that, he's grateful. "Failure is much more important than success," he says.

His view of life and puzzles has a Buddhist feel. "Do not want the answer," he says. "Just enjoy the trial and error."

He even wrote a children's book about his philosophy, which includes the line:

Fail 10 times, small success . . .
Fail 10,000 times, big success.

The book was born out of Miyamoto's struggle with depression and suicidal thoughts. It's called *Irreplaceable Me,* and it uses math to make the argument that your life counts.

If you think of yourself as just one in seven billion
It can make you want to die
But if you think of yourself as an irreplaceable one of one
Doesn't it stir just a little bit of courage?

Miyamoto tells me more about his life when I speak to him over FaceTime one night. After that string of failures, he lucked into a job as an after-school math tutor for students ages ten to fourteen. He's devoted to his students—almost maniacally so. Before he got married, he slept on the classroom floor most nights, waking up at 3 A.M. to prep for class.

His challenge: how to engage the students. His answer: puzzles. He needed a puzzle that taught all four basic operations (addition, subtraction, multiplication, and division). And thus was born KenKen (Japanese for "wisdom squared").

"I call the method 'teaching without teaching,' " he says. Miyamoto hands out the KenKen puzzles at the start of class. And from then on, there's no talking. Just monk-like silence, with kids scribbling away. He says KenKen is so entrancing to his students that not even the earthquake that once rattled his classroom could distract them.

He's a true believer that his method teaches kids tenacity, logical thinking, and independence. And he believes it will eventually be adopted by classrooms everywhere.

"KenKen will conquer the world," he says with a smile.

A few weeks after interviewing Miyamoto, I decided it was time to wrestle with his masterpiece, his 9-by-9 monster. You can see it below:

18		8		17	10		8	
	7		6		9	11		11
	21					14	13	
	21		15					14
3	16	12		12		22		
		19		20	17		15	8
2		23						
				21				24
1		24			12			

Copyright Tetsuya Miyamoto

The solution to Miyamoto's hardest KenKen is found on page 311.

First, I try to do it myself. I fail, and fail, and fail. I fill in a grand total of nine squares.

I need help. I call one former logic-puzzle champion who solves with me for ninety minutes, but then gives up. So I call another: Ellie Grueskin. Ellie is a former KenKen champion, current Harvard junior, and summer intern for the Boston Red Sox statistics department.

"This is definitely the hardest KenKen I've ever done," Ellie says.

Which makes me feel better. Miyamoto had told me that his twelve-year-old students could do it, which had annoyed me. Ellie agrees it's beautiful. She says you can tell it's handcrafted from the unusual and unexpected shape of the cages. We work on it together over Zoom—or really, she works on it, and I make occasional comments. My greatest accomplishment: I pointed out an error in her calculation: 6 × 3 is not 24!

We take a break overnight, and Ellie does some more work on it before we resume the next day. Logic puzzles are like jigsaws. At the end, they get really easy. Ellie lets me fill in the penultimate digit, so I can feel like I contributed.

So did I experience it as art? Was it a Picasso painting or a Beethoven symphony? Well, at times, I kind of glimpsed the beauty, like when we made a breakthrough, and the digits dropped into place like a numerical waterfall.

Though it didn't move me like a great book, it felt like a collaboration with Miyamoto's mind, as if I'm holding a paintbrush and Picasso is peering over my shoulder, telling me where to paint that second asymmetrical eye.

Four Grid Puzzles from History

1) Number Place

Here is the very first Sudoku ever created. Only it wasn't called Sudoku. This is the "Number Place" puzzle that appeared in a 1979 issue of a *Dell* puzzle magazine. Its creator, Howard Garns, died before his invention went viral. The numbers in the circles below the grids are designed to give you a head start. Each of the four circled numbers below a grid belongs in one of the four circles in that grid.

Copyright 2022 by PennyDellPuzzles.com

2) Thomas Snyder Artistic Sudoku

You can go online and find the allegedly hardest Sudoku ever (the AI Escargot). But honestly, it's a slog to finish. Instead, I asked Sudoku master Thomas Snyder to send me a challenging-but-still-fun puzzle. This is from his book *The Art of Sudoku,* which features puzzles with aesthetically pleasing patterns. In addition to creating Sudokus, Snyder is also a Sudoku-solving champion, and has won tournaments everywhere from Hungary to India. (One of his tactics: sugar-loading with a bowl of Cocoa Krispies pre-tournament.) Echoing others I've talked to, Snyder says puzzles are "a more fun example of what life is, which is problem solving." His website is gmpuzzles.com.

				1				
			2	3	4			
		5	6		7	2		
	8	1				3	7	
5	2						4	9
	4	3				8	6	
		8	3		2	4		
			7	4	9			
				5				

3) The first KenKen

Here is the first KenKen that Miyamoto created for his students.

1. In a 4 × 4 grid, you can only use the numbers 1, 2, 3, or 4.
2. No numbers may repeat in any row or column. (Every allowable number must appear in every row and column.)
3. Each "cage" (region bounded by a heavy border) contains a "target number" and usually an arithmetic operation. You must fill that cage with numbers (in any order) that reach the target using the specified arithmetic operation.

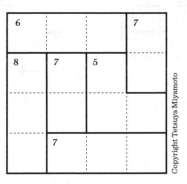

Copyright Tetsuya Miyamoto

4) Star Battle

As I mentioned, there are dozens of variations on the Japanese grid puzzle. This one is called "Star Battle" and was popularized by Jim Bumgardner, who goes by the puzzle name Krazydad (Krazydad.com).

Krazydad explains the rules: In these puzzles, each row, column, and bolded region must contain exactly one star. The stars can't touch each other, not even diagonally. A more advanced version with two stars in each region sometimes goes by the name "Two Not Touch."

Courtesy of krazydad.com

Solutions to Four Grid Puzzles from History begin on page 311.

Chess Puzzles (Chess Problems)

Over the last few months, my obsession with puzzling has caused several spats with my wife. When I insist on finishing the Spelling Bee before scooping out the kibble for our dog? She's not overjoyed.

But so far, puzzles have not ruined my marriage.

The modern artist Marcel Duchamp was not so lucky.

You might remember Duchamp, a Frenchman with a flair for the absurd. He once took a urinal, renamed it *Fountain,* and displayed it as high art. His semiabstract *Nude Descending a Staircase, No. 2* scandalized the art world in 1912 and helped usher in cubism.

What you may not know—I sure didn't—is that Duchamp almost completely stopped creating art at age thirty-six. The reason? He became obsessed with chess, and chess puzzles in particular. Or "chess problems," as they are called by those in the know.

A chess problem consists of a particular arrangement of Black and White pieces on the board. The solver's job is to figure out how White can checkmate Black in a specified number of moves—could be one move, or two, or even fifty-four.

Here's a pretty basic example. In this problem, it's White's turn and White's goal is to checkmate Black in just one move.

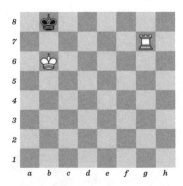

Answer: Move the White rook one space north, to space g8.

Well, Duchamp found these puzzles so addictive, they consumed his life. As author David Shenk writes in *The Immortal Game:* "Even true love could not moderate his fixation. In 1927 Duchamp married a young heiress . . . On their honeymoon he spent the entire week studying chess problems. Infuriated, his bride plotted her revenge. When Duchamp finally drifted off to sleep late one night, she glued all of the pieces to the board. They were divorced three months later."

A type of puzzle so compelling it destroys marriages? I needed to dive in.

I was a bit nervous to do so, not so much out of fear of potential custody hearings, but because I've never been a chess fanatic. I'm not sure why. Maybe it's because chess didn't come naturally to me, un-like Boggle or Scrabble, which felt like they were embedded deep in my DNA. Chess has always been a struggle. If someone asked me to play chess, I'd come up with some cheap excuse. "I'd love to. But in this time when democracy is under threat, I don't think we should endorse anything involving monarchy."

But lucky for me, chess problems and chess matches are totally dif-ferent creatures. They are as distinct as playing tennis and juggling. That tennis/juggling metaphor comes courtesy of novelist Vladimir Nabokov, who was a huge fan of the form.

"Problems are the poetry of chess," Nabokov wrote in his appropri-ately titled book *Poems and Problems.* "They demand from the composer the same virtues that characterize all worthwhile art: originality, inven-tion, harmony, conciseness, complexity, and splendid insincerity."

Chess problems are constrained, unlike open-ended chess matches with their near-infinite options. Chess problems are surprising: they emphasize bizarre sacrifices and out-of-the-box moves. And best of all, there is always one right answer.

Nabokov found composing problems to be a gratifying pastime. *Very* gratifying. He wrote that he often felt "a twinge of mental pleasure as the bud of a chess problem burst open in my brain, promising me a night of labor and felicity." (It's not just me, right? The author of *Lolita* here is kind of making chess puzzles sound dirty?)

Chess problems evolved centuries ago as a method to train for real chess matches. But they've outgrown their original purpose. Chess problems now have their own subculture separate and apart from regular chess. You can root for chess problem superstars, read chess problem magazines, and attend the equivalent of the chess problem Olympics.

There's a whole specialized lingo, with charming words like "Zepler doubling" and "maximummer," as well as the best job title ever: "problematist," which is what you call a chess puzzle composer.

Great problematists are considered artists. "If you don't put their name on their problem, they go berserk," one expert told me. There's a colorful history of such artists, including the Soviet problematist who was executed by Stalin for treason. His alleged sin? He sent chess problems to Western bourgeois chess publications.

THE LIFESAVING POWER OF CHESS PROBLEMS

I lucked into finding the perfect guide to the world of chess problems. His name is Cyrus Lakdawala, and chess problems saved his life. Well, maybe that's a slight exaggeration, but as you'll see, there's a seed of truth in it.

Cyrus was born in Mumbai, India, in 1960, but now lives in San Diego and writes books about chess—a lot of them: fifty-one by last count. His most recent book focuses on chess problems, which is how I found him.

When I called Cyrus, he told me that when he was young, he scratched out a living playing tournaments. "I got PTSD watching *The Queen's Gambit*," Cyrus tells me. "My hands were sweating, my breathing got ragged. It brought back a time when I needed to win a tournament to make rent."

He did well enough to become an international master. But he found his true calling as a chess teacher and writer, an occupation he's pursued for forty years.

So how did chess problems save his life?

Well, in 2018, Cyrus was playing a tournament. He didn't need the money, but he loved the adrenaline rush. While playing in the first round, Cyrus felt a sharp pain in his chest. He considered the possibility that he was having a heart attack . . . but he was winning the match. "If I'm in a winning position and I have a heart attack, I'm playing it out," he says. "And so I kept playing, all four games. And the chest pain worsened. It was the stupidest thing I ever did in my life, and I've done a lot of stupid things."

When Cyrus finally went to the hospital, the doctor told him he was half an hour from death.

On the upside, Cyrus won the tournament.

Following surgery, the doctor told Cyrus he could no longer play competitively. Too stressful. Cyrus was crushed. What could he do? Reluctantly, he turned to chess problems. "I'd always thought that chess problems were for people who couldn't hack tournaments."

Nonetheless, he immersed himself in them. And they surprised him in three ways. First, doing chess problems improved Cyrus's regular chess game by refining his thinking. Second, they filled the void he felt after retiring from competitions and stopped him from disobeying his doctor's orders. And third, chess problems allowed him to fall in love with the game again. "When I was a kid, I didn't play to win, I played for the beauty of the game. And this was a rediscovery of that."

THE HARDEST EASIEST PROBLEM EVER

The easiest chess problems are called "mate in ones." You just have to move one White piece and—voilà—Black is checkmated! It's like a jigsaw puzzle that's nearly finished, just one piece left.

How tough could that be?

Well, pretty damn tough.

"There's this mate in one problem that's so insanely hard—it's just mind-bending," Cyrus warns me. This little nightmare was composed by Leonid Kubbel, the brother of the problematist who was executed by Stalin. Cyrus says a friend of his—an international master no less—struggled with it for half an hour before solving it.

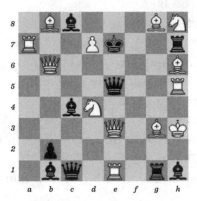

White to Move and Mate in One
Note: In chess problems, White
moves its pawns North, and
Black moves pawns South. For
solution see page 312.

After I hang up with Cyrus, I'm eager to tackle this problem—but when I look at it in Cyrus's book, I accidentally spot the answer at the bottom of the page.

So I ask my son Jasper to try it. Unlike me, Jasper is a very good chess player. He's able to envision four or more moves in advance, and he always shellacs me when we play.

"One move?" Jasper asks. "How is that even a challenge?"

I tell him he'd see. And he does.

"Which way are the White pieces going?" he asks.

"Toward the top of the board."

"Hmmm."

He studies the position. He moves the knight, then pauses.

"Wait, that's not it." He moves it back.

I keep quiet as he studies the board. And studies it. What makes this problem so tricky is that almost every White move allows for Black to make a surprise escape or to capture a piece.

"There are twenty checks, but only one checkmate," I say.

"Don't tell me!"

Jasper is struggling, and so am I. I desperately want to give him a little hint to ease his mental anguish. But I know this would be a mistake. I've heard all the parenting experts talk about how important it is to let your kids struggle so they learn independence and resilience. I've read the books like *The Gift of Failure* and *Grit* and *Go Ahead and Let Your Kid Drown, It's Good for Them* (the last one is not real, but you get the idea). I know that snowplow parents—who knock down all obstacles—are doing their kids no favors in the long term. But still, it's hard. Watching your kid in pain—even if it's voluntary mental pain—is as stressful as the hardest puzzle.

I remind myself that Cyrus is a big fan of the struggle.

"There's no such thing as failure," Cyrus told me, echoing what KenKen creator Miyamoto says. "Just try and fail and fail and fail. What I love about chess problems is that they beat the superficial reality out of you. Things are always more subtle and complex than you dreamt of in your philosophy."

Cyrus comes from a long line of thinkers who say that chess is a great way to learn life wisdom. Ben Franklin wrote an essay called "The Morals of Chess," where he listed four virtues that chess can teach us, including foresight and caution (don't make moves too hastily).

Cyrus says one of the biggest lessons chess has taught him is humility. "The beginner thinks he's brilliant and the master knows he's stupid," says Cyrus. "I've learned over the years, I don't understand one one-millionth of a percent of chess. Chess is like this gigantic universe and you're like this little leaf being blown around in the wind."

I agree with Cyrus. We need more epistemic humility in this world. My own was reinforced when, fifteen minutes later, Jasper solved the problem—in half the time that the international master needed. Jasper smiled broadly. I'm glad I resisted the snowplow.

CHIMPANZEES AND GROTESQUES

I call up Cyrus again a couple of days later. I tell him Jasper cracked the most challenging mate in one problem. Now we want to take it up a level.

"What's the hardest problem of them all?" I ask.

"Well, there's this Russian composer from the 1980s named Genrikh Kasparyan," says Cyrus. "But his problems are just ridiculous. I don't really like them. I can't teach them. They're too difficult. It's like teaching Shakespeare to a chimpanzee."

Now, normally I might be insulted if someone compared my intellect to an ape's. But first, I'm trying to embrace intellectual humility. Second, these metaphors are simply Cyrus's style—and part of why I'm such a huge fan.

As he told me early on, "I'm probably both the most loved chess author *and* the most hated. When chess readers like my style, they are gaga about it. But about 20 percent of readers really, really don't like my style. When there's a post about one of my books on Facebook, they'll respond with the vomit or poop emoji."

Imagine if Hunter Thompson had written about chess instead of drug-fueled trips to Vegas. Consider Cyrus's description of mate in one problems: "These are where the novelist kills off the main character early à la *Psycho*, where Janet Leigh (played by Black's king) is bludgeoned in the shower by a bewigged Anthony Perkins."

I decide to trust Cyrus. My primate brain shouldn't even attempt Kasparyan. (If your chimp intellect wants to torture itself, I've included one of his problems in this chapter's appendix: number 7, Shakespeare for a chimp.) Instead, Cyrus and I choose to work on a genre of chess problems that are charmingly referred to as "Grotesques."

"Grotesques are fun," he says. "We should absolutely try them."

Their name implies that they will be hideous, like a devil-goat sculpture on a Gothic cathedral. But a better adjective is *ridiculous*. Grotesques are the absurdist jokes of the chess world.

In a Grotesque, you're presented a board dominated by Black—an ocean of Black pieces and just a couple of White pieces. You have to figure out how on earth White can pull off a victory. It's David versus Goliath, the Bad News Bears versus that team of rich snobs. Sly wit must triumph over sheer force.

Cyrus shows me one of the most famous Grotesques (written in 1922 by a Hungarian composer named Ottó Bláthy, who in his spare time invented the electric transformer, which makes possible the power grid connected to your lightbulb, FYI).

All sixteen Black pieces versus two White ones?

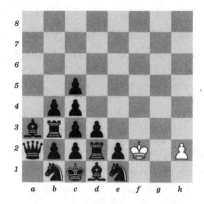

White to Move and Mate in
Several Moves

I laughed out loud when I saw this problem. The setup was so unlikely, with a cluster of Black pieces that would never occur in a real game. Despite Black's overpowering numbers, White can win. This is one of chess's big life lessons. Ben Franklin wrote that chess teaches you it's important not to be "discouraged by present bad appearances in the state of our affairs."

I have mixed feelings about this moral, the one that says even the longest of odds can be overcome, that anything is possible if you just try hard enough.

On the one hand, I've written about the benefits of delusional optimism. I don't think I'd be a writer without it. Delusional optimism gave my twenty-four-year-old self the chutzpah to cold-mail fifty agents with a book idea even though my writing career to date consisted mostly of covering sewage disputes for a small-town newspaper in suburban California.

And yet, I recognize that delusional optimism can have huge downsides. Consider the totally hypothetical case where someone is convinced they would be a great president of the United States despite having zero political experience.

It's a tricky balance between delusional optimism and stark realism. Sometimes, when there are sixteen Black pieces and two White pieces, you should save everyone some time and concede. But sometimes you should fight on.

Back to the Grotesque. There's another important strategy I'm going to need to solve it: don't go with your first thought.

I once interviewed Tina Fey, and I asked her the secret to writing comedy. She told me one rule: Be wary of the first thought that pops into your brain. First thought is often the worst thought. Instead, dig deeper.

In this Grotesque, my first thought is that "queening" is the key to success. In chess, when a White pawn reaches the final row on Black's side of the board, you can "promote" the pawn. In a traditional chess match, you almost always promote the pawn to a queen. After all, the queen is the most powerful and versatile piece.

But here's the twist. To solve this problem, you must resist the temptation to give yourself a new queen. The queen won't win you the game. You must instead promote your pawn to a knight. The knight is much weaker than the queen—but it's the proper tool for the job: a scalpel instead of a hammer. The knight can squeeze out a checkmate because it can threaten the Black king even when pawns are blocking its path.

To figure out exactly how the knight can mate the king, I use another of Cyrus's tips: Start at the goal and work backward.

I find this to be useful advice. While writing, I'll think, *If I can envision the end of this chapter, what will that look like? And how can I get there?* I even worked backward in my love life. After just two dates, I knew I wanted to marry Julie (it took her about four more months to reach a similar conclusion). I knew my goal. How to make it happen? So for this chess problem, I envision the checkmate and work backward.

After twenty minutes of false starts and picturing the endpoint, Jasper and I do it! Checkmate. Down goes Goliath. Two beats sixteen.

THE CHESS KING

A few weeks after my lessons with Cyrus, I get another email from a fan of chess problems: Garry Kasparov.

This is a pleasant surprise. I'd reached out to Garry months ago, but never heard back. I figured he's a busy man. The No. 1 ranked chess player for a record twenty-one years, Garry retired from competitions in 2005. But he still writes books, works on human rights in Russia, runs a chess academy, consults for Hollywood (he was the adviser on *The Queen's Gambit*), and on and on.

But happily enough, Garry has agreed to come to my apartment and talk chess problems.

On the appointed day, I arrange the scene so there will be no wasted time: a chess set on the table, two chairs facing each other. Garry arrives—he has gray hair and is wearing a blue blazer—and accepts my offer of a cup of coffee. He sits down at the table and looks at the board.

"Well, I can see you picked quite a cheap chess set," Garry says.

Oh, man. Embarrassing, but true. It's a small plastic chess set with flimsy lightweight pieces. I bought it for my kids for fifteen dollars. It is not fit for the most famous chess player in the world.

"Um, I can look around and see if I have a better one," I say. We do have a Nintendo-themed set with Mario as King and Luigi as Queen. That was more expensive.

"No, that's all right. I grew up in the Soviet Union," Garry says. "I'm used to cheap chess sets."

"Yes, I was just trying to make you feel at home," I say.

"I'm back in the USSR," Garry says, chuckling.

Okay, crisis averted.

"I read that you first got interested in chess by solving chess problems from a Soviet newspaper," I say.

Garry nods. He was about five, maybe five and a half, he's not certain ("nobody was there to tweet about it," he says), and his parents were working on a chess problem. "I made a suggestion," Garry says. "My mother said I solved the problem. My parents were shocked and pleased, and that's how it all started." Garry says he's not sure he really solved the problem that day, but that's the family lore.

"Should we go over some of our favorite problems?" I ask.

Before Garry arrived, I'd set up the Grotesque—the problem from 1922 with all sixteen Black pieces versus two White ones. Garry looks at the Grotesque for all of five seconds and solves it.

"This is interesting," he says. "But these are not my favorite kind of problems." Garry says Grotesques are too unrealistic. Such an arrangement of pieces would never occur in a game. He prefers chess problems that are more realistic, sometimes taken from actual chess matches in the past. These are often called "endgame studies."

The best endgame studies, though, require the same skill as more artificial problems: the ability to make a counterintuitive move. "The beauty of the studies is when your knowledge from books or common sense is simply being refuted. It looks hopeless, but then there's a kind of miracle."

Garry arranges a few of the (cheap, plastic) pieces on the board.

"In this problem, you have to sacrifice the queen," he says.

This solution doesn't come easily to humans, he says. It feels weird to give up such a powerful piece. "For a computer," Garry says, "this is not a problem. A machine finds it in a split second because a machine doesn't care about the queen. There's no psychological barrier. Machines do not 'sacrifice' anything. For a machine, it's an exchange of one advantage to another. It's all about the bottom line."

So should we try to eliminate our irrational psychological barriers when solving problems?

"You cannot do that," Garry says, "because then we'll lose our humanity." It would, he says, have catastrophic effects in other areas of life.

Computers have another advantage in problem solving. They can see far into the future. Garry tells me about perhaps the hardest chess problem ever created. It's seven pieces on the board. It is possible for White to mate Black, but it takes White an astounding 520 moves.

Garry says he watched a computer solve the problem, and was baffled and awed. "For the first four hundred moves, I didn't understand what was happening. There was no pattern I could recognize," he says.

I tell him that such stories make me nervous for the future in the face of advances in AI.

Garry shakes his head. "I'm more optimistic about the future of humanity," he says.

"You're not worried about AI taking over?"

"Why should I be? I was the first knowledge worker whose job was threatened by machines," he says.

I laugh. It's true. In 1997, Garry was famously beaten in a chess match by IBM's supercomputer Deep Blue.

"I think it's wrong to cry about progress," he says. "The future is not humans fighting machines. The future is humans collaborating with machines. Every technology in history destroyed jobs, but it also created new ones."

Like Tetsuya Miyamoto, the inventor of KenKen, Garry thinks we humans are irreplaceable. This is a relief. Although I still worry that

AI is a threat, Garry's optimism is refreshing. Plus, I remind myself, he's a lot smarter than I am.

"It's all about us being creative and recognizing that humans still have a unique contribution to make, the combining of the decision process of humans and machines," he says.

Garry loves to talk about the decision process. He thinks that's the key to everything—chess, puzzles, and life. A few years ago, he wrote a book called *How Life Imitates Chess*.

The thesis is that chess teaches you how to make decisions by breaking down the problem into its components. In chess, you've got components such as which of your chess pieces remain on the board (the "material," as it's called) and the arrangement of those pieces on the board (what Garry calls "quality"). Garry makes life decisions with a similar lens: When buying a house, he looks at his material (his salary, his bonuses) and the quality (Is it near a good school? How long is the commute? Is there a park nearby?). "You start bringing them together and that's how you make a decision. Our progress in life is always connected to our ability to improve our decision-making formula. And if we train our brains to do puzzles or play chess, it helps us to understand how we can get better."

Garry has finished his coffee, and is ready to leave. I ask him if he likes other kinds of puzzles. He says he's a puzzle fan—he does crosswords in Russian, and can solve a Rubik's Cube in about three minutes. That's good to know. Sure, he can thrash me at chess, but we're about even at Rubik's solving. I'm going to count that as a win.

Eight Chess Problems from History

1) The eight queens puzzle

One of chess's most famous problems is a slightly different type of puzzle.

The goal has nothing to do with checkmate. The goal is to place eight queens on the chessboard so that no two queens threaten each other.

First published by a German composer named Max Bezzel in 1848, it allegedly took two years for someone to figure out the answer. And it is indeed difficult. The eight queens can be arranged in 4,426,165,368 configurations, with only 92 solutions.

Hint: look for L shapes.

2) Guarini's problem

Here's one of the earliest chess puzzles, first published in 1512. Called Guarini's problem, it is set up on a simplified board of 3 × 3. The idea is to switch the positions of the knights. The Black knights should end up where the White knights are, and vice versa. You can move them in any order (meaning you can move two White knights in a row).

3) A manageable problem (As a reminder, White moves its pawns North, and Black moves pawns South.)

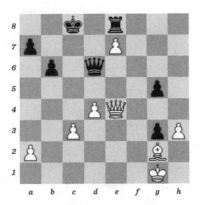

White to Move and Mate in One

4) And another one that isn't too crazy.

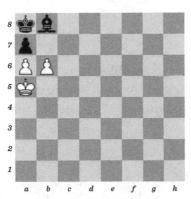

White to Move and Mate in One

5) Nabokov's problem

Here's a problem the novelist wrote in 1969.

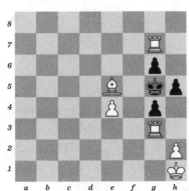

White to Move and Mate in Three Turns

6) Sam Loyd's Excelsior

Remember Sam Loyd? The most famous puzzlemaker in the nineteenth century? And also a bit of a scammer? Before branching out to other puzzle types, he focused on chess puzzles. This one is called "Excelsior," and it was created in 1861 on a dare. The idea was to have the least likely piece deliver the checkmate.

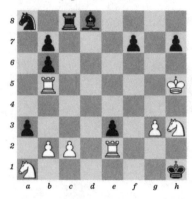

White to Move and Mate in
Five Turns

7) Shakespeare for a chimp (Kasparyan's problem)

Cyrus thinks the problems by Russian Genrikh Kasparyan are the hardest ever created. If you want to torture yourself, be my guest!

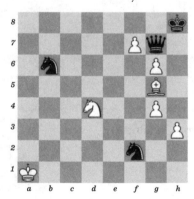

White to Move and Draw in
Several Turns

8) Helpmate

Chess problems have recently taken a turn for the surreal. Problematists are getting creative. There are chess problems in which the flat board is replaced by a cylindrical chessboard. There are fairy problems, in which pieces are granted magical powers—for instance, a rook might be able to fly over pawns.

There's also a genre called "helpmate problems." In these scenarios, the Black and White pieces work together to try to achieve a checkmate.

"I hate those," says Cyrus. "That's not the way chess is supposed to work."

I disagree with Cyrus here. I kind of like the spirit of cooperation. Why shouldn't Black and White be allies? Does chess always have to be such a zero-sum cutthroat operation? Why can't they work out their differences?

Black to Move,
Then White Mates in One

Solutions to Eight Chess Problems from History begin on page 312.

Chess diagrams by Annika Robbins

Riddles

On a fall morning, I call Edward Wakeling at his home on the Welsh border to speak to him about a famous riddle. It's a riddle proposed by the Mad Hatter in *Alice's Adventures in Wonderland.* The riddle is:

Why is a raven like a writing-desk?

Before I reveal the answer, I should mention that Edward is the perfect person with whom to discuss this topic, being one of the world's leading experts on Lewis Carroll, and particularly on Carroll's obsession with puzzles.

To use a phrase that originated in *Alice,* Edward has gone deep down this rabbit hole.

Not only has he written four books on Carroll's riddles and logic puzzles, but his home is a private museum/shrine to Lewis Carroll. We're talking 25,556 Carroll-related books and tchotchkes, stacked and cataloged everywhere you look—bedrooms, attic, stairwells.

Edward takes me on a Zoom tour: an *Alice* translation in Swedish, another in Braille, not to mention more than fifty other languages. A rare copy of *Alice* signed by Alice Liddell herself when she was eighty-one (Liddell was Carroll's inspiration). An original letter from Lewis Carroll written in the author's trademark violet ink. A Cheshire Cat Beanie Baby, a White Rabbit alarm clock.

If the apocalypse comes, Edward could survive for several days on *Alice*-themed food, though it might be a bit stale: biscuits, orange marmalade, and tea, all in their original *Alice* packaging from as far back as the 1970s.

"No doubt, he had one of the greatest minds of all time," says Edward, a retired math teacher with a trim gray beard and a multicolored sweater.

Lewis Carroll—real name Charles Lutwidge Dodgson—a shy math professor and cleric with a speech impediment, is a legend in the puzzle community. He larded his books and private letters with puzzles, some of them obvious, some buried. "He hid puzzles in his writings that weren't discovered for decades after he died."

In fact, a few years ago, Edward himself discovered one of Carroll's secret puzzles. "One of the highlights of my life," he says.

Here's what Edward found: the White Queen in *Alice* says her age is 101 years, five months, and a day. Same as her twin, the Red Queen.

"Carroll was a mathematician," Edward explains, "so I figured that number is likely to be significant. He wouldn't put any old rubbish down."

Taking into account leap years, Edward determined that the Red and White Queens' combined age was 74,088 days old. He thought 74,088 looked intriguing.

"I put it into my calculator, and I fell out of my chair," Edward says. "I was staggered by it. That number is 42 cubed."

And what's staggering about that?

Well, it turns out that Carroll was obsessed with the number 42 and peppered his books with references to it. There are 42 illustrations in *Alice*, the King of Hearts talks about a "Rule 42," and so on.

This was Edward's $e = mc^2$. A meeting of the minds across the expanse of decades. Edward published his findings in the Carroll journal *Jabberwocky*, where it was mostly well received, though disputed by some spoilsports. (Incidentally, it's still a mystery why Carroll loved 42. And also whether Carroll's love of 42 influenced Douglas Adams to choose 42 as the answer to the "Great Question of Life, the Universe, and Everything" in *The Hitchhiker's Guide to the Galaxy*.)

To me, Edward's discovery is perhaps one of the most ridiculous uses of human mental energy I've ever run across, but it's somehow heroic at the same time.

Okay, back to the riddle that inspired me to call Edward in the first place.

Alice is at the Tea Party, and the Mad Hatter asks her:

"Why is a raven like a writing-desk?"

Alice eventually gives up and asks the Mad Hatter for the answer.

"I haven't the slightest idea," said the Hatter . . .
    Alice sighed wearily. "I think you might do something better with the time," she said, "than wasting it in asking riddles that have no answers."

Psych! It's a riddle without a solution. An anti-riddle.

Well, it turned out that Carroll's readers didn't like riddles with no answers. They sided with Alice. They pestered Carroll until he created an answer after the fact.

In the preface to the 1896 edition of *Alice,* a beleaguered Carroll wrote, "I may as well put on record here what seems to me to be a fairly appropriate answer, viz: 'Because it can produce a few notes, though they are very flat; and it is nevar put with the wrong end in front!' This, however, is merely an after-thought; the Riddle, as originally invented, had no answer at all."

("Nevar" is not a typo. It's "raven" backward—more wordplay from Carroll.)

Apparently, this ad-hoc answer didn't satisfy people either, leading to an extremely niche pastime of puzzlers creating alternative answers to Carroll's famous riddle, a game that continues to this day.

Here's a sampling of how other people have decided a raven is like a writing desk:

• Poe wrote on both.
• They both have two eyes (or in the case of "writing desk," two i's).
• The notes for which they are noted are not noted for being musical notes.
• They both involve quills.
• They both slope with a flap.

Such creativity! We humans are rationalization machines. We are great at finding patterns where none exist. There's a term in psychology called the Texas sharpshooter fallacy, which is named for the rifleman who shot up the side of a barn and then painted a target to fit the bullet holes. It's a trait that can have great results (crafting an uplifting narrative out of a chaotic life) or terrible ones (almost any conspiracy theory ever).

Before I end our video meeting, I ask Edward, "What's your favorite answer to the raven/writing desk riddle?"

"There's a *B* in both," he says.

I look at the riddle again.

There's no *B* in "raven," and there's no *B* in "writing desk." What's he talking about?

"You mean there's an *E* in both?" I ask.

"No, there's a *B* in both."

"You mean a *V*?"

"No," says Edward. "There's a *B* in both."

Okay. Duh. The letter *b* in the word "both."

"It's an all-purpose answer to riddles," Ed explains.

Very clever. Kind of irritating, but also clever.

THE ORIGIN OF RIDDLES

Lewis Carroll could deconstruct the concept of a riddle precisely because riddles are such a familiar form of puzzle. In fact, some argue they are the oldest of all forms of puzzles.

Here's a Babylonian stumper from the fifth century B.C.E., one of the first recorded puzzles:

"What becomes pregnant without conceiving and fat without eating?"

The papyrus didn't have the answer, but it's generally agreed that the answer is "rain cloud."

(I'm only going to say this once, but please apply this to all historical riddles in this chapter: you had to be there.)

Riddles are also notable for being so universal. It's hard to find a society in history that didn't have riddles.

Here's a Swahili riddle:

"I am a house without a door."

Answer: an egg.

Or this one from China:

"There is a small vessel holding two different kinds of sauce."

Answer: also an egg!

It seems to me riddles aren't particularly fashionable in modern American culture. They're seen as childish, groan-worthy. They do appear in *Harry Potter* and dozens of escape rooms. But consider how dorky their reputation is compared with their cooler cousin, the joke. Just look at the *Batman* franchise. The Riddler will probably not be winning a lot of Oscars.

But it was not always so. Riddles have had their Golden Age. Or more precisely, several Golden Ages. In ancient Greece, nobles held riddle contests at their villas. These events involved a lot of alcohol and were something like pub quiz meets rap battle. Riddles also appeared in Greek plays, most famously in *Oedipus Rex*. The Sphinx asks the same question to every traveler who dares approach:

"What goes on four feet in the morning, two feet at noon, and three feet in the evening?"

Those who guessed wrong were slain. Oedipus was the first to get the answer correct: a person. At the start of life (that is, the morning), a baby crawls. In the middle (noon), a person walks on two feet. And an elderly person in the twilight of their life walks with a cane.

The Sphinx was so distraught that her riddle was solved that she threw herself over a cliff and died, one of the more memorable overreactions in puzzle history.

The Sphinx used the riddle as an intelligence test. But riddles have served many purposes over the years. They've been didactic—there are plenty of riddles from early Christians meant to instruct solvers about the glory of God. Riddles have been used as spiritual and mystic pronouncements by prophets. And also as a way to parody those pronouncements. Leonardo da Vinci wrote riddles in the form of pseudo-prophecies, mocking supposed mystics. One example:

"Winged creatures will support people with their feathers."

As biographer Walter Isaacson explained, Da Vinci then revealed he wasn't referring to flying machines, but instead to the feathers used to stuff mattresses.

Some historical riddles are, frankly, pretty terrible. In the Bible, Samson tells a riddle at a dinner party he hosts for the Philistines:

"Out of the eater came something to eat, and out of the strong came something sweet."

If you want an awkward five minutes, try this riddle out over dinner on your family or friends, as I did.

"Sugar?" my kids guessed. "Or maybe a bodybuilder who loves candy?"

"Nope! It's a dead lion with honeybees in its corpse!"

Apparently, Samson had once killed a lion and then later noticed that a swarm of bees was making honey in its corpse. Samson's riddle is supremely unfair, an inside joke between Samson and himself. When the Philistines secretly got the answer from Samson's wife, Samson slew thirty Philistines in revenge, making the Sphinx's reaction look restrained.

So Samson's riddle is not good. But what makes a good riddle?

According to the Oxford dictionary, a riddle is "a question or statement intentionally phrased so as to require ingenuity in ascertaining its answer or meaning." To me, the key is ingenuity. The twist can come in different forms. It can be a self-referential twist, something about the words of the riddle themselves, as in this nineteenth-century classic:

"I am at the start of eternity and the end of time."

The answer: the letter *e*.

Sometimes the twist relies on simple one-word puns, like this one posed by the Riddler in the movie *Batman Forever* (Will Shortz alert: the producers of *Batman* hired the *New York Times* puzzlemaster to add riddles to the script):

"If you look at the numbers on my face, you won't find 13 any place."

The answer: a clock.

But to me, the best riddles are the ones that are extended metaphors, like the Riddle of the Sphinx. Or like this, from J. R. R. Tolkien's *The Hobbit:*

"Voiceless it cries,
Wingless flutters,
Toothless bites,
Mouthless mutters."

The answer: the wind.

As riddle scholars point out (yes, there is an academic discipline called riddle studies—more on that in a moment), a good riddle makes you see mundane objects with fresh eyes.

I experienced that with Tolkien's poem, which I read while sitting on my parents' back deck. I paused for a moment and noticed the wind on my cheek. Yes, it does kind of bite. Or at least nibble, since it was a warm day. Wind—it's weird. The riddle was like mild THC.

That's why I love a good metaphor. It makes the familiar strange and the strange familiar. It inspires awe. A stale metaphor does none of that—"make a mountain out of a molehill," for instance, has lost all its power. But a fresh metaphor—there's nothing like it™. I remember when I first heard the phrase "binge watching," it was like a revelation. Yes! That's exactly what it feels like—the screen equivalent of an excessive Thanksgiving feast.

RIDDLING MONKS

Of all the metaphor riddles in history, perhaps the greatest were written in the Middle Ages. They're certainly among the most studied and most controversial puzzles in history.

A week after speaking to Edward Wakeling, the Lewis Carroll obsessive, I make another Zoom call to the United Kingdom, this time to Megan Cavell.

Megan is one of the stars of riddle studies. She runs a website called The Riddle Ages. Her bio lists her PhD, her job as an associate professor at the University of Birmingham, and an impressive slew of publications, but it also says, "I hope this doesn't make me sound stuffy or intimidating, because anyone who has read through a few of my posts will know that I'm a somewhat ridiculous person." Her sense of humor comes through in her writing, which contains references to Alanis Morissette and Gollum.

Megan is wearing big black glasses and a striped sweater. She says she came to medieval riddles partly because of her love of Old English, in which they are written.

"Oh, it's just the most beautiful, guttural language," she tells me. "Sometimes I'll shout bits of Old English at my partner. If I want a glass of water, I might say that in Old English." (It's "Gief me wæter," in case you were wondering.)

Megan has spent much of her time studying the Exeter Book, a tome compiled by monks in the tenth century that contains ninety-five riddles. The riddles in the Exeter Book are famous for two reasons. First, a handful of them are really, really naughty.

Consider the infamous Riddle Number 25 (translated here into modern English).

> My stem is erect, I stand up in bed,
> hairy somewhere down below. A very comely
> peasant's daughter, dares sometimes,
> proud maiden, that she grips at me,
> attacks me in my redness, plunders my head,
> confines me in a stronghold, feels my
> encounter directly,
> woman with braided hair. Wet be that eye.

You know what the answer is, right? Nudge, nudge?

It's an onion, of course. The eye is wet from crying, not from anything X-rated. A classic misdirect.

As a reminder, this is from a book created by monks. Not drunken, damsel-seducing knights. Supposedly celibate monks. How did the monks get away with it?

As Megan explained on a recent podcast, riddles were a "safe space where you could explore taboo topics . . . where you have freedom to explore sexuality even though you are a monk and you're not supposed to be exploring your sexuality." It gives the monks plausible deniability. "If you solve it wrong, if you solve it sexy, then bad on you," she says.

There are other sexy riddles, including one that hints at a leather dildo (seriously), but is actually about a horsewhip. These riddles horrified some prudish Victorian scholars, who refused to translate them and condemned them as "smut and horse-laughter."

But Megan and her colleagues have no such qualms. They adore these riddles. Some are even trying to look at them from a feminist perspective. Megan writes about the slim but real possibility that the riddles could have been secretly written by women. Or at least influenced by them.

For instance, there's the naughty riddle whose answer is dough, but features a woman self-assuredly grabbing that dough as if it were something else. "Did you happen to notice how assertively the 'proud bride' handles the 'boneless thing'?" writes Megan.

The second reason the Exeter riddles are famous is that we can never be sure of the true solutions. There's no answer key. Some answers are obvious (such as the onion). But other answers are a matter of debate. A lot of debate. As in thousands of hours of debate by dozens of scholars hashing it out in journals and conferences.

Consider Riddle Number 4. Based on the amount of bickering it has produced, it might qualify as the hardest riddle in history. Academics have proposed at least thirteen solutions, ranging from a bucket of water to the devil to a phallus (yes, again with the smut and horse-laughter).

The riddle is on the next page, and the proposed solutions are on page 315.

At times busy, bound by rings,
I must eagerly obey my thane,
break my bed, proclaim with a cry
that my lord gave me a neck-torque.
Often a man or woman came to greet me,
sleep-weary; I answer them, winter-cold,
the hostile-hearted ones. A warm limb
sometimes bursts the bound ring;
however, that is agreeable to my thane,
the half-witted man, and to myself,
if I could know anything, and tell my story
successfully with words.

Megan says she's not sure which solution is right. I ask her if it frustrates her that she'll never know the real answer.

On the contrary, she says. "I actually prefer the riddles that have five solutions that all work just as well as each other. I like sparring with friends about them. But I never really care who wins. I don't know whether it's because I'm a lefty academic or it's because of the riddles I study, but I'm fine with holding multiple truths."

In this way, Megan is an outlier in the puzzle community. Most people I've met want definitive answers and closure, not ambiguity. They are like Carroll's readers.

I go back and forth. Sometimes I want a solid answer. We already have enough problems in this alleged post-truth era about what constitutes facts and reality. We're already in a massive epistemic crisis. We're already in a world of wild conspiracy theories and flat earthers. Do I really want to embrace the post-modernism I learned in college, the idea of multiple truths, that everything is just competing narratives?

Other times, I remind myself that accepting uncertainty is a good life skill. And there's so much uncertainty right now to accept. I'm uncertain about the personal (how to raise my kids in the TikTok age) to the global (how best to stop Antarctica from melting). Kryptos, impossible crosswords, and Riddle Number 4 have been excellent practice for me.

Twelve Riddles from History

1) From African folklore

Wherever I go, it closely follows me. What is it?

2) From *The Hobbit,* by J. R. R. Tolkien

This thing all things devours: birds, beasts, trees, flowers; gnaws iron, bites steel; grinds hard stones to meal; slays king, ruins town, and beats high mountain down.

3) From 1900s United States

I am an odd number. Take away one letter and I become even. What number am I?

4) From Chinese folklore

Washing makes it more and more dirty.

5) From tenth-century Jewish poet Dunash ben Labrat

What speaks in all languages in his riding, and his mouth spits the poison of life or death? It is silent when it rests, and it is deaf like a boy or one of the poor.

6) From the United States (circa 1950s)

It can travel anywhere in the world simply by staying in a corner. What is it?

7) From Jane Austen's *Emma*

Note: This riddle is a "charade," a popular form in nineteenth-century England. A charade is broken down by syllables—the "first" refers to the first syllable, the "second" is the second syllable, and "the whole" is the entire two-syllable word.

My first doth affliction denote,/ Which my second is destin'd to feel; And my whole is the best antidote/ That affliction to soften and heal

8) From *Harry Potter and the Goblet of Fire*
Note: This is another charade.

First think of the person who lives in disguise,
Who deals in secrets and tells naught but lies.
Next, tell me what's always the last thing to mend,
The middle of middle and end of the end?
And finally give me the sound often heard,
During the search for a hard-to-find word.
Now string them together and answer me this,
Which creature would you be unwilling to kiss?

9) From Dixie Cups in the 1970s

Where do cows go on Saturday night?

10) From sixteenth-century Europe

Four wings I have, which swiftly mount on high, on sturdy pinions, yet I never fly. And though my body often moves around, upon the self-same spot I'm always found. And, like a mother, who breaks her infant's bread, I chew for man before he can be fed.

11) From eighteenth-century Britain—and also the classic Georgian-influenced film *Die Hard with a Vengeance*

As I was going to St. Ives,
    I met a man with seven wives,
    Each wife had seven sacks,
    Each sack had seven cats,
    Each cat had seven kits:
    Kits, cats, sacks, and wives,
    How many were there going to St. Ives?

12) From *Batman Forever,* a riddle given by the Riddler, written by Will Shortz

Tear one off and scratch my head, what once was red is black instead.

Solutions to Twelve Riddles from History begin on page 315.

(14) *Japanese Puzzle Boxes*

everal months before Covid shut down the world, my family and I took a trip of a lifetime. After years of planning, we went to Japan.

There were many highlights. There was the day we got to participate in a traditional Japanese tea ceremony—where I suspect we might have asked too many questions, because the woman pouring the tea suggested we engage in "silent conversation." Note: I have since adopted the phrase "silent conversation" as a nicer way to tell my kids to shut up. It's quite useful.

There was the amazing food—the sushi that zipped along conveyor belts, the mind-boggling array of pickled vegetables, the authentic Filet-O Ebi (shrimp patty) at the historic Tokyo McDonald's.

But perhaps my favorite stop was at the base of Mount Fuji, where we stumbled onto an unassuming little store that sold wooden boxes. Lots of wooden boxes. They ranged from fist-sized boxes to toaster-sized boxes, and they were dazzling, made with intricate patterns of dark and light wood.

In the back of the store, a middle-aged Japanese man sat on a bench surrounded by half-finished boxes, various saws, and wooden shavings.

The man handed my son Lucas a small box and motioned for him to open it.

Lucas tried to lift off the top, but it didn't budge.

The man took the box back, spun it on the table, and returned it to my son.

This time the box opened.

The man laughed and raised his eyebrows with an almost Groucho Marxist wiggle.

There was nothing inside the box, but that didn't matter. The joy was in the surprising way of cracking it open.

The man took out another wooden box. On top of this one was a tiny wooden figurine of an old man next to a tiny wooden bottle and tiny wooden cup.

Again, the box top was locked.

Our host took the tiny wooden cup with his thumb and index finger and lifted it to the wooden figurine's face.

"Glug, glug, glug," he said. "Sake!"

Now he motioned for Lucas to try to open the box again. This time it did.

Despite the inappropriate pro-alcohol message, I laughed out loud. I didn't know how it worked—magnets maybe? Sleight of hand? But what brilliance!

The man directed us to go next door. There we saw more surprises. Or at least we did once we figured out how to get inside. We tried to open the door by turning the doorknob, which seemed a logical thing to do. No luck.

After two minutes of knocking and jiggling, Lucas realized that it might be a trick door. He tried to open the door from the side with the hinges. It worked, and we entered a three-room museum with dozens of other wooden puzzles, one made to resemble a box of chocolate samplers, another in the shape of an egg.

We didn't know it at the time, but we had stumbled onto the birthplace of a worldwide cult phenomenon: Japanese puzzle boxes—handcrafted, wooden works of art doubling as puzzles.

To open them, you have to crack the code. You have to spin them, twist them, turn them, slide hidden panels on the top and sides of the box. The panels open up to access other hidden panels and drawers. The sequences can get stunningly complicated, requiring as many as 150 moves to open. Inside the boxes are the secret mechanisms that make them work: magnets, gears, cogs, and ball bearings are popular, as are wooden blocks arranged in a 3-D maze.

For the high-end, handmade boxes, collectors pay big bucks. Some go for as much as $40,000. There are secret auctions, rock star designers, and complaints that Russian oligarchs buy up all the good ones.

THE MASTER

Japanese puzzle boxes aren't new. Artisans in Japan have created simple versions of puzzle boxes for centuries, originally as safes for storing jewels, documents, and other valuables. Before 1900, many of the boxes were simpler, often requiring only three or four moves to open. In the 1930s, puzzle boxes containing cigarettes were popular, which I suppose had the healthy side effect of making it harder to chain-smoke.

But the modern puzzle box era began with an Osaka-born man named Akio Kamei. Akio raised the boxes to new levels of complexity and playfulness. In 1981, he formed the Karakuri Creation Group, a team of box designers, many trained by Akio himself. It's based in the town we visited, the one near Mount Fuji.

I call Akio one summer day from New York. The language barrier is big (he speaks a little English, I speak zero Japanese), so it isn't my most in-depth interview, but I still get a sense of his personality.

I ask Akio, who is now seventy-four years old, how he got interested in puzzle boxes.

"From my childhood, I like to laugh with many people. So I want the humor and joke to appear in the box."

"What is the favorite box you've ever made?"

Akio tells me he's fond of one of the first boxes he designed. It had dots on each side, like a die. To solve it, you have to turn the die's sides from one to two to three, and so on. On six, the box will open up. When you turn the die, you are causing a small steel ball inside the box to make its way through a maze to release a latch.

Akio says it's not about difficulty. It's about cleverness.

I ask him how he's able to keep coming up with ideas.

"I have no new ideas now," he says, with a laugh. "If possible, please teach me."

THE POPULARIZER

While Akio may be the most famous Japanese puzzle box designer, the most famous solver is probably a heavily tattooed Canadian magician named Chris Ramsay.

Chris, who is thirty-eight years old, has a YouTube channel where he records himself trying to open puzzle boxes. His videos get up to 10 million views. (See image in color insert.)

Not everyone is happy about his channel. Some in the puzzle box community think it's bad form to reveal the boxes' secret solutions to the world. It's seen as a betrayal. But his fans love to watch him suffer and sweat. He sighs, he complains, he says, "I'm going nuts here" or "Are you enjoying watching me struggle my life away?"

But he also exudes joy when he solves one. "This is so cool!" "Yes! I'm a genius!" he says with a wide smile.

I call up Chris to get some hints on solving. He says what he loves about these puzzles is that they force you to use all your senses. "Sequential discovery puzzles are cool because often you're relying on sound and touch, not so much the visuals of a puzzle."

He embraces the unexpected. He talks about one box that cost $2,500 and was designed to look like an old radio with knobs. To open it, you had to smash down on the top. "It's really counterintuitive when you pay so much money for a puzzle."

THE JOYS OF FRUSTRATION

Some weeks after talking to Chris, I attended the New York Puzzle Party. This is an annual gathering for fans of mechanical puzzles; it was held in the classroom of a Manhattan school a few months before

Covid hit. As one attendee promised, it's about three times geekier than Comic-Con, which was all the enticement I needed.

The idea is to hear puzzle-related talks, trade info, and buy and sell puzzles. I listened to a lecture from a man—who was wearing a blazer decorated with images of Darth Vader, incidentally—about how he hacked a giant jigsaw puzzle.

I heard tales of the best and worst mechanical puzzles. One collector and blogger, Brett Kuehner, told me about a puzzle box that only opened when it was frozen. The problem? The puzzle box arrived in the mail already solved. It was delivered to a Boston home in the middle of winter.

They talked about the best ways to solve puzzle boxes: taking photos, writing flow charts, even X-raying.

On one of the desks in the classroom, a man was selling his late father-in-law's collection for bargain prices. Wooden puzzle boxes for $10 each. I went home with two.

After a week of fiddling, I did finally get one of the two boxes open. It required sliding about ten panels in the correct order and turning the box upside down.

But the other box—one with a gorgeous wooden inlay of Mount Fuji on the top—stymied me. I was able to move one little wooden slat, and then . . . nothing. Hours and hours. Spinning, squeezing, sweet-talking, threatening—nothing.

Failing to open a puzzle box is more frustrating than failing to solve other types of puzzles. At least for me. I'm not sure why. Maybe it's an evolutionary thing. Maybe I'm like a monkey who really *really* wants to open that coconut. Maybe it's the physicality of it—it's always there, in your face, teasing you. Even if there isn't something special inside, it seems that there is.

I try to remind myself that some amount of frustration is good for me. I need to eat my mental broccoli.

I've been reading an excellent book by a professor named Bret Rothstein at Indiana University. It's called *The Shape of Difficulty: A Fan Letter to Unruly Objects*. It's a scholarly take on the profundity of mechanical puzzles, including puzzle boxes. Bret says that mechanical puzzles are beneficial for us: "Objects of this sort keep us humble with their refusal to satisfy expectations."

They teach us important lessons about the dangers of certainty. By depriving our faculties of the "certitude we so crave," they render the world "suddenly surprising, unexpectedly complex."

They teach us to get out of our ruts. "The culprit is habit, which in this case derives from the stickiness of common sense."

Humility, lack of certainty, fresh perspectives—these are some of my favorite lessons from other puzzle genres as well.

I tried to embrace the frustration, as Bret suggested. But at a certain point, the frustration turns into loathing. I began to despise that box. That box became my nemesis.

Finally after a month, I was fiddling with the box while walking through the kitchen, and I accidentally dropped it on the tile floor.

And it popped open!

The fall had jarred something inside. This was not like Chris's box that you were supposed to smash. No, I just broke the box. Does that count as solving or cheating? I'm not certain. Certitude is dangerous.

Regardless, inside was a yellowed piece of paper with a handwritten note in blue pen, dated August 1990:

"To open, slide small piece in front to left. Take small pencil and push to the bottom and end will pop open."

Interesting. The solution is INSIDE the puzzle box, put there thirty years ago. It was a paradox worthy of Escher. Or maybe, since it's Japanese, a Zen koan: the solution is inside the puzzle, but you can't get inside without the solution.

THE GENIUS

Everyone in the puzzle box world said I had to get in touch with a Colorado-based designer named Kagen Sound. "He's on another level," wrote Jerry Slocum, who has authored several books on puzzle history. "He's really, really brilliant," said film director and puzzle fan Darren Aronofsky. "His craftsmanship is insane."

I reach out to Kagen. He is happy to talk. Kagen tells me he got hooked on puzzle boxes after his parents bought one for him as a kid in San Francisco's Chinatown. He offers to give me a video tour of his workshop.

"You can't smell the hints of cedar over the Internet," he says. "And I can't smell it either; I've gotten so used to it."

But the visuals are stunning. One wall holds 159 different-sized clamps, all with bright orange handles. There are saws and sanders and giant Willy Wonka–like steel tubes for sucking up the stray sawdust.

But most of all, there is wood. Cubbyhole after cubbyhole of wooden slats, ranging from dark chocolate to cream colored, from common oak to exotic fifty-thousand-year-old Kauri wood dug out of peat bogs in New Zealand.

"Each wood is different—they all have distinct personalities," Kagen says. "They all have their own density, curliness, color, sliceability."

I spot no less than eight types of maple, one labeled "super curly." Kagen selects the woods for his boxes like a composer selecting notes for a song. "I can look at a board and see it getting subdivided into pieces and folded into a box, like origami."

I ask Kagen what makes a good or bad box. He says it's a lot about the rhythm. The biggest sin for a puzzle box designer? A box without hints or signs of progress. A good box gives solvers a series of aha moments, allows them to open parts that yield to other parts. It has rhythm. As another beloved designer, Robert Yarger, told me, boxes need ups and downs, just like "movies, songs, and sex." This goes for all great puzzles, no matter the genre.

When I speak with Kagen, he is friendly and jovial. But he tells me it was in this very workshop that he almost lost his mind. In 2004, Kagen got a call from Darren Aronofsky, director of such twist-filled movies as *Pi* and *Black Swan*. Aronofsky asked Kagen if he would design a desk with built-in puzzles.

He told Kagen, "It can be whatever you want it to be. You just have to make it perfect."

"I had no idea what I was getting into," Kagen says.

The desk consumed Kagen's life for four and a half years. "I struggled with anxiety and depression at the time. I got cabin fever from being locked in the workshop with that project."

He stopped going out with friends and dating. He gave up his hobbies of hiking and volleyball. He just stayed in the workshop, designing and redesigning, as obsessed as the protagonist of Aronofksy's *Pi*.

But what resulted is Kagen's Sistine Chapel. It's an unbelievable piece of work.

A few weeks later, Darren got on Zoom with me to show off the desk. "I kind of felt guilty for how long the desk took him," he says. "So I asked him to make a bench for the desk, and I overpaid for a bench."

The desk contains twenty-two puzzles, and it took Darren and his son months to solve. On the top is a panel of sliding wooden slats that look like a maze. Move the slats in the right order, and it turns into a checkerboard, which pops open a drawer.

There are puzzles inside each drawer that allow you to open other drawers. The desk isn't ideal if you're in a hurry to find a stapler, but Aronofsky says he loves writing screenplays on it.

But wait, the desk has another level: when you solve all the puzzles, the desk turns into a wooden pipe organ that plays one of Aronofsky's favorite songs, Irving Berlin's "Blue Skies." The notes play when you pull the drawers.

Hold on, there's more! The pipe organ is actually similar to a programmable computer. You can rearrange the pegs in a wooden motherboard and it will play a different song.

Despite the fact that it almost drove him insane, Kagen says he's glad he made it. "I'll get emails from Darren, like 'David Blaine loves it,' or 'Mike D from the Beastie Boys thinks it's great.' It makes my day."

SAVED BY SONDHEIM'S STRATEGY

At the end of my chat with Kagen, I did a foolish thing. I asked Kagen if he would send me the hardest puzzle he ever designed.

He chose a demonic little stumper called the Rune Cube. The cube is about the size of a Rubik's Cube, but it's made of blond wood with metal pins, and it has mysterious symbols carved on the top. Kagen can set it up to be solved relatively easily (6 moves), or he can make it nearly impossible (116 moves). He did the latter.

I made no headway on it. For months. I'd fiddle with it, get frustrated, put it away for a few days, then pick it up again and repeat.

And then I was saved by Stephen Sondheim. Sondheim was a huge puzzle-head, and he collected boxes, including ones from Kagen.

Kagen emailed me that Sondheim gave him a shout-out in a *Games* magazine interview. I read it. And Sondheim said that, to him, solving puzzle boxes is not the point. "I have absolutely no three-dimensional imagination at all . . . I just love the objects. I can almost never open them without looking at the solution sheet. But I don't really care." Sondheim added that he just loves the feel of the boxes. "They're satisfying even if I have to be told how to do them."

Aha! I will be like Sondheim. I will not care about finding the solution myself. I'll just embrace the beauty.

I asked Kagen for the solution, and he sent it to me with a warning: "Even decoding the algebra notation in the solution is a beast." He was right. But after a few days, I was able to tame that beast.

Sure, I didn't solve it in the traditional way. But I tell myself following instructions has its own pleasures. As a kid, I used to spend hours supergluing plastic model cars from elaborate step-by-step directions. It's more like origami, line dancing, or cycling classes—a different experience from puzzling, but still satisfying.

(15) *Controversial Puzzles*

"I didn't send this puzzle out because it was too controversial."

The speaker is mathematician Peter Winkler. He's giving a talk for the National Museum of Mathematics about stumpers he sent to puzzle fans every week during the course of the pandemic. There were a lot of difficult puzzles—but there were some that were just too tricky for public consumption.

One of those: the Sleeping Beauty problem.

It's not controversial in the offensive-to-sensibilities way, he explains. It's controversial in that it's led to a ridiculous, unprecedented amount of debate and is still unsettled.

"This is a puzzle so baffling, it has spawned one hundred philosophy papers," Peter says, among them papers arguing that the puzzle has direct implications about the apocalypse.

It's crazy-making, perhaps literally, as you'll see. It reminds me of the Monty Python sketch about the joke that's so funny, it's dangerous: people who hear it die from laughing.

I'm including a short chapter on the Sleeping Beauty problem because I want to explore puzzles that are so tricky, we may never get a definitive answer. I've researched other unsolved puzzles, like Kryptos and the medieval riddles. But those are slightly different. The Sleeping Beauty problem seems like another level of mystery—one that involves wrestling with profound philosophical ideas.

The Sleeping Beauty problem is a distant cousin of the Monty Hall problem, which is more famous but less controversial. For those who haven't heard or need a refresher: the Monty Hall problem gained notoriety in 1982, when it was featured in a column in *Parade* magazine by the supposedly smartest person in the world, Marilyn vos Savant, who scored 228 on her IQ test. It's called the Monty Hall problem because it is loosely based on the game show *Let's Make a Deal,* hosted by Monty Hall. Here it is:

> Suppose you're on a game show, and you're given the choice of three doors: Behind one door is a car; behind the others, goats. You pick a door, say no. 1, and the host, who knows what's behind the doors, opens another door, say no. 3, which has a goat. He then says to you, "Do you want to pick door no. 2 instead?" Is it to your advantage to switch your choice?*

Pause here if you want to figure it out yourself, spoilers ahead.

Marilyn said yes, you should switch (assuming you want a car, and not a goat).

Marilyn's answer triggered a deluge of angry letters. In fact, several professional mathematicians wrote condescending notes to Marilyn explaining why she was wrong.

Except the twist is: Marilyn was absolutely correct. It's counterintuitive but true. The reason is that when Monty opened the door, he gave you new information. He didn't just pick a random door. He knew what was behind all three doors, and he picked one with a goat.

So now you know that one of the doors hides a goat and one hides a car. If you switch, you have a 2 in 3 probability of winning, which is better than your initial odds of 1 in 3.

One way to visualize it is to take it to the extreme.

Imagine there are 100 doors, with 99 goats and just one car.

You pick a door—say door number 55.

Then the host opens 98 other doors to reveal 98 goats.

All that's left is the door you picked, no. 55, and one other, door no. 73.

Now it's clearer why you should switch doors. It's a 99 in 100 chance, not a 1 in 100 chance.

The Sleeping Beauty problem also deals with counterintuitive

---

* By the way, both the player and the host know beforehand that the host will reveal a goat after the player's first guess.

probabilities. The difference is, the answer to the Sleeping Beauty problem has no universally agreed-upon solution. Mathematicians and philosophers continue to debate in peer-reviewed articles with opaque names such as "The Measure of Existence of a Quantum World and the Sleeping Beauty Problem," and the "Everettian Illusion of Probability and Its Implications for Doomsday and Sleeping Beauty."

As Peter Winkler says, "It is indeed a beauty of a problem."

If you dare, here is the problem (wording courtesy of Wikipedia):

Sleeping Beauty volunteers to undergo the following experiment and is told all of the following details: On Sunday she will be put to sleep. Once or twice, during the experiment, Sleeping Beauty will be awakened, interviewed, and put back to sleep with an amnesia-inducing drug that makes her forget that awakening. A fair coin will be tossed to determine which experimental procedure to undertake:

If the coin comes up heads, Sleeping Beauty will be awakened and interviewed on Monday only.

If the coin comes up tails, she will be awakened and interviewed on Monday and Tuesday.

In either case, she will be awakened on Wednesday without an interview and the experiment ends.

Any time Sleeping Beauty is awakened and interviewed she will not be able to tell which day it is or whether she has been awakened before. During the interview Sleeping Beauty is asked: "What is your credence now for the proposition that the coin landed on heads?"

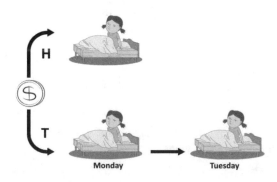

What should Sleeping Beauty say?

Well, many mathematicians and philosophers think she should say the chance of heads is 50 percent. Sleeping Beauty gets no new information when she is awakened, so she should assume the odds of the coin remain those of a fair coin flip: 50/50.

This is the position of the "halfers."

On the other hand, there are the "thirders." These are the folks who argue she should say the chance of heads is 1 in 3. They say: imagine this experiment being done many times to Beauty, week after week. In this case, two-thirds of the times when she wakes up, the coin will have landed on tails (since she is woken up twice as many times when it lands on tails).

But that's just the start. There's a profusion of factions, as Peter Winkler has charted out: besides halfers and thirders, there are dualists, objectors, Lewisian halfers, and double halfers.

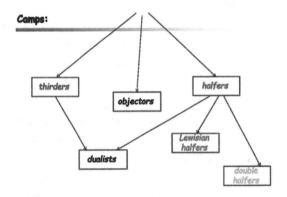

And that's not all.

"The two biggest groups, both underrepresented in journal articles, are those who don't know, and those who don't care," Peter deadpans.

And maybe even another faction, such as my niece: those who think Sleeping Beauty is a creepy fairy tale with consent issues and that the puzzle should be reworded and ditch the cultural baggage.

I didn't read all the papers, but I read enough to know they introduce all sorts of bizarre elements. Some argue the answer depends on the multiverse theory. Or it depends on whether there's a device in the room that records the time. Or it depends on how Sleeping Beauty is feeling—literally, like does she have indigestion.

I don't understand all these, but my gut leans toward the thirder side.

Or more precisely, I'm a thirder who believes the problem might be semantic. I think many arguments can be solved with semantics. Such as the old classic: If a tree falls in a forest, does it make a noise?

If you define noise as the human act of hearing, no, it doesn't make a noise.

If you define noise as air particles bumping into each other, yes, it makes a noise.

So maybe it's the same with Sleeping Beauty.

If you ask her simply, "What are the odds of the coin flip being heads?" That's 50 percent.

If you ask her, "What are the odds the coin flip is heads, taking into account all you know about this experiment and its history?" That's 33.3 percent.

I call Peter up to tell him my solution, aware that I probably didn't settle the debate for all time. I was correct. Peter says the halfers wouldn't buy that. I ask him if he can refer me to a halfer who can give me a clearer argument on their side. Peter refers me to a man named Mike Gefers.

Mike is happy to talk. He's a former high school math teacher who does a lot of tutoring. He read about the Sleeping Beauty problem two years ago, and he went all in.

"It was my white whale," Mike says. "I thought about it all the time. I would spend hours just staring at the wall, trying to figure it out. My wife would come in and say, 'You're still staring at the wall.' And I'd say, 'Would you rather I put a television in front of the wall so that it looks more normal?'

"Two weeks ago, I decided I had worked on it enough. It wasn't healthy for me or my family or my work. I put all my Sleeping Beauty papers in an accordion file, wrapped it in duct tape, and put it in the closet." I'm relieved when I hear this.

"And then your call came," he says. "And I got them out again."

Oh no. What have I done? I'm an enabler. I'm the bartender who keeps pouring bourbons for the alcoholic.

I tell him I'm very uncomfortable being the one to bring the Sleeping Beauty problem back into his life.

"No, no, it's good," he says. "Your interest in this makes me feel like I've got someone to share these ideas with."

I'm still not sure how I feel about the situation, but we spend an hour talking about it.

"I am a halfer because I believe there is a lot of mathematics to support the view," he says. Mike explains the halfer position to me using a variety of metaphors. He references *Groundhog Day* and a cheese cube and Peoria versus Poughkeepsie. He talks about geometry and calculus and the book *Flatland*. I understand about 40 percent of what Mike says. Occasionally, during our hour of conversation, I have a flash of insight. I'll see the halfer position. I'll see it like the vase in the vase/face illusion. And then a minute later it's gone, vanished. (Since I'm not mathematically sophisticated enough to accurately summarize Mike's argument, I've posted a memo from him on thepuzzlerbook.com, for those who want a more in-depth explanation.)

I thank Mike for the crash course in the halfer worldview. I keep in touch with him over the next few months and he assures me that he's less obsessed with the problem.

Is it a massive waste of time for philosophers to argue about this bizarre fictional scenario? Maybe. But maybe not. If you ask them, it has implications for higher math and epistemology, the study of knowledge.

It might even say something about the future of humanity. Or so goes one line of reasoning. In this perspective, your birth is analogous to Sleeping Beauty's waking up. Just as Sleeping Beauty doesn't know what day of the week it is, we don't know where we are in the timeline of human history.

Homo sapiens have been around for about three hundred thousand years. How much longer will humanity last? Another few thousand years? Another million? Another billion? If it's a billion, then you are existing in the first 0.1 percent of humanity's reign. Isn't that kind of weird? And improbable? It'd be like randomly picking a word out of the *Oxford English Dictionary*, and it happened to be aardvark.

I don't know if the analogy holds. Sometimes I buy it, sometimes I don't. Whatever the answer to the Sleeping Beauty experiment, I do hope humanity is in the first Monday of a very long experiment.

CHAPTER

(16) *Cryptics*

I t's been several months since I first heard about the fearsome cryptic—that British puzzle that Brendan Emmett Quigley described as a colonoscopy combined with an organ transplant. I've decided I'm ready to take it on. I've been preparing myself for a range of emotions: bafflement, frustration, despair, and anger.

I'm especially concerned about anger.

I've experienced anger when grappling with several puzzles this year. I've crumpled up a bunch of Japanese logic puzzles, and I've thrown a Rubik's-type polyhedron across the room.

But the truth is, anger is counterproductive to puzzle solving. And to problem solving in general. This is not just me talking. This is the current wisdom in psychology. Several studies indicate we are better able to solve problems when we are in a good mood. Positive emotions enhance our creativity. Anger, on the other hand, dampens our ability to make mental leaps. Plus, getting angry makes me feel like hell and ruins my day.

Recently, I was watching a webinar from a child psychologist. The topic was something like "a parent's guide to surviving quarantine," and I figured I could use all the help I could get.

During the webinar, the psychologist gave the following advice: "Don't get furious. Get curious."

I don't think a phrase is automatically true just because it rhymes. For instance, if the glove doesn't fit, you don't have to acquit. But this particular rhyming phrase seems both wise and true.

The psychologist was suggesting that, if your kid is throwing a tantrum because, say, she painted her balsa wood boat the wrong color, don't get furious at her. Get curious.

Get curious as to why it makes her so upset. Get curious as to whether there's a deeper underlying issue. Get curious about what concrete steps we can take to solve this problem and prevent it in the future.

It's a hard mantra to employ. Kids often act like little psychopaths whose only job is to infuriate us. But I think it's a deep insight. And not just in parenting. Why not try to approach almost all life problems and societal problems with the same idea, from politics to health to romance to friendship?

This is the puzzle mindset. We should look at a problem and figure out potential solutions instead of just wallowing in rage and doubling down on our biases. I didn't come up with this idea, of course. It's a theme that has popped up over and over in my reading and conversations this year. The idea is expressed using different metaphors.

The author and podcaster Julia Galef talks about the scout mindset versus the soldier mindset. Scouts explore the intellectual terrain looking for truth, for information that counters their biases, for evidence one way or the other. Soldiers, on the other hand, are looking to win the intellectual battle by any means necessary. They are looking to confirm their biases using motivated reasoning.

Meanwhile, the popular website LessWrong published a viral post a few years ago about mistake theory and conflict theory. These are two ways of seeing the world. Conflict theorists see society through the lens of a zero-sum struggle between classes or ethnicities or political parties. Mistake theorists see society through a non-zero-sum lens. They argue many of society's problems are the result of mistaken practices and beliefs, and we can fix them with the proper tools and approach. While both are valuable lenses, I think placing more emphasis on mistake theory would do us good.

Psychologist Adam Grant uses a different schema in his bestseller *Think Again*. He categorizes thinkers into scientists, preachers, prosecutors, and politicians. Only one of them, the scientist, is open to changing her mind; the others are using motivated reasoning. Finally, I interviewed David Bornstein, the cofounder of Solutions Journalism Network—a group that advocates for more articles exploring solutions to social ills instead of just pointing them out. He says we need to think more like engineers and less like lawyers, because engineers look for solutions, while lawyers look for evidence that reinforces their side.

All these metaphors have in common the idea of trying to turn down the volume on motivated reasoning and anger, while turning up the volume on curiosity and the search for solutions.

It's a daily battle, but I have decided to attempt to be more curious and less furious in every part of my life, from puzzles to politics to raising my kids. It could be a small problem, like what ingredients should I stock up on for the coming week. Or it could be a big one, like an argument over politics. If I'm talking to someone with different politics, I try not to think of it as a battle of words but rather as a puzzle: What is the root of the disagreement? And is there anything we can do to resolve it?

It's a powerful way to frame problems. Even just inserting the word "puzzle" can make a difference. If I hear about the climate crisis, I want to curl up in a fetal position in the corner. But if I'm asked about the climate puzzle, I want to try to solve it. That, to me, is the only way out of our current mess.

We could all use more curiosity, one of the greatest human virtues. I once interviewed the late *Jeopardy!* host Alex Trebek for a magazine article, and he told me something I think of often. He said, "I'm curious about everything—even those things that don't interest me." It's a bit paradoxical, perhaps even nonsensical. But I think it'd be a better world if everyone was more like Alex. ABC: Always be curious.

GO TIME

Okay, back to this potentially infuriating British cryptic. As I mentioned in the crossword chapter, American crosswords and British cryptics are different. With cryptics, it's all wordplay. Crazy, esoteric wordplay, including homophones, puns, and coded language.

Those who don't like them say British cryptics are elitist, impenetrable. One puzzler compared them to getting shoved into a locker in middle school. And there is surely some extra sadism. One of the most famous cryptic makers proudly went by the pen name Torquemada.

But cryptics have plenty of fans. As Brendan put it, American crosswords seem kind of boring and one-dimensional in comparison. Stephen Sondheim was an early supporter of cryptics. Many years ago, he wrote an article for *New York Magazine* with the headline: "What's a Four-letter Word for 'East Indian Betel Nut' and Who Cares?"

His point was that he didn't give a hoot about weird trivia. Wordplay, on the other hand, is a treat. He wrote: "A good clue can give you all the pleasures of being duped that a mystery story can. It has surface innocence, surprise, the revelation of concealed meaning, and the catharsis of solution."

Over the years, American crosswords have become a bit more like cryptics. They've toned down the obscure trivia and ramped up the wordplay. But there's still a big gap between crosswords and cryptics.

So for all you Yanks, grab a Pabst Blue Ribbon and a refrigerated egg and read this admittedly oversimplified intro.

A cryptic clue has two parts: the straight-ahead definition part, and the wordplay part. The straight-ahead definition is a synonym for the answer. The wordplay part is about homophones or anagrams or other manipulations of the letters.

Here's a sample of a cryptic clue:

"Only about five do the puzzle."

What?

Okay, let's break it down.

Take the first three words of the clue: "Only about five."

Well, "only" is a synonym for "sole."

"Five" means the Roman numeral V.

And "about" is cryptic-speak that tells you the letter V is inside the word "sole."

Hence: SOL(V)E.

Or Solve.

Remember, the other part of the clue is a straight-ahead definition. In this case, "Do the puzzle."

Which is also: Solve.

Why have cryptics taken off in Britain but are still niche in the United States?

One cryptic maker I interviewed suggested that "perhaps Americans are more straightforward thinkers, while British have a more convoluted, tortured, how-can-I-make-my-life-more-difficult mind." I appreciate him calling us straightforward thinkers, which sounds better than dum-dums.

Now just to make things more complicated but also more accurate: There is a separate category of American-style cryptic puzzles. These puzzles are similar to British cryptics, but the answers are usually less obscure, more accessible. American cryptics have a growing fan base, and can be found in *The New Yorker, The Wall Street Journal,* and, occasionally, in *The New York Times.* In fact, the sample cryptic clue above is from an American cryptic by Richard Silvestri. So if you like wordplay, but find the British cryptics too much, American cryptics could be your cup of tea (to use a British idiom). You can find an original American-style cryptic by Sara Goodchild on page 285 of this book.

THE ORGAN TRANSPLANT

I retrieve the email where Brendan sent me the British cryptic that almost broke his spirit. Brendan suggests that it's important to work on cryptics in pairs. It's hard to go it alone. So I recruit as my co-solver my twenty-five-year-old niece, Andrea, who is a better crossworder than I am (not to be confused with my other niece, Ally, who is a better jigsaw solver).

I open the cryptic. As Brendan warned, it is nearly impenetrable. A word salad. I'm tempted to use Google. I have no moral objection to people solving crosswords with Google. But I've kept up a no-googling policy for myself for years, so I resist. Finally, my niece and I crack one clue, 23-Across.

"Fans backing style of print"

We figure out that the "style of print" refers to serif.

The word "backing" in the clue means to spell serif backwards, so: "Fires."

"Fires" is a synonym for "fans." Both can mean to increase something's strength.

So the answer is "fires."

The next few hours bring zero other breaks. I won't look at Google, but what if I called the editor for help? Is that cheating? Probably. But desperate times. He can at least tell me how to think about the puzzle.

I track him down on LinkedIn. Turns out he is a lovely man named Tom Johnson who is as British as sticky toffee pudding. Example: when his computer froze, he said, "Crikey!" Also, he moved our interview time because it conflicted with the British soap opera *Coronation Street.*

Tom edited the puzzle, but he didn't create it. The creator goes by the pseudonym of "Pabulum."

"Pabulum always makes puzzles which are fair, but they are the extreme end of fair," Tom says.

Others might argue he left fair far behind.

I ask Tom about a couple of clues. Tom is stumped. "The trouble is, I forget about them as soon as I'm on to the next."

Aha! So even the editor of the puzzle has trouble. That makes me feel better.

"What about 20-Down?" I ask.

The clue is:

"Slaughtering hectic shah is wrong."

Tom goes to retrieve the answer sheet.

"Ah, the answer is 'Schechitah.' "

I've never heard of this word. I ask Tom to decode the clue.

Here's the explanation: "Slaughtering hectic shah is wrong."

Well, "wrong" is a code word for "there's an anagram in the clue."

If you do an anagram of the phrase "hectic shah," you get the word "Schechitah."

Schechitah is a Hebrew word for when you kill an animal according to kosher laws. And this is a synonym for the first word in the clue, "slaughtering."

Easy!

Just so you know: I'm Jewish and I also wrote an entire book about Judaism and the Bible, and I'd never heard the word. Tom sends me on my way with a piece of advice: "Look at the clues from every possible angle."

I return to the Pabulum cryptic with my niece. We tag-team it, texting each other hypotheses every day, trying out paths, backtracking. I remind myself to be curious, not furious. My desk is sprinkled with pink eraser bits.

It takes longer than the nine days I worked on Peter Gordon's Fireball crossword. Finally, after five weeks, on a Friday afternoon, we finish. At least part 1. Then we have to do the meta-puzzle, which is equally absurd (rearrange the letters of the answers to make them into obscure animals, such as MARTIAN into TAMARIN).

After the experience, my niece tells me that she is officially removing British cryptics from her puzzle diet. But I want to keep trying, at least with the more reasonable ones. I want to resist being furious at cryptics, and to be curious. I ask myself: What are the redeeming qualities of cryptics? I reflect upon a few.

First, the aha moments, as in most good puzzles, were powerful. After all that work, the reward of cracking a clue seems particularly well deserved.

Second, I remember that cryptics saved the world. Or at least helped the Allies win World War II. In 1942, the British newspaper *The Daily Telegraph* held a cryptic contest at its offices. Competitors who solved the cryptic in less than twelve minutes apparently received a letter offering them a job at the Bletchley Park codebreaking operation. The puzzle was a secret recruiting tool to find brilliant brains to help crack the Nazis' Enigma code. (See next page for the puzzle.)

The Telegraph printed the cryptic in the newspaper the day after the contest. I tried it, and it took me far longer than twelve minutes. So if I had any fantasies of being a codebreaker, this took care of them.

The final virtue I found in cryptics is that they are so punny. I have a complicated relationship with puns. Unlike most of my puzzling compatriots, I wasn't born a pun fanatic. I often found them more wince-inducing than pleasurable. My father-in-law was a chronic punster—I can't remember most of them, but one of the more painful ones involved "olive" and the first letter of the Hebrew alphabet "aleph"—and I usually reacted by staring at the carpet, so as not to encourage him. This year of puzzling, however, has made my mind more punny. I've started to see puns all over. I can't help it (but unlike my late father-in-law, I try not to say them out loud). I see pun opportunities I missed in my past. I recently realized that I wrote an entire book organized by body part—heart, lung, and so forth—and I didn't end with the appendix.

I now have decided that puns get an unfairly bad rap. For one thing, puns remind us of the trickiness of the English language. The heart of a pun is that one word can mean two different things. Often wildly different things. English is particularly prone to multiuse words. The word "run" has more than six hundred definitions in the *Oxford English Dictionary,* and that's just for its verb form.

This ambiguity can be used for harmless (if groan-inducing) reasons, like word

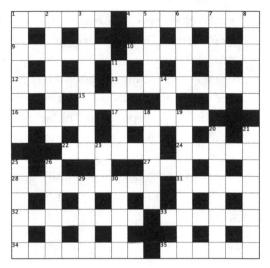

Across

1. A Stage company (6)
4. The direct route preferred by the Roundheads (5,3)
9. One of the ever-greens (6)
10. Scented (8)
12. Course with an apt finish (5)
13. Much that could be got from a timber merchant (5,4)
15. We have nothing and are in debt (3)
16. Pretend (5)
17. Is this town ready for a flood? (6)
22. The little fellow has some beer; it makes me lose colour, I say (6)
24. Fashion of a famous French family (5)
27. Tree (3)
28. One might of course use this tool to core an apple (6,3)
31. Once used for unofficial currency (5)
32. Those well brought up help these over stiles (4,4)
33. A sport in a hurry (6)
34. Is the workshop that turns out this part of a motor a hush-hush affair? (8)
35. An illumination functioning (6)

Down

1. Official instruction not to forget the servants (8)
2. Said to be a remedy for a burn (5,3)
3. Kind of alias (9)
5. A disagreeable company (5)
6. Debtors may have to this money for their debts unless of course their creditors do it to the debts (5)
7. Boat that should be able to suit anyone (6)
8. Gear (6)
11. Business with the end in sight (6)
14. The right sort of woman to start a dame school (3)
18. The "war" (anag.) (6)
19. When hammering take care not to hit this (5,4)
20. Making sound as a bell (8)
21. Half a fortnight of old (8)
23. Bird, dish or coin (3)
25. This sign of the Zodiac has no connection with the Fishes (6)
26. A preservative of teeth (6)
29. Famous sculptor (5)
30. This part of the locomotive engine would sound familiar to the golfer (5)

Solution on page 316

puzzles and puns. But it can also be exploited and muddle our thinking on important matters. The word "free" is an example. "Free" has multiple definitions. Mostly, it's got a positive aura to it. So when you say "free market," for instance, you're immediately disposed to like a free market. But if a market is totally "free" in this sense—zero government regulations whatsoever—it may cause the opposite of freedom in other ways: monopolies thrive, customers lack freedom of choice, workers lack freedom to negotiate.

This kind of puzzle trains us to be more skeptical, more wary of how a series of letters can mean different things in different contexts (the word "mean" has sixteen definitions, by the way, from "nasty" to "average" to "cheap" to "signify").

One Cryptic from History

This is one of the most heartbreaking puzzles I've ever seen. In it, longtime cryptic creator the Reverend John Graham (known as "Araucaria") announces to his readers that he has a fatal disease. It appeared in *The Guardian* in 2013. Graham, ninety-one, died a few months later. He told *The Guardian,* "It seemed the natural thing to do somehow," he said. "It just seemed right."

Araucaria has 18 down of the 19, which is being treated with 13, 15.

Copyright Guardian News & Media Ltd 2021

ACROSS

1 Subject to town hall causing milieu's panic (12)
9 Encounter dog's home (5)
10 Araucaria beginning to recite old poetry books, bringing Christmas cheer (9)
11 Man with a first having common sense? That's terrible (7)
12 Scouse blues go green in time for energy supplier (7)
13,15 Friendly (say) vicar at ease (say) with arrangement for coping with 18 down (10,4)
18 101° under the ice? (4)
19 Food transporter heard to gradually reduce an endless effusion (10)
22 Place(s) of non-vintage vintage? (7)
24 Food related to cake of soap? (4,3)
25 Complete very large reproduction with look at 19 etc (9)
26 See 1 down
27 Bargain keeping mum to deal with 18 down (12)

DOWN

1,26 18 down worker gives coat to factory girl and father of archbishop's killer? (9,5)
2 Northern ocean hides love which could give ultimate 13, 15 (8)
3 French writer passed, only first out of university (5)
4 Overplay muddle over old Frenchman (9)
5 Hang about to see the Queen of Italy (6)
6 Scamp item to expand 19, for example (5)
7 Accident on motorway summit? (6)
8 Case lacking in posture (6)
14 Corrupt dealing with crime, the French abandoning the leader of the march? (9)
16 Gray's works (in two volumes?) contain opening of Byzantine controversy (4-5)
17 Plant reported to be enemy to skin complaint (8)
18 Sign of growth (6)
20 Fat found Poles at end of day (6)
21 Beast of Oz whose subject was cats (6)
23 Dimension accompanying outside number (5)
24 Cook said to be lawman and impresario (5)

Solution to One Cryptic from History is found on page 316.

(17) **Scavenger Hunts and Puzzle Hunts**

In January of 2020, I found myself on a train to Boston to compete in the biggest puzzle event of the year, the Ironman Triathlon for Nerds. Well, that's what I think of it as. The official name is the MIT Mystery Hunt.

And my analogy is only semi-accurate. The MIT Mystery Hunt is actually much longer than an Ironman Triathlon: seventy-two hours of excruciating mental anguish, punctuated by joyous aha moments.

Founded in 1981, the Mystery Hunt attracts about two thousand of the world's smartest people to the campus of the Massachusetts Institute of Technology to wrestle with some of the most difficult puzzles ever designed. I'm talking crosswords with no clues, fortune cookies containing baffling symbols, riddles that require algebraic topology.

If your team is the first to solve all of the 150 or so puzzles, the answers will lead you to the prize: a coin hidden somewhere on the MIT campus. The teams are huge. Some have more than fifty people. This is because it helps to have a variety of minds—engineers, astronomers, experts on mid-'90s hip-hop. You never know what you'll need.

The puzzles themselves contain no instructions. You just have to figure out what the heck the puzzle creator is getting at. Most often, solving the puzzle requires an insight linking two wildly different realms. For instance, a series of numbers turns out to be longitude and latitude, which then turns out to be a list of towns on Justin Bieber's last tour.

The MIT Mystery Hunt is legendary. It has spawned a slew of off-spring. Colleges and corporations host puzzle hunts. There's a monthly national puzzle hunt called Puzzled Pint held at local bars.

There are escape rooms, which have been heavily influenced by the MIT Mystery Hunt. More on them later.

I'm going to MIT for two reasons. First, to test my skills. But I have another motive: I want to learn some secrets to puzzlemaking.

As I mentioned in the introduction, my wife, Julie, is president of an event company called Watson Adventures. They put on games and scavenger hunts for the public and for companies. Julie figured if I'm writing a book on puzzles, she should at least get some free labor out of it. So I have been tasked with creating a puzzle hunt for Watson Adventures.

I'm on the lookout for lessons at MIT, and I learn my first one soon after arriving:

Lesson 1

The real goal is NOT to stump the solvers. The real goal is to bond the puzzlers together through a shared struggle.

On Friday morning, I join hundreds of other hunters in the campus auditorium. The puzzlemakers stage a skit that serves as an introduction to the hunt. To everyone's surprise, this year's skit includes a wedding. A legally binding wedding. The bride and groom are two puzzlers who had met and fallen in love at a previous event.

The groom says: "This weekend, as we celebrate this art form, which is about creating fun and joy to share with your friends and loved ones, I promise to be your partner. I promise to fill your life with puzzles and puns. I KEN-KEN promise you never to DOUBLE ACROSTIC you. Simply because you a-MAZE me."

The audience responds with a mix of groans, laughter, and "awwws." I remind myself of the upside of puns.

After the skit, the teams disperse and gather at their respective headquarters. My team's home base is a skylit MIT classroom filled with whiteboards, dozens of laptops, and a tangle of computer cords.

I've been invited onto the team by my friend Alex Rosenthal, a puzzler who works at TED-Ed. The team is called Setec Astronomy, which is an anagram of the phrase "Too Many Secrets." And when the teammates see each other, it's like a family reunion. They hug each other, catch up on kids and work and one teammate's lawsuit against a computer company for spamming his email.

Coincidentally, Greg Pliska—the man who created the puzzles for this book—is a teammate, as is his wife, Jessica, who is also a puzzler, though not quite as obsessed. She says, "I once said to Greg, 'These are some of the smartest people in the world, and they're here doing these ridiculous puzzles. Shouldn't they be curing cancer?' And Greg said, 'A lot of them do spend the other 362 days trying to cure cancer. But these three days they are here.'"

I'm reminded of the aforementioned Cass Sunstein's talk about the challenge of bridging cultural gaps. Cass did research involving groups of liberals and conservatives. Debating the issues just drove them further apart. When they did a crossword puzzle, however, they were able to work well together.

So maybe we need to have the United Nations do an MIT puzzle hunt. I'm only half-joking.

Lesson 2

Choose a theme, and go all in.

The MIT Mystery Hunt isn't just a random collection of 150 crazy-hard puzzles. The puzzles are linked by a story, a theme.

This year's theme: an amusement park. The real-life newlyweds will be spending their honeymoon at the fictional Penny Park. It turns out, Penny Park is on the verge of bankruptcy, and the teams need to find the magic coin that will restore the park to solvency.

The puzzlemakers have committed to this theme and committed hard. They've dressed up as characters in Penny Park—a clown, a wizard, a wolf—and spent the weekend walking from room to room in full costume.

I was too oblivious to realize, but one of my teammates points out the character names in the opening skit were references to foreign coins—other countries' versions of pennies. Kopek the Clown is named for the Russian currency, Luma the Astronaut is Armenian. It was the first of many times that weekend I'd say, "Ooooh."

Lesson 3

Stretch the very idea of what a puzzle can be.

The puzzles start relatively sanely. The first puzzle pops up at exactly 1 P.M. on Friday. It is a list of jobs, and we have to figure out the common link between pairs of jobs. Who "performs Hail Marys"? Well, a priest *and* a quarterback.

The Setec Astronomers crack the puzzle in about half an hour. They submit the solution—which, as usual, is a single word—to the puzzlemakers' website. Correct. That unlocks the next set of puzzles.

As the weekend goes on, though, the puzzles become weirder and more creative. One puzzle involves following complex knitting directions. In the end, you're supposed to get an elaborate object out of red yarn. Another puzzle is reminiscent of Pictionary, but instead of drawing pictures, you must communicate with teammates via pancakes. You use multicolored batter to create identifiable images in the pancakes, which your teammates have to guess.

Interestingly, MIT Mystery Hunters are allowed to use Google in their attempts to solve the puzzles. But the puzzles are so out-of-the-box that Google will only get you so far.

The puzzles are invariably brilliant and difficult, but also sometimes gross. A few years ago, one puzzle was in the form of a fudge-filled diaper. The clues were buried in the fudge.

This year's grossest puzzle is based on the board game Operation and carries the warning "Not for the squeamish." Not being particularly squeamish, I think this could be my big break. So far, I have contributed barely anything. Well, that's not quite true. The first puzzle did involve cutting up pieces of paper, and I'm decent with scissors, so I did that. But as for aha moments? Not much.

I clicked the not-for-the-squeamish puzzle on my laptop. The image is a cartoon drawing of a naked, paunchy, and genital-free man like the one in Operation.

If you click on the cartoon's various body parts, up pops a video of real-life surgery. Real blood-and-guts close-ups.

Someone on the team—not me—figures out that we first need to identify the precise types of surgeries. We recruit one of the surgeons on the team. "That's an umbilical hernia. That's a lung transplant. And a craniotomy."

Someone—again, not me—figures out that each of these surgeries has an official code number in the insurance industry. Somehow, these yield a series of letters and we start filling in the blanks at the bottom of the page.

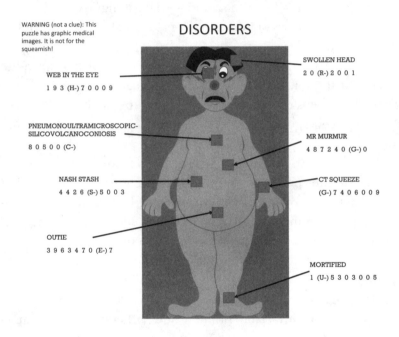

WARNING (not a clue): This puzzle has graphic medical images. It is not for the squeamish!

DISORDERS

WEB IN THE EYE
1 9 3 (H-) 7 0 0 0 9

SWOLLEN HEAD
2 0 (R-) 2 0 0 1

PNEUMONOULTRAMICROSCOPIC-
SILICOVOLCANOCONIOSIS
8 0 5 0 0 (C-)

MR MURMUR
4 8 7 2 4 0 (G-) 0

NASH STASH
4 4 2 6 (S-) 5 0 0 3

CT SQUEEZE
(G-) 7 4 0 6 0 0 9

OUTIE
3 9 6 3 4 7 0 (E-) 7

MORTIFIED
1 (U-) 5 3 0 3 0 0 5

B _ _ C K _ _ E

"What if the word is blockage?" I ask.

A pause.

"Nice!"

"You 'Wheel of Fortuned' it!" says one of my teammates.

Yes I did. I didn't do any of the high-level work, but I did fill in the letters like a basic game show contestant. What a relief. With my Operation insight, I feel I contributed perhaps 0.04 percent to the greater effort.

(Note: Blockage is not the final answer. We needed to do about fourteen other permutations to get the final answer, which is Tracheostomy.)

Lesson 4

Avoid puzzle clichés.

As I mentioned, the MIT Mystery Hunt has had a great influence on escape rooms. Escape rooms, which first appeared about fifteen years ago, are smaller in scope and much shorter than the Mystery Hunt— usually involving no more than a dozen people, who spend an hour or so solving puzzles. The gimmick is that the puzzlers are trapped, and solving the puzzles will reveal the code that will let them unlock an escape door in the room. Or in the igloo or coffin, depending on the theme.

If you like nerdy inside puzzle jokes, the Mystery Hunt is the place for you. One of the MIT puzzles is a parody of an escape room. It's not a real escape room. Instead, we are given an audio recording of several drunk escape room contestants trying to solve puzzles. We have to re-create the puzzles and solve them based on the ramblings of the (fictional) contestants. It's very meta.

The fake escape room mocks many of the clichés found in real escape rooms, such as answers exposed by black light.

"I love escape rooms, but you tend to see a lot of the same puzzles in them," says one MIT puzzler. "I don't think I ever need to see another puzzle where you have to use semaphore flags."

It turns out that one of my teammates works at an escape room. It's a challenging job. You have idiot clients who sabotage the props. You have people sticking their fingers in electrical outlets thinking it might be a puzzle. You have nudist groups who like the privacy a closed-door activity affords.

Many escape rooms have the sleazy bachelor problem. This is a guy who comes every week with a different woman and pretends it's his first time at that escape room. His hope, apparently, is that his date will be awed by his mastery of anagrams and the NATO alphabet.

Two of the Mystery Hunt competitors happen to be the world's foremost experts on escape rooms. They are a married New Jersey–based couple named David and Lisa Spira. They've done, at last count, more than nine hundred escape rooms, and they have a witty blog *(Room Escape Artist)* where they review rooms.

David tells me that he fell in love with escape rooms early on, after doing his first one in New York in 2014.

When he finished that first room and walked back onto the street, David says he was in an altered state. "It's almost like you're on a drug. You're in this state of hyper-awareness, almost a primal state, like you're back in the Neolithic era and you have to be aware because there might be something in the grass that wants to jump out at you." You notice things you never noticed before. David says he had this feeling after his first few dozens of rooms, but no longer gets this rush. "I miss it so much," he says. I flash back to that feeling I had after the riddle about the wind. I know what he means.

David and Lisa tell me some people are creating brilliant and innovative escape rooms, but there are also lazy escape room designers. There's even a lingo for common blunders. "Lock orgy" means the room has too many locks. "Number soup" means there is an overload of numerical codes. So, as always, avoid clichés.

Lesson 5

Limit the busywork.

At one point during the weekend, I am working on a puzzle with a teammate, when he declares, "I am so angry at this puzzle. I really have a lot of hatred toward it." He is furious, not curious.

The anger-inducing puzzle contains 150 seemingly unrelated images (a teddy bear, a sailboat, a house) that somehow need to be connected. It's too random, too unclear. Even MIT puzzlemakers can miss the mark sometimes.

One big problem is when a puzzle requires too much grinding busywork and not enough moments of revelation. One puzzle this year, for instance, required a spreadsheet with thousands of cells.

You want to give solvers "checkpoints"—occasional wins that will keep them motivated throughout the frustration.

Lesson 6

Provide closure.

On Monday, we gather again in an MIT auditorium. The emcee announces the winner: a team called ✈✈✈ Galactic Trendsetters ✈✈✈ (the airplane emojis, incidentally, are an important part of the team name, which is pronounced "wooosh Galactic Trendsetters neeoooowh").

Surprisingly, most members of Setec Astronomy are not crushed. This is because winning is a mixed blessing. The winning team gets to (or has to) create the following year's hunt, which involves thousands of hours of work. My team, having won twice in the last five years, is ready for a break.

An emcee reveals that the winning coin was hidden in a machine in one of MIT's classrooms. They've brought the fridge-sized gadget onstage. It is, naturally, a ridiculously intricate device made from a discarded electron microscope, adorned with vacuum tubes and flashing multicolored lights. If you put sixteen other coins in the proper slots, a latch on the machine opens up, releasing a puff of dry-ice smoke, and out pops the prize coin.

The honeymoon has been a success. Penny Park has been saved!

The newlyweds stand up in the front row, to a roar of approval. The groom goes in for a kiss. The bride pulls her head away (one last misdirection!), then they kiss for real.

MY ADVENTURES IN PUZZLEMAKING

With the lessons I learned at the MIT Mystery Hunt, I am ready to face my assignment: make a virtual puzzle hunt for Watson Adventures, my wife's company. "I'll be your boss, and I'll be a real hard-ass," Julie says. "That'll be good for your book."

Watson Adventures was founded twenty years ago by our friend Bret Watson, who worked with us at *Entertainment Weekly* magazine. Bret loves museums, but he couldn't get his friends to go with him. So he turned museums into a game. He created clever, often tricky clues, and had his friends scour the museum looking for surprising details in the paintings and sculptures (the image of a potato peeler on the back of a Van Gogh self-portrait, for instance). It was a scavenger hunt, but for obscure information.

His friends liked it. They were so enthusiastic that Bret decided to go pro. Julie was the first employee and head of the business side. The two of them turned Watson Adventures into a real business, with employees, an office, a photocopier, the whole deal. I've watched proudly from the sideline as they grew their company.

They've now run thousands of scavenger hunts all over the country. Some are for corporate team building, others are for the public or weddings or bar mitzvahs. I've done a bunch of them. I can objectively say they are loads of fun.

My game will have to be virtual. With museums shut down because of Covid, Watson Adventures pivoted to online games. Julie and Bret want to create a murder mystery for teams to solve on Zoom.

Following the MIT lessons, the first thing I need is a theme. Julie and I love board games, so what if that was the theme? Puzzles based on Monopoly, Settlers of Catan, Operation (though mine would skip the gruesome surgery footage).

I pitch it to Julie. "What if it was based at the Parker Brothers headquarters," I say. "But we could call it something else. Barker Brothers. And the two Barker brothers are both in love with the same woman. And it leads to this twisted murder-suicide at the board game factory."

"Um," Julie says. "You know a lot of our clients are companies, right? Doing team building? You sure a creepy family love triangle is the way to go?"

Point taken. Along with my co-writer—a Watson Adventures staffer named Ryan Greene—we decide on a more G-rated murder at a board game store, love triangle not included. Competitors would be given ten puzzles, each with a one-word answer. Those ten answers feed into a meta-puzzle (like the one in this book). Put them together and you figure out the murderer.

Ryan and I start brainstorming. We take a board game—Othello— and try to figure out how to turn it into a puzzle. How can we hide a code in that? What if the black and white pieces were dots and dashes of Morse code? Nah, that doesn't sound fun.

One thing becomes clear very quickly: it's hard to find the Goldilocks zone. You want to create puzzles that aren't too easy but not impossible either. As Greg Pliska once told me, "There's nothing easier than creating a puzzle no one can solve."

You need to try to see the world from the solver's point of view. You need to avoid what psychologist and author Steven Pinker calls "the curse of knowledge," which is the problem writers face from knowing too much about a topic. You need to try to look at the puzzle as if it's your first time. For instance, I created one puzzle that led to a bunch of words: thimble, iron, race car, Scottish terrier, wheelbarrow.

Solvers have to find the link among them. (Pause here if you want to try it yourself.)

I couldn't decide: Is it too obvious that they are all Monopoly tokens? Or too obscure?

Another challenge: the sheer number of constraints. As I've mentioned, I'm a firm believer that constraints yield creativity. There's nothing more overwhelming than giving someone a blank page and telling them to write whatever they want.

But maybe there's such a thing as too many constraints?

As a puzzlemaker, I'm constrained by copyrights—my idea to have a puzzle linking hammerhead sharks and MC Hammer is a no-go, because we can't get the rights to MC Hammer's photo.

I'm constrained by appropriateness. For one puzzle involving songs and body parts (for instance, "Under My Thumb" by the Rolling Stones, and "Poker Face" by Lady Gaga), I had to reject my friends' suggestion that I include "Baby Got Back."

Finally, after a week, we have ten puzzles we think are decent. Not groundbreaking, like the MIT puzzles are. But, I hope, solid and entertaining. And at least none of them uses black light.

Then comes the most stress-inducing part of puzzlemaking. The test run. Watson Adventures recruited a couple of dozen volunteers to be guinea pigs. And on a Tuesday night, they all Zoom in, get their instructions, and go off to their team Zoom rooms.

I drop into Team 2's room to observe. It's a family from Virginia, and they are struggling with the first puzzle—a Scrabble-like puzzle where you have to fill in letters to make words.

"Is it *pears*?" one guesses.

I make a face. I hate seeing them flailing.

"Tears?" another says.

I break my silence: "Lions and tigers and . . ."

"Bears!" one says.

Not exactly a subtle hint.

This happens several times throughout the night. I go into a room, see them struggling. I start to sweat and then blab the answer.

It is then that I realize, sadly, I'm not cut out to be a puzzlemaker. In the book *Puzzlecraft*, which is about how to make puzzles, co-author Mike Selinker talks about the people he hires to help run puzzle events:

> *The ones that don't get invited back are those that cannot bear to see a solver in pain. The solver will come up, eraser worn to a nub, and say, "I can't solve this!" The puzzle staffer who says "Here, I'll show you the answer" is failing in her job. Because the solver doesn't want to know the answer. People solve puzzles because they like pain, and they like being released from pain, and they like most of all that they find within themselves the power to release themselves from their own pain. What the solver wants from you is acknowledgment that she is not wasting time.*

The bottom line is, I'm not sadistic enough to be a puzzlemaker. I prefer masochism.

It's the same reason I'm no good at pulling practical jokes. When my dad is telling a stranger that the whole family was born on February 29, I can tolerate the awkwardness only so long before I shake my head and confess the truth.

I can't wait to return to the land of the tortured, not the torturer.

Three Puzzles from Scavenger Hunt History

1) Here is one of the puzzles I made for Watson Adventures. The instructions are:

Each drawing in Column A pairs with a drawing in Column B to represent a common phrase. Fill in the phrases to reveal the one-word answer.

Doodlepalooza

A	B

1. _ _ _ _ _   _ _ _ _ _□_

2. _ _ _ _□_   _ _ _ _ _

3. _ _ _ _ _ _   _ _□_ _ _

4. _ _ _□_ _ _   _ _ _ _ _ _

5. □_ _ _ _   _ _ _

6. _ _ _ _ _ _   _ _ _ _□

2) The very first MIT Mystery Hunt was held in 1981 and was written by MIT student Brad Schaefer. It was just twelve questions on a double-sided sheet of paper. The winning team got a keg of beer. It included a complicated mathematical equation, a Chinese logogram, and a message on a flagpole located on the MIT campus. Here are a sample of the questions, which were a lot harder pre-Google. The full hunt (all two pages!) can be found on the MIT Mystery Hunt website.

    a. Nearest globular cluster to Cor Caroli
    b. Tweedledum's rank
    c. "He that plays the king shall be ____; his majesty shall have tribute of me."
    d. First word of the Bible.

3) This is one of the 152 puzzles at the 2020 MIT Mystery Hunt. As is customary, there are no instructions. The answer is a single word. Don't try it alone. Find a partner—or fifty. It was constructed by Justin Graham.

Bobcat

Fun fact about bobcats: their yowls sound like cheering and screaming. Maybe that's why all the other animals in their enclosure like entertaining them.

1. These animals worship flights of fancy

2. These animals are glad to be all in the same place.

3. Please spill your sweetener on this animal.

4. This animal likes rosé homes.

5. This animal shouts out a warning when a tree is falling.

6. This animal set itself on fire on your behalf.

7. These animals are also known as the monarch of precipitation.

8. These animals can be found just a few kilometers above the troposphere.

9. These animals have marshmallow all over their noggin.

10. These animals may lose their teeth after eating one of Mackintosh's confections.

11. These animals have organized themselves into a euphoric corporation.

12. Look out! This animal is starting to do it another time.

13. These animals would like to express their happiness to the entire globe.

14. These animals will shake you as if you were in a tropical storm.

15. These animals operate an inn on the West Coast.

Solutions to Three Puzzles from Scavenger Hunt History begin on page 316.

(18) *Infinite Puzzles*

It has arrived.

A cardboard box about as tall as your average Olympic gymnast. It's covered in yellow packing tape, stamped "fragile," and has a return address of a town in the Netherlands.

I've been waiting for it for weeks.

Inside this box is a thing of beauty—and absurdity. It's a one-of-a-kind puzzle created just for me by one of the greatest puzzlemakers in the world.

It is, almost surely, the hardest puzzle ever to exist.

And it's a fitting end to my puzzle journey.

Before I open the box, let me tell you how it came to be. And for that, I need to rewind several months to a meeting I had with a puzzle collector named Wei Zhang.

Wei and her husband, Peter Rasmussen, live in the Bay Area and are famous in the puzzle community for having one of the best collections of Chinese puzzles in the world. When I contacted Wei a few months ago, she told me she was visiting New York to attend an antiques show and research some puzzles. She agreed to meet me at her friend's apartment in midtown.

Wei answers the door and ushers me in.

"I brought you a gift," she says, handing me a white box.

I open it and lift out a green ceramic pot with a spout on the side. This pot—which was made in China—is meant to hold wine. But it's not an ordinary container. It's actually a puzzle.

"Come to the kitchen and fill it up with water," Wei says.

I put the pot under the faucet and try to fill it—but the water rises to a certain height and then just drains out.

"It's a moderation pot," explains Wei. "It's supposed to teach the dangers of greed."

The trick is that if you put too much wine in the pot, the wine will flow into a hidden pipe inside the pot and all the wine will empty out. If you want the wine to stay inside, you can only fill the pot halfway.

Wei explains there's a whole category of puzzles called puzzle jugs or puzzle vessels. You have to figure out how to fill them or drink from them without spilling.

As you know, I'm a sucker for a puzzle with a life lesson. I thank Wei, and I promise to be less greedy (I didn't even complain about not getting any wine).

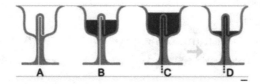

Cross Section of the Moderation Cup. Fill to the level in B and you can drink it. Fill to the level in C and it will all siphon out. By Nevit Dilmen, courtesy of Creative Commons.

Wei opens a laptop and clicks on the catalog featuring the favorite puzzles in her collection. It includes examples of the two most famous types of Chinese puzzles.

First, the tangram. The tangram is a wooden square chopped up into seven shapes—triangles, a parallelogram, and so forth. From these shapes, you must figure out how to make thousands of figures—birds, farmers, boats, you name it. When the tangram was exported to Europe in the nineteenth century, it became one of the first puzzle

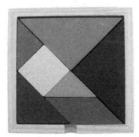

fads in the West. Napoleon himself was a fan. A French cartoon from 1818 depicts a mother neglecting her crying baby, too entranced by the tangrams, like a nonalcoholic version of the painting *Gin Lane* and a foreshadowing of the crossword panic a hundred years later.

The other most famous Chinese puzzle is the Chinese ring puzzle. Wei showed me a photo of one in her collection: a wooden stick surrounded by nine brass rings. The Chinese ring puzzle, also called a patience puzzle, dates back more than two thousand years, at least in its simplest form. The goal is to slide rings until they are all removed from the bar.

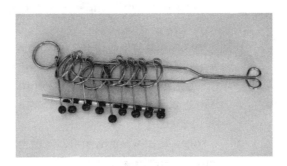

Wei, who was born in China and moved to the United States in 1985, tells me she first became aware of the ring puzzle when she was eleven. It was 1966, right at the start of China's Cultural Revolution. Wei's school had been shut down, and her father had been taken to another city.

Wei says math and puzzles kept her sane during this scary time. They even kept their food safe from the rats. Wei says she locked the family's grain container with a wire puzzle. The lock was so secure that Wei's mom couldn't solve it and had to wait till Wei got home.

One day, Wei spotted some other kids playing with a ring puzzle. "I was so intrigued," she says. She asked to borrow it. The other kids said no.

"You know how kids are," Wei tells me, laughing. "So I had to make my own." To make her own nine-ring puzzle, Wei used plastic curtain-rod rings and scraps of metal from a tin can.

The Chinese ring puzzle is particularly fascinating to me because it's a special kind of puzzle. It's recursive: it gets much, much harder the more rings you add to it.

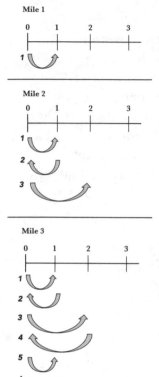

Mile 1

Mile 2

Mile 3

The goal is simple: to move the rings off the stick. But the catch is that, for each additional ring, there is an exponentially greater number of moves you have to make.

To solve a three-ring puzzle, it takes only 9 moves.

But a four-ring puzzle takes 43 moves.

A nine-ring puzzle takes 341 moves.

This is because to remove the ninth ring, you first have to repeat the entire process of removing the first ring, the second ring, the third ring, and so on.

Imagine if you had to run a marathon, but at every additional mile, you had to return to the starting line and repeat the entire sequence that got you there. It'd look like the diagram on the left.

You see how many miles you have to run to get to even the third mile marker? If I actually did the diagram for the twenty-six miles, this book would be taller than the Empire State Building.

That's a recursive pattern.

Wei flips the page to show me another one of her Chinese ring puzzles. This one is a beast: it's as long as a pool cue, and has sixty-four rings.

How many moves would be needed to solve it? Billions and billions and billions. That's insane. The opposite of the moderation pot!

GENERATION PUZZLES

When I get home from visiting Wei, I research more about the Chinese ring puzzle. Turns out, the ring puzzle has several cousins in the puzzle family tree. They are called generation puzzles, since they take generations to solve. You're supposed to pass them on to your kids, who pass them on to their kids, who pass them on to their kids, and on and on.

This is great! I love the idea of a generation puzzle—the ambitious scope, the idea of connection to my descendants. I've always wanted an heirloom I can hand to my sons on my deathbed. The closest I have is a blazer my grandfather gave me—it's red-and-white checkered and could double as a tablecloth at an Italian bistro. It's fraying and won't last.

But a generation puzzle? That would be perfect.

The question is: What kind of generation puzzle? There's the ring puzzle, but there's also something called the Tower of Hanoi. You might have seen this one. It's sometimes sold as a children's toy. It features three rods and a series of disks. The goal is to move the disks from one rod to another, but the catch is that you cannot put a bigger disk on top of a smaller disk.

The Tower of Hanoi is sometimes known as The End of the World Puzzle. This is because it's the centerpiece of an Indian legend about, well, the end of the world.

According to this legend, on the first day of creation, the priests in a temple are given an enormous version of the puzzle. The rods are made of diamonds, and the disks—all sixty-four of them—are made of gold. All day and all night, the priests' only job is to move the disks from one rod to another. And when all sixty-four disks have been moved, the world will disappear with a burst of thunder.

Now *that's* a puzzle!

Which gives me an idea: What if I make a Tower of Hanoi puzzle that one-upped the legend. One that has sixty-five disks?

"And the point of that would be?" asks Julie, when I tell her my plan.

"Just trying to prolong the life of the universe," I say. "In case that legend is true."

But the truth is, I'm attracted to the idea for several reasons.

First, as I mentioned, I'm genetically programmed to attempt absurd world records, such as my dad's record for most footnotes in a law article.

Second, I want that heirloom.

And third, I think it'd be an amazing reminder of the vastness of time. Remember Tanya, the Russian mathematician who told me that gazing at space made her feel like she was touching infinity? This would be my version.

JACOBS' LADDER

First, I need a collaborator. I find a carpenter through a friend who says that he could do it, but with that many disks, the puzzle would have to be huge: eighteen feet long. To fit in our apartment, we'd have to get rid of the couch. A bit of a long shot, knowing my family.

A friend suggests I contact a man named Oskar van Deventer, a Dutch puzzle creator. I'd heard Oskar's name dropped in puzzle circles many times. He's considered one of the greats. He has made many famous puzzles, including a fractal jigsaw and a Rubik's-type cube with gears and cogs on the outside.

Oskar caused a minor kerfuffle when he posted a video of a puzzle he made for the sex research center the Kinsey Institute. It was in the shape of a penis. Some more prudish puzzlers were shocked. But aside from that silly controversy, Oskar is almost universally respected, even revered.

I call Oskar in the Netherlands and ask him if he could create a generation puzzle for me.

"Let me think about it," he says, with a hint of a Dutch accent. "I don't want to just create a big Chinese ring puzzle or Tower of Hanoi. That would be boring."

A few days later, Oskar emails me a plan: The puzzle would be made of sticks and a metal rod, and the goal would be to remove the rod. To do that, you'd have to turn a series of pegs. And it'd be recursive. Even more recursive than the Chinese ring puzzle. Instead of doubling with every new level, it'd go up by a factor of four.

"We could call it Jacobs' Ladder," Oskar says.

I'm sold.

"Would it break the record?" I ask.

"I don't know if I can do that," he says. "But I can try."

The current record for hardest-to-solve generation puzzle is a sixty-five-ring Chinese puzzle owned by collector Jerry Slocum. It'd take 18 quintillion moves. That's 18 followed by 18 zeros.

In the following weeks, Oskar sends me updates. Things are not going well. He tried to 3-D print the puzzle out of gold-colored plastic, but it melted and warped. He's worried it will be too big to ship to the United States. He has to take off a week to paint his house.

And then, on a Friday morning, I wake up to an email from Oskar. He finished making the puzzle—and it works.

He has made a fifty-five-pin Jacobs' Ladder. It will take 1.2 decillion moves to solve (the number 1 followed by 33 digits).

Or, if I were to write it out, that'd be:

1,298,074,214,633,706,907,132,624,082,305,023 moves.

We crush the old record by thirteen orders of magnitude.

Oskar followed up the next day with an amazingly nerdy email explaining just how long it would take to solve this puzzle. For example:

> If you move one peg per Planck interval (the universe's shortest time interval), then the whole universe will have decayed into Hawking radiation by the time the puzzle is solved. This includes the puzzle itself, even when presuming that the puzzle was moved away from earth before the sun turns into a red giant.
>
> Moreover, if only one atom rubs off per move during friction, the puzzle has eroded away before it is solved.

THE UNBOXING

On a summer day, in our living room, with my wife and sons assembled, we slice open the cardboard box.

I pull out the Jacobs' Ladder and put it on the floor. It's about four feet tall, and looks like a Jenga tower mated with a giant corkscrew and then mated again with a girder from a skyscraper.

"Ta-da!" I say.

"More than one decillion moves to solve it," I say. "It's impossible for our brains to conceive of how many that is."

My son Zane begs to differ. He tells me he saw a video on how to conceptualize mega-huge numbers. He explained: Imagine trying to fill the Grand Canyon one grain of sand at a time. When the Grand Canyon is full, you take one grain of sand and put it on a field. Then you empty the Grand Canyon and start filling it again. When it's full, you add another grain of sand to the field. And repeat.

Keep going until the pile of sand in the field is the size of Mount Everest. The number of seconds it took you is still less than 1 decillion.

I'll give it to him. "That's the best metaphor I've heard," I say.

As I mentioned in the Rubik's Cube chapter, I love enormous numbers. They keep me humble. If we humans manage not to blow ourselves up, there could be billions, trillions of beings to come.

It's not just that, though. Jacobs' Ladder is a physical manifestation of so much of what I love about puzzles. Over the course of this project, I've learned that doing puzzles can make us better thinkers—more creative and more incisive. Jacobs' Ladder may not offer the same logical and creative challenges as cryptics or chess problems, but like all great puzzles, it contains lessons about ingenuity, fresh perspectives, and optimism. And for me, it has one more thing I value in puzzles: it's got a meditative angle.

I'm terrible at just-sitting-and-breathing meditation, but Jacobs' Ladder will be my version of meditation. I'll let my thoughts flow in and out of my brain as I calmly twist the pegs. And it will teach me to be okay with lack of closure. As Maki Kaji—the late godfather of Sudoku said—puzzles are a journey:

$$? \rightarrow !$$

Kaji said the key is to embrace the middle part, the arrow, the journey. Don't be obsessed with endings and perfection.

"It's about the journey, not the destination!" Lucas says, with a roll of the eyes.

"Exactly!" I say. "Except without the eye-roll part."

I twist one of the plastic pegs. It doesn't turn easily. It gives resistance, like a cap on a soda bottle, then makes a soft clunking sound and locks into place.

I turn to Julie. "Okay, it's your turn."

Each member of the family dutifully twists another peg—Julie, then Lucas, then Jasper, then Zane.

At least to me, it feels like a sacred ritual, like we are lighting the candles on a menorah, or ringing bells in a temple. I pledge to turn a peg every day. Or at least every week. Maybe every month. But we will do it.

"We're on our way," says Zane.

It's true.

Only 1,298,074,214,633,706,907,132,624,082,305,018 moves to go.

After that, I promise to quit puzzles.

The Puzzler *Contest*

For the official rules and details on *The Puzzler* contest, see thepuzzlerbook.com.

In the introduction, the authors have hidden a secret passcode that will give you access to a series of puzzles on the website thepuzzlerbook.com. The first reader to complete the contest will win $10,000.

The contest can be accessed starting May 3, 2022, at noon Eastern U.S. time, using a password hidden in the introduction to this book. The introduction can be accessed for free at ajjacobs.com or thepuzzlerbook .com.

An Original Puzzle Hunt by Greg Pliska

You've tackled Babylonian riddles and World War II codes. Now it's time to return to the present with the official all-new original puzzle hunt by Greg Pliska. (The footnotes throughout this section are also courtesy of Greg.)

In the following pages, you will find a series of nineteen puzzles— each one themed to a chapter in the book. There's a crossword-themed puzzle, a Rubik's one, a chess one, and so on.

When solved, each of these puzzles will lead to a word or phrase. Sometimes the puzzle gives you that word or phrase directly; other times you extract a hint to what the final word or phrase is.

There will be a total of twenty answer words or phrases, all of which are essential to solving the final metapuzzle, located on page 288. (Note: Puzzle 12, Greeks vs. Romans, and Puzzle 13, Who Are We?, each lead to *two* separate answer words.)

To clarify: This is separate from the $10,000 contest. You won't get any money for solving this series of puzzles, though you will get bragging rights and a lot of aha moments.

A few tips from Greg on how to maximize your enjoyment and success when solving these puzzles (or, indeed, any puzzles):

- It's okay to use references. More than anything, these puzzles rely upon lateral thinking, moments of inspiration, and careful analysis. But often they also depend upon facts or allusions with which you might not be familiar. If that happens, go look up the answer! It's not a final exam, it's not a competition; it's meant to be fun, and if you're stuck because you don't know the name of the 1942 Preakness winner, go websearch it.*

---

* The winner of the 1942 Preakness Stakes was a horse named Alsab. Not knowing this fact (nor the name of the author of *Gil Blas*) is the reason I stared for five

- If you're stuck, try looking at the puzzle a different way. If you're not getting anywhere, put the puzzle down, have a cup of coffee, go for a run, take a nap—anything to knock your brain out of the rut and hopefully put you on the road to inspiration.
- If you're still stuck, check the back of the book for hints, starting on page 319. Or visit our website, thepuzzlerbook.com, for more hints. Or ask a friend—sometimes two heads really are better than one.
- The title and the italicized text at the top of the page are clues. Ask yourself why we chose that title for the puzzle, or used that specific language in the italicized text (also known as flavortext). Those choices weren't random, and more often than not the specific language is meant to be a nudge toward the solution of the puzzle.*
- The puzzles can be solved in any order you want. With the exception of the final puzzle, the metapuzzle Big Secrets, which should be solved last.
- When you have a set of things, sometimes you take a letter from each one to spell the final answer. In an acrostic, you take the first letters of each word to spell another word. In some of these puzzles, there will be a number indicating which letter to take— it's not always the first!—to spell out your answer.
- Numbers in parentheses are your friends. When you see a clue like "Author AJ (6)" that number is an enumeration, an indicator of how long the answer is. In a few puzzles, you get both an enumeration and an indication of which letter you want to take, so "Puzzlemaker Pliska (2/4)" tells you to use the second letter of a four-letter answer (the R in GREG).

---

competition-losing minutes at a final-round puzzle at the American Crossword Puzzle Tournament, where, of course, we weren't allowed to look things up.

* I once sat with one of my cleverest solving friends, Guy Jacobson—also a test solver for this book—to do a puzzle hunt called Intercoastal Altercations. The introductory flavor was all about a flock of birds that had dispersed across the country, and our job was to track down the various cities they'd gone to. Guy turned to me and said, "I bet the answer to the metapuzzle is PHOENIX." A couple hours later, after doing all the puzzles together, we solved the metapuzzle . . . whose answer was, indeed, PHOENIX.

- Go to thepuzzlerbook.com for PDFs of puzzles. Two of the puzzles (the Rubik's Cube and the jigsaw puzzle) might be easier to solve in color. There are color PDFs of these available on the website. If you download and print the jigsaw puzzle, this will also save you from having to cut up your book with scissors!
- When all else fails . . . drop us a line via thepuzzlerbook.com website. We want you to be challenged, but we also want you to have fun. And if you've tried everything else and you're stuck—or if you think you've found an error or an ambiguity in a puzzle—let us know! We're here to help.

Puzzles by Greg Pliska https://exaltation-of-larks.com
With Puzzle 16 by guest puzzlemaker Sara Goodchild (@sarathegood)

1) GREG'S "THE PUZZLE OF PUZZLES" PUZZLE
The "The Puzzle of Puzzles" Puzzle
In which the puzzlers are puzzled about the puzzle of what keeps us together.

1 African antelope
2 Common crossword clue for ERST
3 "_____ and away!"
4 Tourist destination in the Leeward Islands
5 Renowned Chinese classical pianist
6 Newsboy's shout
7 German spa town
8 Words before "brief candle" in a Shakespeare soliloquy
9 Dance move paired with the whip in "Watch Me"
10 Ramones member who played the bass

2) GREG'S CROSSWORD-THEMED PUZZLE

Data Error

In which A.J. and G.P. appear together in a crossword puzzle for the first time!

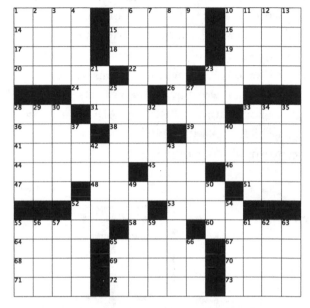

ACROSS

1 Broadway title role originated by Heather Headley
5 Less-played part of a 45
10 Quiet before a storm
14 Related (to)
15 Eyeball-bending painting style of the 60s
16 Specialty
17 Arctic hazard
18 Bacall's love, informally
19 Symbol on a screen
20 "___ alive!"
22 Winter mo.
23 Single-handedly
24 Enjoy a book
26 Earth goddess in the *Ring Cycle*
28 ___ de los Muertos
31 Went by
33 Ten percent, for an agent
36 Draft classification
38 ___ for Innocent (Grafton novel)
39 Added or removed powder
41 Some socks, after washing, or a description of twelve cells in this crossword (the 13th of which might describe the kind of error these represent)
44 Person with "I" trouble?
45 It crosses a st., in Manhattan
46 Early Ron Howard role
47 Yuletide beverage
48 Not too swift
51 ___-A-Mouse, early singjay stylist
52 Car horn sound
53 PC key
55 Curling or hurling, e.g.
58 Tolkien creature
60 Black Friday events
64 ___-Seltzer
65 Diarist Nin
67 Organ in tadpoles but not in frogs
68 Jazz pianist Allen or singer Halliwell
69 Bus station
70 Stone or Thompson of *Cruella*
71 ___ Clayton Powell, Jr., New York's first African-American Congressman
72 Sedative, for short
73 Underpart of a plant or a tooth

DOWN

1 What over 91m Brits got in 2021
2 Company founded by Ingvar Kamprad
3 Nowitzki who played 21 seasons with the Mavericks
4 Lewis Black in *Inside Out*
5 Steal from
6 Having two stressed syllables, in poetry
7 Character in *Othello* or *Aladdin*
8 Takes the wheel
9 When the French fry?
10 Spelling bee winner Avant-garde
11 With the bow, in music
12 Boxer Spinks
13 Horse hair
21 Reason for an R rating, often
23 Make sense
25 Kinda
27 Most embarrassed
28 In 2021, 24 U.S. Senators
29 Montoya of *The Princess Bride*
30 Famous fabulist
32 Old-time expletive
33 Michael of R.E.M.
34 Like *American Horror Story*
35 Famous Ford failure
37 "What Kind of Fool ___?"
40 ___ Paulo, Brazil
42 Balance-sheet entry
43 Landlord's threat
49 Act before the headliner
50 12-mo. periods
52 Cranium contents
54 Beer variety
55 Extended yarn
56 Said "not guilty," perhaps
57 Gumbo ingredient
59 Valley known for its vineyards
61 Star's car
62 Ticklish Muppet
63 Czech or Slovak, e.g.
65 Big inits. in home security
66 R-V hook-up

3) GREG'S RUBIK'S CUBE–THEMED PUZZLE

Rubik's 3 × 3 × 3

In which we discover some colorful magic.

This unfolded Rubik's Cube has six faces with the traditional colors: white, green, red, blue, orange, and yellow. Combine the three-letter combinations (known as trigrams) to spell out four or five words or phrases related to each color. These words will be in alphabetical order as you string the trigrams together; the box below tells you how long each word in each color-related set will be.

For example, BRE and ADC can be combined to make BREAD (which goes with white), leaving a C that starts the next white-related word, which is nine letters long.

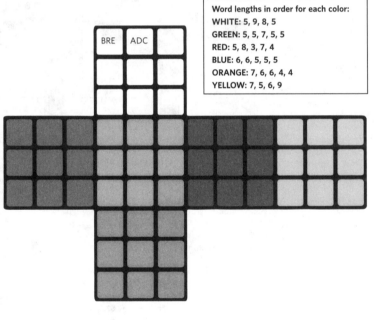

Word lengths in order for each color:
WHITE: 5, 9, 8, 5
GREEN: 5, 5, 7, 5, 5
RED: 5, 8, 3, 7, 4
BLUE: 6, 6, 5, 5, 5
ORANGE: 7, 6, 6, 4, 4
YELLOW: 7, 5, 6, 9

ACK	~~ADC~~	ALA	APE	BEL	BER	BLO	BON	~~BRE~~	CEN	CHI	DES	DFE	DTH	EBL
EHE	ELZ	ERW	EST	ETG	HAM	HAN	HAR	HOC	HOE	IAN	INE	INO	ITH	IZA
LAG	LEP	LIE	LIU	MAR	MCO	MER	NAC	NAM	NET	NGT	NTE	OLA	OON	OTH
OTT	RDW	RES	RNS	RRI	RYP	SPE	SSO	STO	SUB	SUE	SUR	TEE	TEY	TLA
TRH	UMB	UNT	VER	YJU										

The colored grid for this puzzle can be found on page 16 of the color insert.
You can also enter your answers into the black-and-white image above.

Once you have figured out the words, place them into the Rubik's face of the appropriate color, one trigram per cell, to fill up the cube. We've started the white face for you.

When the cube is full, the remaining trigrams can be rearranged to spell a clue (5 6 6 4 7 5) to this puzzle's answer.

(You can also download a color version of this puzzle at thepuzzlerbook.com/rubiks.)

4) GREG'S ANAGRAM-THEMED PUZZLE
Flatfoots

In which we investigate all kinds of dastardly wordplay.

National Puzzlers' League "flats" are a unique style of verse puzzle in which several words have been replaced by "cuewords," capitalized words that function as placeholders for the answer words.

Combine the six boxed answer words, in order, to form the clue for the anagram puzzle below.

1. HOMOPHONE

Homophones are words that sound the same but are spelled differently, like *right* and *write*. Several of these homophones are borrowed from other languages.

I was born the wrong time and I've got a passé social attitude.
Some songwriters saved me. I B them a real debt of gratitude.
"A, Lady Be Good," wrote the Gershwins—I fully agree!
It's good to drink deeply a snifter of fine C-de-vie!
When Crosby and Kelly sing gaily the joys of D monde,
I love to join in, for of Cole Porter's work I am fond.
And nothing will send me like music from Irving Berlin.
If "Top Hat" and tails is so wrong, well, I'll happily sin!

A = _ _

B = _ _ _

C = _ _ _

D = _ _ _ _

2. PADLOCK

In this puzzle the last five letters of FIRST are the same as the first five letters of SECOND. When you remove those overlapping letters from both words—as if they overlapped and were "padlocked" together—the remaining four letters (two from FIRST and two from SECOND) form THIRD. For example, RUSHING + SHINGLE = RULE.

Back in the '70s I was a FIRST,
In mind-body-spirit was fully immersed.

Tried Ram Dass and Buddha, and old Edgar Cayce,
Theosophy, tantra and anything spacy.
If you were a bettor you'd surely have SECOND
That if it was kooky to me it'd've beckoned.
What caused this behavior, this passion absurd?
These fads filled a void in me, met some deep THIRD.
Today I'm more grounded, these trends I've reversed,
But back in the '70s I was a FIRST!

FIRST = _ _ _   _ _ _ _
SECOND = _ _ _ _ _ _ _
THIRD = | _ _ _ _ |

3. CURTAILMENT

A longer word (in this case a proper noun) has its last letter removed (curtailed) to make a new word.

"If a thing isn't yours, son, you cannot just take it!"
Or so Putin's mother would scold her young Vlad.
When Russia took LONG, though, no country could make it
Retreat. It's a SHORT, but says Putin, "Too bad!"

SHORT = | _ _ _ _ _ |
LONG = _ _ _ _ _ _

4. FIRST-LETTER CHANGE (LOON, MOON)
DELETION (MOST, MOT)

In a first-letter change, the first letter of a word is changed to another to form a new word. In a deletion, one letter is deleted from inside a word to form a new word.

While MOST and LOON are MOT in nature
Friendship isn't out of MOON,
Like when they're animated creatures
In that 80's Disney 'toon.

MOST = _ _ _ _ _
MOT = | _ _ _ _ |
LOON = _ _ _ _ _ _
MOON = _ _ _ _ _ _

5. PROGRESSIVE TRANSDELETION

The title sounds complicated, but the wordplay isn't. Start with a seven-letter word, in this case a capitalized word. Remove one letter and rearrange the rest to make a new word. Continue removing a letter, then rearranging, to form a series of new words, the last of which is three letters long. (The five-letter word is a proper noun; the six-letter answer is two words, often capitalized.)

Although you won a Tony for The Rink,
And Spider Woman *was your second score,*
It's West Side Story *that's your biggest THREE.*
For sixty years you've scratched your theater FOUR.
Dear FIVE Rivera, you should take a break!
Try yoga, SIX, Qigong—or go abroad,
Sip SEVEN 'neath a setting Tuscan sun.
Such well-earned recreation we'd applaud!

SEVEN = _ _ _ _ _ _ _
SIX = _ _ _ _ _ _
FIVE = _ _ _ _ _
FOUR = _ _ _ _
THREE = | _ _ _ |

6. REPEATED LETTER CHANGE

Every instance of a letter that appears more than once in the first word is changed to a new letter to form the second.

My books are alphabetical
By SECOND on my shelf.
To mix them is heretical.
I check them all myself.
Today I see a lack—oy!

What to do? I fear the worst!
'Twixt Beowulf *and* Black Boy
Something's missing. It's The FIRST!

FIRST = _ _ _ _ _
SECOND = [_ _ _ _ _]

ANAGRAM

Clue, formed from the boxed answer words above:

_ _ !	_ _ _ _	_ _ _ _ _	_ _ _ _	_ _ _	_ _ _ _ _
A	THIRD	SHORT	MOT	THREE	SECOND

This is a clue to a five-word '90s television show. The letters in the clue can be rearranged to form the title of that show, which is _ _ _ _ _ _ _ _: _ _ _ _ _ _ _ _ _ _ _ _ _ _ _ .

5) GREG'S REBUS-THEMED PUZZLE
Signs and Symbols

In which we attempt to interpret the signs.

The images below clue eleven words or phrases that have something in common. Solve each rebus, then take the indicated letters to spell out a clue to this puzzle's final answer.

The numbers below each rebus indicate which letter to take out of the total length of the word. For example, (2/6) under the first rebus indicates you need the second letter of a six-letter word.

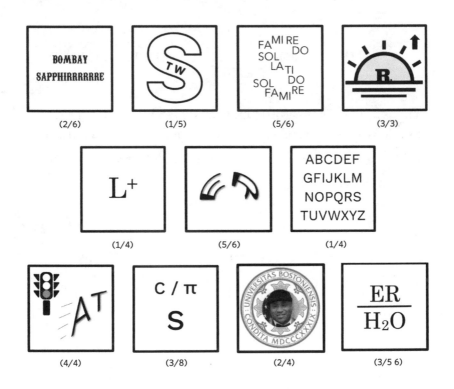

6) GREG'S JIGSAW-THEMED PUZZLE

A Perfect Match

In which even frenemies can go glamping and chillax.

(You can download a color version of this puzzle at thepuzzlerbook.com/jigsaw.)

On the following page are twelve square puzzle pieces, with an image on each edge. The numbers in parentheses indicate the lengths of the words clued by the images.

Cut out and reassemble the pieces in a 4 × 3 grid so that each pair of bordering images clues a pair of words that can form a common portmanteau, a word that blends the sounds and meanings of two other words. For example, *friend* and *enemy* can combine to make *frenemy*.

There are seventeen portmanteau pairs in the completed grid. We've given you brief descriptions of each one, listed below in alphabetical order of the portmanteau. When the pieces are properly assembled, the words clued by the images on the outer perimeter will spell out a message that clues the final answer to this puzzle.

Portmanteau descriptions (in alphabetical order by answer):

- Transportation service
- Cocktail
- Political term
- Children's novel series
- Drink brand
- Unit of time
- U.S. federal holiday
- Dog breed
- Game and entertainment franchise
- Dessert
- Online game platform
- Film title
- Meat product
- Utensil
- Vegetable
- Sports term
- Reviews website and app

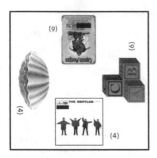

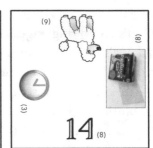

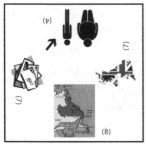

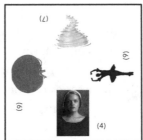

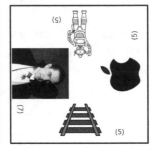

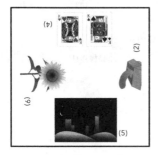

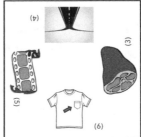

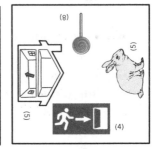

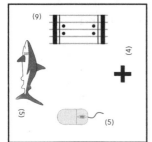

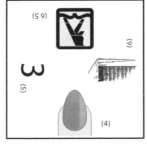

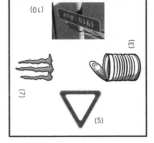

7) GREG'S MAZE-THEMED PUZZLE

We Aim to Please

In which we thread our way through several mazes but get all knotted up.
In each maze below find the shortest route—the one that traverses the fewest number of squares—between the two heavy-bordered cells, starting at the arrow and ending at the target. Begin in the direction of the starting arrow and move from square to square according to the following rules:

Mazes 1–3: You may move to any square in the direction of the arrow you are standing on, visiting each square you pass through along the way. In cells with two arrows you may go in either direction.

Mazes 4–6: Same as 1–3, except that you must alternate black and white arrows.

Maze 7: You can only move <u>one</u> square in the direction of the arrow you are standing on. In cells with two arrows you may go in either direction.

We recommend marking your path by filling in each square you visit, including the first and last.

1.

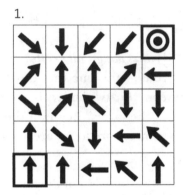

2.

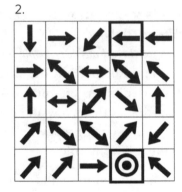

3.

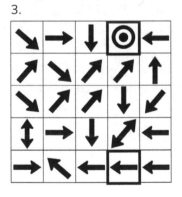

4.

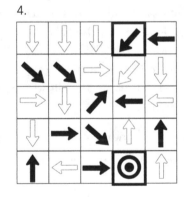

5.

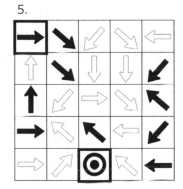

6.

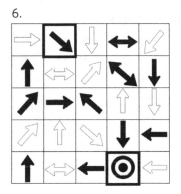

7.

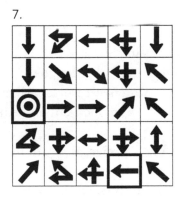

8) GREG'S MATH- AND LOGIC-THEMED PUZZLES

A. The Latest Fashion

In which it matters who goes when, and how much of what they show.

Five fashion designers (Bautista, Kwame, Meifeng, Nikita, Salman) revealed their latest designs this afternoon, each working with a single fabric (cashmere, corduroy, cotton, muslin, or taffeta). They presented each hour from one to five, and each showed a different number of outfits, from one to five each.

Using the five statements below, determine which designer had which time slot, and the number of outfits they showed in their chosen fabric. Then use all that information, reading row by row in the completed grid, to extract the final answer to this puzzle.

Time	Name	No. of Outfits	Fabric
1:00			
2:00			
3:00			
4:00			
5:00			

1. Salman, who designs in cotton, showed twice as many outfits as the person before him, who designs in corduroy.
2. Nikita and Kwame (who never works with taffeta) showed six outfits between them, and one went immediately after the other.
3. The person showing cashmere debuted three hours after the person showing five outfits.
4. Bautista's time slot was the same as the number of outfits he showed, which was even.
5. There were more outfits in taffeta than in muslin.

B. Real Numbers

In which we do a little a-rhythm-etic on some hit singles.

For this puzzle, we began by compiling a list of some of our favorite songs that have at least one number in their titles. Then we abbreviated those titles, leaving the numbers intact but using only the first letter of each word. So, for example, "99 Bottles of Beer on the Wall" would be presented as 99 B O B O T W.

Finally, we replaced one letter or number from each abbreviated title with a blank. The characters that belong in those blanks will spell, in the given order, a clue to this puzzle's ten-letter solution. As an extra solving aid, we've given you a list of the artists—but in alphabetical order, not necessarily aligned with the songs they performed.

1 S F, 3 S ___	Ariana Grande
9 I T ___	The Beatles
___ O 69	Bob Marley and the Wailers
___ O 17	Bryan Adams
3 L ___	Chicago
__ 1 B T D	Dave Brubeck
50 W T ___ Y L	The Four Seasons
___ O 1000 D	Jay-Z
99 ___	Lynyrd Skynyrd
2 ___ O 3 A B	Meat Loaf
G 3 ___	Olivia Rodrigo
___ G B (500 M)	Panic! at the Disco
___ 5	Paul Simon
__ W D 4 U	Prince
25 ___ 6 T 4	The Proclaimers
19th ___ B	Queen
___ N A	The Rolling Stones
___ D A W	The Searchers
D 63 (___ W A N)	Stevie Nicks
7 ___	The White Stripes
L P N ___	Wilson Pickett

9) GREG'S CIPHER AND CODE–THEMED PUZZLE
Remix

In which the rule is you have to figure out the rules.

We've taken eleven clues, removed the spacing and punctuation, then transformed each clue according to a particular rule. You must figure out the transformation rule and restore the original clue, then perform the same transformation on the clue answer to make a new word.

These eleven new words will have something in common. The numbers in parentheses indicate which letter to take from the new word, as well as how long that word is. (3/6), for example, indicates that you need the third letter of a six-letter word. The letters you extract will spell an apt two-word name.

1. CORNCTRLONDELTHEESCBLANKTAB (3/6)
2. TINGERXHOSECIGIITXASLISSGROMBSOSE (2/4)
3. GLYDEDOWNHYLLLYKELYNDSEYVONN (1/3)
4. PNOITATIPICERMGNIXIRNIAADNSWON (1/5)
5. USAUTRALIANILWIDOGDOROFRMAMFAOUSERMEYL TRSTEEPINLIE (1/6)
6. LZUNDMZUASUREEZUUALLING4ZU40SZUUAREY ZURDS (5/5)
7. PRESIDENTPOFPMOSCOWPORPSTPPETERS BURG (4/8)
8. WODRIGHTTHTAIGHTCNAIGHTFOLLWOIGHTHIEVI GHTMASTREIGHTROIGHTNEVREIGHT (1/8)
9. PEOIBTOXPERITEATMENTPEAITRGET (4/10)
10. ANBCYDOEFMESTICFEGHLINE (5/5)
11. HAPPOBBITSHAPPOMEIAPPNLAPPORDOAPPFTAPP HERAPPINGS (5/8)

10) GREG'S VISUAL PUZZLE
Border Crossings

In which we show that one thing can be in two places at the same time.

The outline maps of thirteen pairs of countries have been overlaid below with their capital cities overlapping. The names of those capitals have been similarly intermingled, with the letters of each capital remaining in order in the mashed-up result.

The names of the countries in each pair are the same length (ignoring spaces and punctuation). Once you've identified each pair of countries you can extract a letter from each pair to spell a phrase that is appropriate to what is going on here.

(Note: The countries in each pair are shown roughly to scale with each other, but not necessarily with other pairs.)

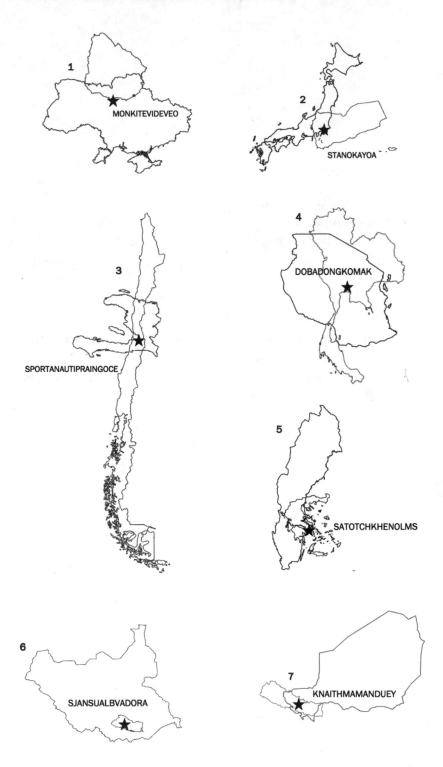

1 MONKITEVIDEVEO

2 STANOKAYOA

3 SPORTANAUTIPRAINGOCE

4 DOBADONGKOMAK

5 SATOTCHKHENOLMS

6 SJANSUALBVADORA

7 KNAITHMAMANDUEY

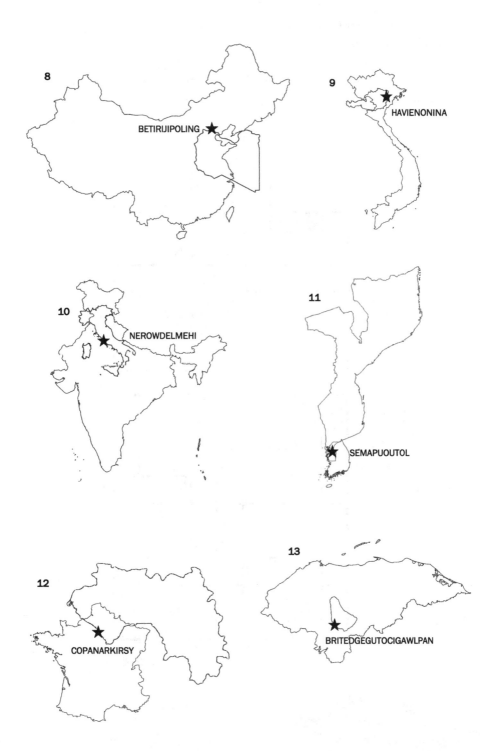

8 BETIRIJIPOLING

9 HAVIENONINA

10 NEROWDELMEHI

11 SEMAPUOUTOL

12 COPANARKIRSY

13 BRITEDGEGUTOCIGAWLPAN

11) GREG'S SUDOKU- AND KENKEN-THEMED PUZZLES
Coming to Terms

In which our heroes reach agreement about a few things.

A.J. loves KenKen; Greg prefers Sudoku. But there are a few things they discover they can agree on, including that both puzzles are . . .

				6	8			
2			7			6		3
	8		1	9			4	
9	7					3		
		5		3		9		
		4					7	2
	4			8	6		9	
8		2			3			6
			4	5				

2/		2×	15×		840×		3/	
315×	72×		24+		42×			3+
				32×		48×		
		18×				30×		
3+		24×		18+	15+		24+	
30×		7−			17+			
	8−	60×	42×				29+	13+
21+				2−				
			27×		3+			

12) GREG'S CHESS-THEMED PUZZLE

Greeks vs. Romans

In which we decide: infight or insight?

(Note: This puzzle has **two** separate answers.)

The chessboard on the next page represents a competition between the Greeks, represented by the White knight, and the Romans, represented by the Black.

The two knights move according to normal chess rules, from square to square, gathering letters as they go. No square is landed upon more than once, and the two knights always move symmetrically relative to each other. So if the Black knight moves to the A, then the White knight moves to the V, and so on.

The letters landed upon by the White knight spell out the Roman clue phrase, which has a seven-letter answer.

The letters landed upon by the Black knight spell out the Greek clue phrase, which has a six-letter answer.

H	E	E	H	I	I	E	♘
A	P	T	R	M	I	W	L
H	B	A	L	S	F	V	I
L	T	E	E	N	N	L	O
C	T	E	W	C	R	R	F
D	A	A	T	N	H	A	A
O	H	M	O	N	O	I	U
♞	R	N	E	L	H	I	R

ROMAN (White knight):

_ _ _ _ _ _ _   _ _ _   _ _ _ _ _   _ _ _ _   _ _ _-_ _ _   _ _   _ _ _ _

GREEK (Black knight):

_ _ _ _ _ _ _   _ _ _ _   _ _ _   _ _ _   _ _ _ _ _ _   _ _   _ _ _ _ _ _

13) GREG'S RIDDLE-THEMED PUZZLE
Who Are We?

In which the sum of the parts is two wholes.

Each riddle below clues a string of letters (word, abbreviation, suffix, et al.) whose length is in parentheses. String all the answers together to form a clue to this puzzle's **two** solutions.

1. Together we're in your metabolism,
   Alone or in pairs, in your blood.
   Seen seaborne and found in lavabos,
   But never in liquid or mud. (3)

2. I'm drunk, I'm exciting,
   I'm not pitch-black.
   You enjoy my fine writing
   'Til I go back. (3)

3. Add me to a pot, I'll make a magical drink.
   Add me to your bill, you'll owe more than you think.
   Make a pass at me and with desire I'll fill,
   But wed me with Eros and it all goes downhill. (3)

4. It's surely this simple: our initial appearance.
   But then, at the end, we will make you adherents. (4)

5. Black or White, you've surely seen
   Me on the stage or on the screen.
   Higher than ten, I still bow to the Queen. (4)

6. She looks at a photo, a moment of thought, her
   Comment is "Brothers and sisters I've none,
   But that man's mother is my mother's daughter."
   Relation of that man to her? (That's the one!) (3)

7. Fanboys are here, but one of them's missing,
   Yet folks might not guess, for they don't always get it,
   Nor will it be easy, or that's what we're guessing,
   So read the first word here to never forget it. (3)

8. In 4/4 time, the speed of light?
   Around 100, copyright. (1)

9. In South African capital your errand is done,
   While Capitol Hill Paul has randomly begun. (4)

10. Gobbled by the alligators, eaten by the swallows,
    Never in the deep end, always in the shallows.
    Exhibited in galleries, but never seen in zoos,
    Digitally captured, it's the answer that you'll choose. (3)

14) GREG'S JAPANESE PUZZLE BOX–THEMED PUZZLE
Japanese Puzzle Boxes
In which we meet a famous manipulator of puzzle boxes.
Each column represents a set of items in the same category, with lines connecting boxes that contain the same letter. The arrows indicate the three places where a single word branches off, starting a new column for each new category it belongs to.

Start with JAPANESE, PUZZLE, and BOX and fill in the boxes until you determine the ten letters that make up this puzzle's final answer.

JAPANESE PUZZLE BOXES

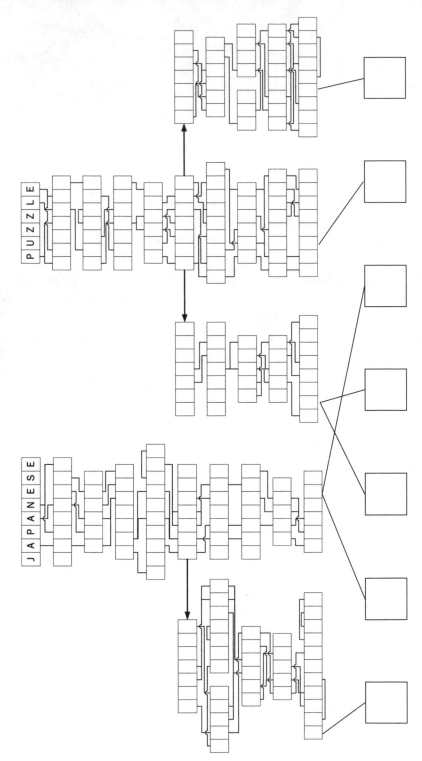

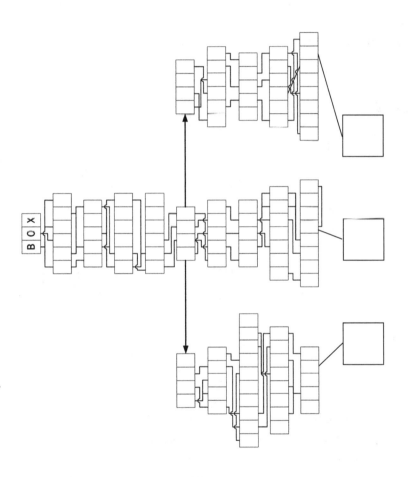

15) GREG'S CONTROVERSIAL PUZZLE–THEMED PUZZLE
Thirders and Halfers

In which we take a hatchet to the Sleeping Beauty problem.

The clues below have been chopped up to represent two schools of thought regarding the Sleeping Beauty problem. The Thirders clues are in three parts, while the Halfers are in two. Reassemble the clues using one item from each column, then perform another connection process with the answers to make five more clues. These will lead you to your final answer.

(Note: The numbers in parentheses indicate the length of each answer.)

Thirders

1	French	a	today (4)
2	Lakers'	Antoine-	Leona (4)
3	Desegregation	definite	check (4)
4	Surgeon	in	karaoke (4)
5	Participate	lyric	Jerry (4)
6	Endorse	owner	Hippolyte (4)
7	NWA	pioneer	contraction (3)
8	"America"	Sudan,	article (3)

Halfers

1	500, in	___ (fish sauce) (3)
2	Symbol for	a chair (3)
3	Opposite of	acid, chemically (4)
4	Event for	an ump's call (3)
5	Nam	carbon (1)
6	With "out"	Cinderella (4)
7	Took	coffee server (3)
8	Big	Fozzie (4)
9	Winter time zone in	Haile Selassie (3)
10	Royal title for	Nova Scotia (3)
11	Golfer's	Roman numerals (1)
12	Paddington or	shout (4)

16) GREG'S CRYPTIC-THEMED PUZZLE

By guest constructor Sara Goodchild

Transatlantic

In which this originally British crossword type finds a home in the USA.
Five across clues have one word each that does not contribute to the
wordplay or definition. Identify the extra words for a helpful instruction.

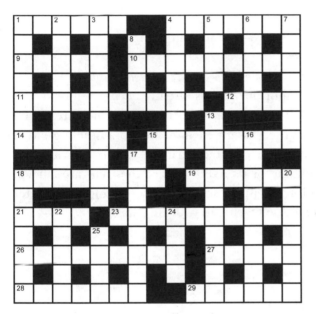

Down

1 MAC's reformulated top-quality, semi-rare cosmetic (7)
2 Missing finals, US territory sounded off with empty promise (9)
3 Song "Row, Row, Row Your Boat," for example, led by Instagram character in Greek (1,3,6)
4 Neglected chance after dropping in (8)
5 Wacky person, either way (4)
6 Initially miniature avatar running in overalls! (5)
7 Idly move griddle, getting pair of tweezers for half of grub (7)
8 Hostilely express point (4)
13 Mall Elinor different lubricant (7,3)
16 Famous Russian environmentalist-politician welcomes composer at five (9)
17 Disgrace southern sweetheart wearing French designer (8)
18 Stupidly considers job joker offered up (5,2)
20 Dress rehearsal disturbed rest at university in Tennessee (4,3)
22 In favor of surrounding lake with a group of plants (5)
24 Reportedly regretted lacking manners (4)
25 Climbing weed's termination (4)

Across

1 Doctor that is following mother bird (6)
4 Messy contents of bunk emptied (7)
9 Saint consumed these, say (5)
10 Cracked up prior to medley (9)
11 Sandler not in favor of northeastern firm (10)
12 "Use glue," answers 007 (4)
14 Make gold Marvel character pen (6)
15 Confection regimen somehow gets you in the end (8)
18 Spooner's slim courage endorsed (8)
19 Mammal runs twice into dogs? (6)
21 Nintendo console includes full networking option (2-2)
23 Frauds blacken the French bronzes (10)
26 Another abridged novel: "The Drones" (9)
27 "Yellow" singer pursuing Oscar (5)
28 Traditional hunter rejected agent role (7)
29 Number of Rivendell denizens grasping essentially every clue (6)

17) GREG'S INFINITE PUZZLE–THEMED PUZZLE

Skyscrapers of Hanoi

In which A.J. and Greg visit some of the world's most famous buildings.

This Skyscrapers of Hanoi puzzle has already been assembled, but the ring labels were left off. First answer the clues, which are sorted by answer length, and then assign each answer to a building based upon rules which are left for you to determine. (Hint: The rules will be related to the building or its name.) Once the rings are labeled appropriately, from longest up to shortest, take the indicated letter from each ring label to spell a clue to your final answer.

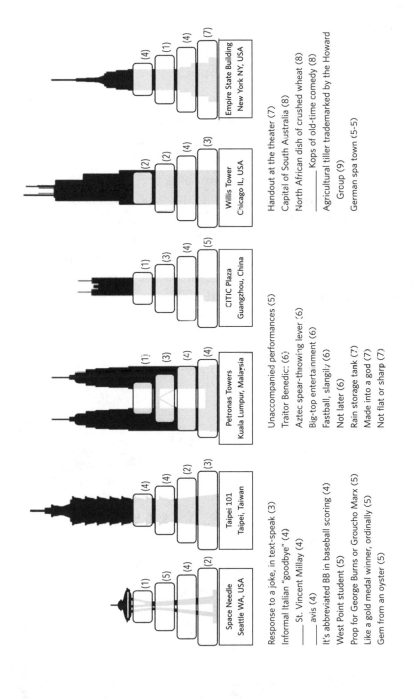

Empire State Building
New York NY, USA

Willis Tower
Chicago IL, USA

CITIC Plaza
Guangzhou, China

Petronas Towers
Kuala Lumpur, Malaysia

Taipei 101
Taipei, Taiwan

Space Needle
Seattle WA, USA

Handout at the theater (7)
Capital of South Australia (8)
North African dish of crushed wheat (8)
_____ Kops of old-time comedy (8)
Agricultural tiller trademarked by the Howard
    Group (9)
German spa town (5-5)

Unaccompanied performances (5)
Traitor Benedict (6)
Aztec spear-throwing lever (6)
Big-top entertainment (6)
Fastball, slangily (6)
Not later (6)
Rain storage tank (7)
Made into a god (7)
Not flat or sharp (7)

Response to a joke, in text-speak (3)
Informal Italian "goodbye" (4)
_____ St. Vincent Millay (4)
_____ avis (4)
It's abbreviated BB in baseball scoring (4)
West Point student (5)
Prop for George Burns or Groucho Marx (5)
Like a gold medal winner, ordinarily (5)
Gem from an oyster (5)

18) GREG PLISKA'S PUZZLE HUNT–THEMED PUZZLE
Big Secrets
In which A.J. and Greg learn the secret of successful puzzling.

(Note: This is the metapuzzle, which combines the answers to all the other original puzzles in the chapter.)

A.J. approaches his work with joyful exuberance, willing to step into the unknown without fear of failure or embarrassment. Greg, on the other hand, is a clever trickster, conjuring mental delights from thin air. Together, they have set out to discover what kinds of people inhabit the world of puzzles, and you have accompanied them on this journey, solving many puzzles along the way.

When joined with A.J. and Greg, your twenty puzzle answers can be associated with a complete set. Put those answers in the canonical order in the blanks below and take the indicated letter from each to spell out exactly what kinds of people are the happiest and most successful in the puzzle-solving world.

A.J.
GREG

_____	3
_____	11
_____	2
_____	1
_____	3
_____	4
_____	3
_____	3
_____	3
_____	1
_____	5
_____	1
_____	6
_____	8
_____	2
_____	3
_____	1
_____	2
_____	3
_____	13

Puzzle Resources

I've compiled an (I hope) interesting and (I know) non-comprehensive list of helpful puzzle books and websites.

Resources on Puzzle-like Thinking and Problem Solving in General

The Puzzle Instinct: The Meaning of Puzzles in Human Life **by Marcel Danesi (2004).** An anthropology professor from the University of Toronto argues that the urge to solve puzzles is hardwired into our species.

The Sweet Spot: The Pleasures of Suffering and the Search for Meaning **by Paul Bloom (2021).** A psychology professor's exploration of why we embrace painful things such as crosswords and marathons.

A Brief History of Puzzles: Baffling Brainteasers from the Sphinx to Sudoku **by William Hartston (2019).** A concise and fun collection of puzzles, including ancient math problems about fertile rabbits and grazing oxen.

The Scout Mindset: Why Some People See Things Clearly and Others Don't **by Julia Galef (2021).** Julia is one of my favorite thinkers and podcasters. This book is a paean to curiosity and rational inquiry, as opposed to motivated reasoning.

Problem-Solving Techniques That Work For All Types of Challenges **by Spencer Greenberg.** https://www.spencergreenberg.com/2017/06/1514/. A great guide to thinking about real-life puzzles by a mathematician and scientist.

Wired to Create: Unraveling the Mysteries of the Creative Mind **by Scott Barry Kaufman and Carolyn Gregoire (2016).** Psychologist and podcaster Scott Barry Kaufman teams up with science writer Carolyn Gregoire for this insightful guide to creative problem solving.

Think Again: The Power of Knowing What You Don't Know by **Adam Grant (2021).** As with Julia Galef's book, this one by organizational psychologist Adam Grant extols the virtues of an open mind. He argues that we should strive to think like scientists, not preachers, prosecutors, or politicians.

Gödel, Escher, Bach: An Eternal Golden Braid by **Douglas R. Hofstadter (1979).** A nonfiction classic that dives deep into cognition and logic—and the minds of the three titular geniuses.

Crossword Resources

Fireball Crosswords
https://www.fireballcrosswords.com
Peter Gordon's "blazingly" hard crosswords.

Inkubator Crosswords
https://inkubatorcrosswords.com
Laura Braunstein and Tracy Bennett edit this ongoing collection of crosswords by women.

Two Nerdy Obsessions Meet—and It's Magic
TED Talk by David Kwong (2014)
https://www.davidkwongmagic.com
David Kwong is one of my favorite crossword makers, and I loved his off-Broadway show *The Engimatist,* which combined crosswords and magic. His TED talk is also great.

Queer Qrosswords
https://queerqrosswords.com/
Constructor Nate Cardin puts out this collection of crosswords by LGTBQ+ puzzlemakers, with proceeds going to LGTBQ+ charities.

Thinking Inside the Box: Adventures with Crosswords and the Puzzling People Who Can't Live Without Them by **Adrienne Raphel (2020)**
A fun exploration of the crossword world, including Adrienne's trip on a crossword puzzle–themed cruise.

Deb Amlen's Crossword Coverage in *The New York Times*
Deb is the *New York Times* chief puzzle writer, and her articles are as clever and entertaining as the puzzles themselves. For starters, there's her article "How to Solve the New York Times Crossword," a must-read for be-

ginners. She also edits the Wordplay column, which dissects that day's crossword and offers other puzzle-related articles.

Gridlock: Crossword Puzzles and the Mad Geniuses Who Create Them by Matt Gaffney (2006)
https://xwordcontest.com
A fun guide inside the minds of constructors. Matt also posts a weekly contest with crosswords and metapuzzles.

The Curious History of the Crossword: 100 Puzzles from Then and Now by Ben Tausig (2013). The noted cruciverbalist writes about the evolution of the puzzle, along with samples for you to solve.

Brendan Emmett Quigley
https://www.brendanemmettquigley.com
Puzzles from the brilliant (and masochistic) crossword maker.

From Square One by Dean Olsher (2009)
A lovely exploration of crosswords and life.

Rubik's Cube and Other Mechanical Puzzle Resources

Cubed: The Puzzle of Us All by Ernö Rubik (2020)
An ode to twisty puzzles and messy rooms by the man who kicked off the craze.

Sydney Weaver
http://www.sirwaffle.com
Sydney is a great Rubik's instructor, whether you're an accomplished solver or me.

That Guy With the Puzzles website
http://www.thatguywiththepuzzles.com
Puzzle designer and collector Brett Kuehner was one of my most trusted guides while exploring mechanical (and other types) of brainteasers. His website has photos of his collection, a guide to designing escape rooms, and more.

The Shape of Difficulty: A Fan Letter to Unruly Objects by Bret L. Rothstein (2020)
An erudite guide to the history and philosophy of mechanical puzzles by a professor at Indiana University.

The Jerry Slocum Mechanical Puzzle Collection
https://libraries.indiana.edu/lilly-library/mechanical-puzzles
Jerry has amassed one of the largest collections of mechanical puzzles in the world, and donated most of it to Indiana University. You can see images of thousands of historic puzzles (including French entanglement wire puzzles that I didn't include in this book because they weren't as exciting as I'd hoped. But there are plenty of other more interesting puzzles).

Rob's Puzzle Page
http://robspuzzlepage.com
Collector Rob Stegmann shares photos and history of more than 6,600 puzzle items and 250 puzzle-related books that he owns. Rob has vast knowledge of mechanical puzzles.

Chinese Puzzles
The website https://chinesepuzzles.org from Wei Zhang and Peter Rasmussen is an excellent resource, as are their books *Chinese Puzzles I* and *II*.

OskarPuzzle
https://www.youtube.com/c/OskarPuzzle
Dutch genius Oskar van Deventer, who designed Jacobs' Ladder, has a YouTube channel with hundreds of videos of his other creations.

Anagram and Word Game Resources

The National Puzzlers' League
https://www.puzzlers.org
The world's oldest puzzlers' organization (founded in 1883) hosts conferences and publishes *The Enigma*, which contains famously tricky word puzzles.

Word Ways
https://digitalcommons.butler.edu/wordways
A journal of "recreational logology" covering "puzzles, novel poems, palindromes, games, magic, unusual lists, etc."

Beyond Wordplay
https://beyondwordplay.com
News and puzzles for fellow word nerds from linguist and *Wall Street Journal* columnist Ben Zimmer, among other illustrious contributors.

Puzzlesnacks: More Than 100 Clever, Bite-Size Puzzles for Every Solver by **Eric Berlin (2019)**
A collection of accessible and creative word puzzles by one of the modern masters.

Sunday NPR Puzzle
Every Sunday, Will Shortz presents a word puzzle on NPR. The puzzles can be found here: https://www.npr.org/series/4473090/sunday-puzzle. One fan has archived them along with discussions here: https://puzzles .blainesville.com.

Jigsaw Resources

Stave puzzles
https://www.stavepuzzles.com
Home to devious, beautiful (and expensive) wood-cut jigsaw puzzles.

USA Jigsaw Puzzle Association
http://usajigsaw.org
A good resource for tournaments and tips. One of the founders is Guinness World Record jigsaw holder Tammy McLeod, who has been an excellent source of wisdom during this book on jigsaws and other puzzles.

The World Jigsaw Puzzle Federation
This is the group that puts on the world championship, where my family did not finish in last place.
https://worldjigsawpuzzle.org

Karen Puzzles
https://www.youtube.com/c/KarenPuzzles
Jigsaw solving tips and oddly satisfying time-lapse videos from a popular YouTuber.

The Jigsaw Puzzle: Piecing Together a History by **Anne D. Williams (2004)**
The most comprehensive book I found on jigsaw history, including facts like this one: a Canadian company in the 1990s agreed to send updated pieces to its world map puzzles as countries' borders changed.

Maze and Labyrinth Resources

The Labyrinth Society
https://labyrinthsociety.org
The best resource for all things labyrinthine. They hold conferences, put out a publication, and will help you find labyrinths near you.

Eric Eckert's Mazes
http://www.ericjeckert.com/mazes
Eric Eckert creates pencil mazes featuring celebrities (Bob Ross, Pam Grier), as well as personalized mazes of yourself or your friends.

***The Curious History of Mazes: 4,000 Years of Fascinating Twists and Turns with Over 100 Intriguing Puzzles to Solve* by Julie E. Bounford (2018)**
A good book covering everything from Pompeii maze graffiti to the 1980s Japanese wooden maze craze and more.

Adrian Fisher
https://www.mazemaker.com
The insanely prolific maze designer and author.

***Labyrinths & Mazes: A Complete Guide to Magical Paths of the World* by Jeff Saward**
A photo-filled book spanning Egyptian inscriptions to labyrinths created from ultraviolet light. The book is from the founding editor of *Caerdroia*— the Journal of Mazes and Labyrinths.

Math and Logic Puzzle Resources

Tanya Khovanova's Math Blog
https://blog.tanyakhovanova.com
Fourteen years' worth of entertaining posts about math and puzzles from MIT's Dr. Khovanova.

TED-Ed riddles
https://ed.ted.com
A wonderful collection of videos (sixty-three at last count) featuring logic puzzles with names like the "Egg Drop Riddle" and the "Cuddly, Duddly, Fuddly, Wuddly Riddle."

***Mathematical Puzzles: A Connoisseur's Collection* by Peter Winkler (2020)**
Puzzles featuring everything from cake slicing to coin-flipping to spiders on a cube. They are not easy, but are great.

The Moscow Puzzles by **Boris Kordemsky (1992)**
Originally published in the Soviet Union during the Khrushchev era, this classic contains iconic logic puzzles, including one about Communist youth decorating a hydroelectric powerhouse!

Tokyo Puzzles by **Kōzaburō Fujimura (1978)**
A great collection of logic and math puzzles, including some classic matchstick-rearranging problems.

Entertaining Mathematical Puzzles by **Martin Gardner (1961)**
The late and legendary *Scientific American* columnist has written a raft of books. This is just one. But almost any of them are worth reading if you are a math and logic puzzler.

The Riddle of Scheherazade: And Other Amazing Puzzles by **Raymond Smullyan (1998)**
Smullyan was a mathematician and a master of paradoxes and recreational logic. This is one of my favorites of his many books.

Cipher and Code Resources

Elonka Dunin's Kryptos website
https://elonka.com/kryptos
The ultimate Kryptos resource from ultimate expert Elonka Dunin.

Codebreaking: A Practical Guide by **Elonka Dunin and Klaus Schmeh (2021)**
An exceedingly useful book for novices and experts interested in codes and ciphers.

The Codebreakers: The Comprehensive History of Secret Communication from Ancient Times to the Internet by **David Kahn (1996)**
A 1,200-page, nearly four-pound classic that is worth reading if you love codes and ciphers (even if it is a little dated).

Cipherbrain blog by **Klaus Schmeh**
https://scienceblogs.de/klausis-krypto-kolumne
One of my favorite people in the cryptography community, Klaus runs a blog that features unsolved historical ciphers and codes—and a passionate audience that often solves them.

American Cryptogram Association

cryptogram.org

An organization devoted to recreational ciphers with conventions and a bimonthly publication called *The Cryptogram.*

Visual Puzzle Resources

Quest for the Golden Hare by **Bamber Gascoigne (1983)**

A fascinating look at the Masquerade madness in the UK in the early '80s, and the cult that it created.

The 12-Hour Art Expert: Everything You Need to Know About Art in a Dozen Masterpieces by **Noah Charney (2022)**

This book by art historian Charney is a good intro to art in general, but also has some nuggets about hidden symbols.

Sudoku, KenKen, and Other Grid Puzzle Resources

The Art of Sudoku by **Thomas Snyder (2012)**

The World Sudoku Champion shares 120 puzzles that, as the book says, "could never have been produced by random computer generation."

The 15 Puzzle Book: How It Drove the World Crazy by **Jerry Slocum and Dic Sonneveld (2006)**

A detailed look at the puzzle fad of the 1880s, and the trickery of Sam Loyd.

Puzzles Old & New: How to Make and Solve Them by **Jerry Slocum and Jack Botermans (1986)**

A photo-filled book of puzzles dating back centuries, often with excellent names such as the "Zornbrecher Puzzle" and "The Loculus of Archimedes."

Chess Problem Resources

Rewire Your Chess Brain: Endgame Studies and Mating Problems to Enhance Your Tactical Ability by **Cyrus Lakdawala (2020)**

One of Cyrus's fifty-plus books, this is a highly entertaining guide to chess problems, ranging from easy to mind-melting.

Prepare With Chess Strategy **by Alexey W. Root (2016)**
My other favorite chess writer. A great intro to chess strategy, with problems sprinkled throughout.

The Immortal Game: A History of Chess **by David Shenk (2007)**
A fascinating book, and the source for the story in my book about Marcel Duchamp. I'm also a fan of the extended subtitle *How 32 Carved Pieces on a Board Illuminated Our Understanding of War, Science and the Human Brain.*

Riddle Resources

The Riddle Ages website
https://theriddleages.com
A trove of scholarly but surprisingly fun writing about medieval riddles (some of which are naughty). It was started by University of Birmingham's Megan Cavell.

Lewis Carroll's Games & Puzzles **by Lewis Carroll and Edward Wakeling (1992)**
Acrostics, ciphers, and wonderful, excruciating wordplay from one of the masters.

The Curious History of the Riddle **by Marcel Danesi (2020)**
A chronology of riddles from ancient Greece to the middle ages to Harry Potter.

Puzzle Box Resources

Karakuri
https://karakuri.gr.jp/en
The originals. This is the group of designers that started the Japanese puzzle box craze.

Kagen Sound
https://kagensound.com
The designer of Darren Aronofsky's puzzle desk, Kagen makes puzzles as beautiful as they are perplexing.

Stickman
stickmanpuzzlebox.com
Home to Oklahoma-based designer Robert Yarger's intricate and innovative boxes.

Chris Ramsay
https://www.youtube.com/c/ChrisRamsay52
A video collection of the tattooed Canadian magician who grapples with the hardest (and most expensive) puzzle boxes.

Boxes and Booze
https://www.boxesandbooze.com
Steve Canfield's website with an unusual premise: each puzzle box is paired with a cocktail. (FYI there is a modicum of evidence that a small amount of alcohol can help with problem solving, but diminishing returns kick in soon.)

Sleeping Beauty Resources

The Best Writing on Mathematics, 2018 edited by Mircea Pitici
Perhaps the clearest introduction to the Sleeping Beauty problem is Peter Winkler's essay in this anthology of math-related writing.

The Halfers' side
Fans of the Sleeping Beauty problem mostly fall into two camps: halfers and thirders. If you want to learn more about the halfer arguments, Mike Gefers has provided a memo on this book's website, thepuzzlerbook .com.

Scavenger and Puzzle Hunt Resources

Watson Adventures
https://watsonadventures.com
This event company puts on delightful highbrow scavenger hunts, both in person (at museums and in historic neighborhoods) and virtually. They have done hunts in all fifty states and several foreign countries. They also offer Puzzled to Death, co-written by me. The company was founded by Bret Watson, and its president happens to be an awesome human named Julie Jacobs.

MIT Mystery Hunt
Here's the official site for the MIT Mystery Hunt, the famously challenging puzzle marathon that occurs every January.
puzzles.mit.edu

Another site archives more than three thousand MIT Mystery Hunt puzzles, starting in 1994.
https://devjoe.appspot.com/huntindex

Room Escape Artist
https://roomescapeartist.com
This website on escape rooms accurately describes itself as "well-researched, rational, and reasonably humorous." Founded by David and Lisa Spira, it has reviews of hundreds of escape rooms, both real and virtual, as well as history and tips on puzzles.

How to Puzzle Cache by Cully Long (2019)
I didn't have room in the book to talk about geocaching, but as you might know, it's sort of a worldwide treasure hunt where you find boxes hidden under trees, in the cracks of walls, and so on (the treasures are stickers, plastic trinkets, notes—not diamonds or gold). Many of the caches require you to solve a puzzle, and this book is an excellent guide.

The Joyful, Perplexing World of Puzzle Hunts by Alex Rosenthal
A great TED Talk from one of my Setec Astronomy teammates and TED-Ed team member.

Puzzled Pint
http://www.puzzledpint.com
An in-person monthly event that takes place in dozens of pubs across the U.S. and other countries. Participants are given a series of challenging puzzles to solve with friends (or alone). It happens on the second Tuesday of every month, but to find your local pub, you have to solve a puzzle posted on the website the Friday before.

Solutions

CHAPTER 1 · *Crosswords*

From page 7: **The first crossword puzzle ever**

Solutions to Four Crossword Puzzles from History

1. A More Diverse Crossword

G	O	R	P		M	A	M	A	S		L	S	D
M	A	Y	A		L	U	N	A	T	E		U	M	A
C	H	A	M	B	E	R	D	O	O	R		M	E	N
S	U	N	G	E	A	R			P	E	B	B	L	E
		R	V	P	A	R	K		N	O	E	L	S
S	O	C	I	E	T	Y	A	F	F	A	I	R
E	T	H	E	L			G	E	O			J	I	B
C	O	U	R	S	E	D		D	O	I	D	A	R	E
T	E	N			L	A	M		N	A	N	A	S
		K	E	Y	I	N	G	R	E	D	I	E	N	T
S	T	Y	L	E		K	R	O	N	U	R	
T	O	K	L	A	S		L	U	C	Y	L	I	U
A	N	N		S	A	U	C	E	R	E	C	I	P	E
S	K	I		T	I	P	T	O	E		O	K	A	Y
H	A	T		S	L	A	Y	S		W	E	D	S

2. The World War II puzzle

ACROSS: 1: AFTERTHOUGHTS, 10: ALL EARS, 11: BLADDER, 12: BUCKET, 15: SET OFF, 16: DECIDED, 17: UTAH, 18: FEAT, 19: DECORUM, 20: MACE, 22: AMEN, 24: GALAHAD, 26: SAMPAN, 27: RITUAL, 30: EQUALLY, 31: CHABLIS, 32: REINSTATEMENT

DOWN: 2: FELUCCA, 3: ELATED, 4: TEST, 5: ORBY, 6: GRADED, 7: TADPOLE, 8: HARBOURMASTER, 9: PROFIT AND LOSS, 13: TEHRAN, 14: BIVOUAC, 15: SECULAR, 21: COMPUTE, 23: MAUDLIN, 24: GALLON, 25: DISARM, 28: SYLT, 29: SCUT

3. Scandinavian Crossword

4. Peter Gordon Fireball Crossword

The six longest Across answers in the puzzle end with the last names of Hall of Fame baseball players whose uniform numbers have been retired by their teams. From top to bottom, they are the following: Rollie FINGERS (#34 retired by the Brewers and A's), Jim RICE (#14, Red Sox), Johnny BENCH (#5, Reds), Bob LEMON (#21, Indians), Nellie FOX (#2, White Sox), and Mike PIAZZA (#31, Mets). The numbers in order from top to bottom are these: 34, 14, 5, 21, 2, 31. Looking at the letters in the grid in the correspondingly numbered squares (highlighted in the answer grid) yields J, A, C, K, I, E.

There is only one Jackie whose number has been retired: Jackie Robinson. The Brooklyn Dodgers infielder made his debut on April 15, 1947, breaking baseball's color barrier. He batted .311 in his 10-season career and was elected to the Hall of Fame in 1962, his first year of eligibility. The Dodgers retired his number in 1972, and on April 15, 1997, the fiftieth anniversary of his historic first game, his number was retired throughout the majors.

Jackie Robinson Day is celebrated each year on April 15. In recent years, every player, coach, and umpire in every game in the majors wears Robinson's uniform number on that day. That uniform number (which also happens to be the answer to the great question of life, the universe, and everything, according to the Douglas Adams book *The Hitchhiker's Guide to the Galaxy*) is the final answer to the puzzle: 42.

19D: M. Patate, the French name for Mr. Potato Head, has a NEZ (nose) piece.

35D: Max BAER's technical knockout of Max Schmeling at Yankee Stadium was *Ring* magazine's 1933 Fight of the Year.

CHAPTER 4 · *Anagrams*

1. MOON STARERS = ASTRONOMERS

2. BAG MANAGER = GARBAGE MAN

3. A STEW, SIR? = WAITRESS

4. MR. MOJO RISIN' = JIM MORRISON

5. ONE COOL DANCE MUSICIAN = MADONNA LOUISE CICCONE

6. GENUINE CLASS = ALEC GUINNESS

7. RADIUM CAME = MADAM CURIE

8. CASH LOST IN 'EM = SLOT MACHINES

9. BUILT TO STAY FREE = STATUE OF LIBERTY

10. DIRTY ROOM = DORMITORY

11. VIOLENCE RUN FORTH = FRENCH REVOLUTION

12. Cartoonist Bil Keane (*The Family Circus*) turns into Bike Lane

13. Virgin Wool turns into Virginia Woolf

14. 5,280 Feet in a Mile

15. 3 Sides in a Triangle

16. 5 Fingers on a Hand

17. 14 Days in a Fortnight

18. 6 Feet in a Fathom

19. 9 Lives of a Cat

CHAPTER 5 · *Rebuses*

From page 61: **Sam Loyd's Famous Trick Donkeys**
    For further explanation of the Trick Donkeys puzzle, see thepuzzler book.com.

SOLUTIONS TO SEVEN REBUSES FROM HISTORY

1. Potatoes (Pot plus eight Os)

2. The escort card reads:

    May I see you home my dear?

3. The answer to the newspaper rebus is "Horace Greeley."

    The hints are:
    The male spectator is shouting "Ho!"
    They are watching a "race."

The dog is saying "Grrrr."

The runner has an "E" on his shirt.

The female spectator is cheering on "Lee."

4. The bottle cap rebus is

Book R T Washing Ton

or

Booker T. Washington

5. The ball is in your court.

6. Travel overseas

7. For once in my life

CHAPTER 8 · *Math and Logic Puzzles*

From page 113: **The Rhind Papyrus puzzle Problem 79**

The total is 19,607.

From page 113: **The first known river-crossing puzzle**

1. Take the goat and leave it on the other side.
2. Return to the original side alone.
3. Take the wolf across and leave it on the other side, but retrieve the goat.
4. Return with the goat.
5. Leave the goat on the original side and take the cabbage to the other side.
6. Return alone and bring the goat to the other side.

Solutions to Nine Math and Logic Puzzles from History

1. If you move the I from "IX" to the minus sign and turn it into a plus sign, you get a correct equation.

VI + IV = X

2. The girls are not twins. They are triplets (or quadruplets).

3. The answer is one. Here is Carroll's diagram of how this is possible:

In this genealogy, males are denoted by capitals, and females by small letters.

The Governor is E and his guest is C.

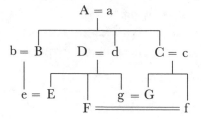

4. The missing yen puzzle

FROM *THE TOKYO PUZZLES:*

This puzzle is a play on words. If you analyze the problem correctly, you will find the right answer.

The 27,000 yen is the sum of the 25,000 that the cashier received and the 2,000 yen that the maid took. Therefore, it does not make sense to add once again the maid's 2,000 yen to the 27,000 yen. It does make sense to add the 3,000 yen that the maid returned, in which case the two amounts equal 30,000 yen.

5. According to William Poundstone's book *Are You Smart Enough to Work at Google?,* from which this Fermi problem was taken, it would take about 250 billion toilet paper rolls to cover Texas.

6. Pour wine from the vessel with 8 pints into the 5-pint vessel (leaving 3 pints).

Then take the 5-pint vessel and pour it unto the 3-pint vessel (leaving 2 pints).

So now we have 3 pints in the 8-pint vessel, 3 pints in the 3-pint vessel, and 2 pints in the 5-pint vessel.

Pour all the wine from the 3-pint vessel into the 8-pint vessel. The 8-pint vessel now has 6 pints.

Now pour the 2 pints from the 5-pint vessel into the empty 3-pint vessel.

Now take the 8-pint vessel and pour all you can into the 5-pint vessel, leaving 1 pint.

So we've got 5 pints of wine in the 5-pint vessel, 2 pints of wine in the 3-pint vessel, and 1 pint in the 8-pint vessel.

Now pour what you can (1 pint) from the 5-pint vessel into the 3-pint vessel, which has 2 pints already. The 5-pint vessel now has 4 pints!

Now pour the 3 pints from the 3-pint vessel into the 8-pint vessel.

Now the 8-pint vessel also has 4 pints, and you have some well-aerated wine.

Enjoy!

7. Two slices on top and one horizontal slice through the middle give you eight pieces.

8. 3, 4, 5 doesn't belong because it is the only one with consecutive numbers.

> 8, 10, 12 doesn't belong because it is the only one that isn't a Pythagorean triple. It also doesn't belong because it's the only one where the numbers are all even.
>
> 6.9, 11.5, and the $\sqrt{84.64}$ doesn't belong because
> it is the only one with decimals
> or it is the only one with a radical sign
> or it is the only one where the sum of all the digits isn't 12 (3 + 4 + 5 = 12, 8 + 1 + 0 + 1 + 2 = 12; 5 + 1 + 2 + 1 + 3 = 12).

There are many other solutions. These are just a few.

9. The first man is a knave, and the second man is a knight.

We know the first man is a knave because a knight cannot lie, so a knight could never say that he was a knave. We know the second man is a knight because if the second man was also a knave, the first knave would be speaking the truth when he says, "We are both knaves." Knaves cannot tell the truth. So, one knave and one knight.

CHAPTER 9 · *Ciphers and Secret Codes*

1. Victorian love ciphers

A.B. to M.N.—Tn dvcr trw rhtn yltcfrp drtln yln srsd t s uy dn trw t uy.

The secret is that the cipher omits vowels and spells the words backward. So the message is (something like):

"Not Received. Write another, perfectly unaltered. Only desirous to see you. Need write to you."

2. Newspaper cryptograms

a) Alaska is the only state whose name can be typed on one row of a keyboard.

b) Pink Floyd's lyric "We don't need no education" is a self-defeating argument.

c) Here comes Santa Claus, here comes Santa Claus, right down Santa Claus Lane. What are the odds?

d) George Washington's boozy eggnog recipe included this instruction: "Taste frequently."

3. Edgar Allan Poe's ciphers

I am a word of ten letters. My first, second, seventh, and third is useful to farmers; my sixth, seventh, and first is a mischievous animal; my ninth, seventh, and first is the latter's enemy; my tenth, seventh, and first supports life; my fourth, fifth, seventh, and sixth is a fruit; my fourth, fifth, and eighth is a powerful implement; my whole indicates a wise man.

The answer is "Temperance."

The words indicated in the riddle include "team," "rat," "cat," "eat," and "pear."

The cipher is below:

A 9 / C 6 / D: / E 8 / F s / G; / H 7 / I o / L n / M? / N 5 / O a / P! / R d / S—/ T 3 / U h / V x / W 2 / X g / Y †

4. The NASA code

The rays of the sun contain Morse code (in the form of alternating long and short rays) that reads "Explore as one."

The phrase is a slogan of NASA's Jet Propulsion Laboratory.

CHAPTER 10 · *Visual Puzzles*

Hidden logos

1. Baskin Robbins—The lighter parts of the letters "BR" resemble the number 31, as in their trademark 31 flavors.

2. Toblerone—There is a silhouette of a bear in the mountain. A bear is a reference to the Swiss city Bern, where Toblerone was created and which features a bear in its coat of arms.

3. Tour de France—The R resembles a rider, and the two circles resemble the wheels of a bicycle.

4. Sun Microsystems—The diamond pattern contains the word "sun."

5. Pittsburgh Zoo—The faces of a gorilla and a lion can be seen on either side of the tree.

6. The Missing Square puzzle
   The two figures may look like triangles, but they are actually not triangles. The hypotenuse in these figures is not a straight line. One is slightly convex, the other slightly concave. The difference in area is enough to create a gap the size of the square. This puzzle is often given to geometry classes as a warning to not trust your eyes.

7. The Soviet camping puzzle

   a) There are four tourists. See the four sets of cutlery on the picnic blanket and four names on the duty list.
   b) They arrived a few days ago—long enough for a spider to build a web between their tent and a tree.
   c) They got there by boat, judging by the oars next to the tree.
   d) The closest village is not far—the chicken wouldn't be walking around in the area otherwise.
   e) The wind is blowing from the south. The flag on top of the tent shows the wind direction and, looking at the trees, branches on the southern side are normally longer.
   f) It's morning. The shadows show the sun is to their east.
   g) Alex is catching butterflies—see the scoop net behind the tent.
   h) Colin was on duty yesterday. He's looking for something in his backpack, which is marked with a "C." Alex is catching butterflies. James is taking pictures. Peter is on duty today, and Colin was on duty yesterday.

i) It's August 8th—because Peter is on duty and there is a watermelon in the ground. Watermelons ripen in August.

Bongard problems

8. The left side has spirals that curve counterclockwise; the right side has spirals that curve clockwise.

9. The left-side shapes have horizontal necks; the right-side shapes have vertical necks.

10. On the left side, the dots inside the shape outline are grouped more densely than the dots outside the contour. On the right, it's the opposite.

11. The second and third panels are identical, as are the first and fourth.

CHAPTER 11 · *Sudoku and KenKen*

Ben Franklin's Magic Square

From page 163:

From *The Gentleman's Magazine:*

Surprizing Properties of Numbers placed in Dr. Franklin's Magic Square of Squares.

The great square is divided into 256 small squares, in which all the numbers from 1 to 256 are placed in 16 columns, which may be taken either horizontally or vertically. The properties are as follows:

The sum of the 16 numbers in each column, vertical or horizontal, is 2056.

Every half column, vertical and horizontal, makes 1028, or half 2056.

Half a diagonal ascending, added to half a diagonal descending, makes 2056; taking these half diagonals from the ends of any side of the square to the middle thereof, and so reckoning them either upward or downward; or sideways from left to right hand, or from right to left.

The same with all the parallels to the half diagonals, as many as can be drawn in the great square: for any two of them being directed upward and downward, from where they began to where they end, their sums will make 2056. The same downward and upward from where they begin to where they end; or the same if taken sidewise to the middle, and back to the same side again.

N.B. One set of these half diagonals and their parallels is drawn in the figure upward and downward. Another such set may be drawn from any of the other three sides.

The four corner numbers in the great square added to the four central numbers make 1028, equal to half the sum of any vertical or horizontal column, which contains 16 numbers, and equal to half a diagonal or its parallel.

If a square hole (equal in breadth to four of the little squares) be cut in a paper, through which any of the 16 little squares in the great square may be seen, and the paper be laid on the great square; the sum of all the 16 numbers, seen through the hole, is equal to the sum of the 16 numbers in any horizontal or vertical column, viz, to 2056.

From page 169:

Miyamoto's hardest KenKen solution

6	5	9	1	8	3	7	2	4
7	6	1	2	9	4	8	3	5
8	7	2	3	1	5	9	4	6
4	3	7	8	6	1	5	9	2
9	8	3	4	2	6	1	5	7
3	2	6	7	5	9	4	8	1
2	1	5	6	4	8	3	7	9
1	9	4	5	3	7	2	6	8
5	4	8	9	7	2	6	1	3

Copyright Tetsuya Miyamoto

Solutions to Four Grid Puzzles from History

1. Number Place

1

4	2	3	9	8	1	7	5	6
7	5	8	4	6	3	2	1	9
9	1	6	2	5	7	3	4	8
5	8	4	3	1	9	6	2	7
6	9	2	8	7	5	1	3	4
1	3	7	6	2	4	9	8	5
3	7	5	1	4	6	8	9	2
8	4	1	7	9	2	5	6	3
2	6	9	5	3	8	4	7	1

2

6	8	7	2	5	3	4	1	9
4	1	2	7	8	9	6	5	3
3	9	5	6	4	1	2	8	7
7	2	4	9	3	5	8	6	1
9	5	8	1	6	2	7	3	4
1	6	3	4	7	8	5	9	2
8	7	6	3	9	4	1	2	5
5	3	1	8	2	7	9	4	6
2	4	9	5	1	6	3	7	8

Copyright 2022 by PennyDellPuzzles.com

2. Thomas Snyder Artistic Sudoku

2	6	4	9	1	5	7	3	8
8	1	7	2	3	4	9	5	6
3	9	5	6	8	7	2	1	4
9	8	1	4	2	6	3	7	5
5	2	6	8	7	3	1	4	9
7	4	3	5	9	1	8	6	2
1	5	8	3	6	2	4	9	7
6	3	2	7	4	9	5	8	1
4	7	9	1	5	8	6	2	3

Courtesy of Thomas Snyder

3. The first KenKen

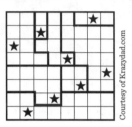

4. Star Battle

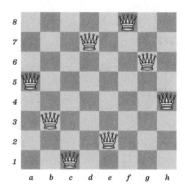

CHAPTER 12 · *Chess Puzzles (Chess Problems)*

From page 178: Kubbel's hardest mate in one problem:

Move the White queen to a3.

Solutions to Eight Chess Problems from History

1. The eight queens puzzle

There are twelve solutions. All are readily found on the Internet. Here's one of them:

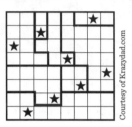

2. Guarini's problem

Black knight (BK) from a3 to c2

BK from c3 to b1

White knight (WK) from c1 to a2

WK from a1 to b3
BK from c2 to a1
BK from b1 to a3
WK from a2 to c3
WK from b3 to c1
BK from a1 to b3
BK from a3 to c2
WK from c3 to b1
WK from c1 to a2
BK from b3 to c1
BK from c2 to a1
WK from b1 to a3
WK from a2 to c3

3. Mate in one problem no. 1
Move the White queen to b7

4. Mate in one problem no. 2
Move the White pawn to b7

5. Nabokov's problem
1. h3 Kh4 2. Rxg6 gxh3 3. Bf6#

1. White pawn moves to h3, Black king moves to h4 2. White rook takes on g6, Black pawn takes on h3 3. White bishop checkmate on f6

Other variations include:

1. h3! h4 2 Rh7! hxg3 3 h4 mate, and

1. h3! Kh6 2 h4! g5 3 hxg5 mate

6. Sam Loyd's Excelsior
1. b4!

Threatening 2.Rf5 *any* 3.Rf1# or 2.Rd5 *any* 3.Rd1# (with possible prolonging of both by 2 . . . Rc5 3.bxc5 *any* 4.R mates). White cannot begin with 1.Rf5 because Black's 1 . . . Rc5 would pin the rook. Now there are multiple possible moves defending only one of the threats and one secondary non-thematical defense: 1 . . . Rxc2 2.Nxc2! a2 3.Rd5 (or Rf5) a1=Q 4.Nxa1 *any* 5.R mates.

1 . . . Rc5+ 2. bxc5!

Threatening 3.Rb1#.

2 . . . a2 3. c6!

Again with the same threats as on move one, i.e. 4.Rf5 *any* 5.Rf1# or 4.Rd5 *any* 5.Rd1#.

3 . . . Bc7

Because both Rd5 and Rf5 are threatened; the alternative moves 3 . . . Bf6 and 3 . . . Bg5 would only defend against one or the other. The given move does defend against Rd5 in the sense that 4.Rd5 Bxg3 5.Rd1+ Be1 6.Rdxe1# takes more than the required five moves, and similarly for 4. Rf5 Bf4.

4. cxb7 *any* 5. bxa8=Q/B#

The mate is delivered with the pawn that starts on b2.

Solution courtesy of Wikipedia.

7. Shakespeare for a chimp (Kasparyan's problem)

1. Bh6!!

Deflection. White puts the bishop en prise as well. When I see a move as insane-looking as this, all that registers within my brain is gibberish. It seems almost a joke that White would play on, yet Fritz 17 assesses the position at -0.57 (soon to go to 0.00) where Black is barely up half a pawn. And that is an overestimation!

Not 1 Ka2? Nd7 and Black consolidates.

1 . . . Qxh6 A similar result occurs after 1 . . . Qxd4+ 2 Ka2 Qa4+ (2 . . . Nd7 3 g7+ Qxg7 4 Bxg7+ Kxg7 is a theoretical draw) 3 Kb1 Qb3+ 4 Ka1 Qa3+ 5 Kb1 and as long as the White king keeps to a1 and b1, Black has nothing better than perpetual check.

2. Nf5! This way the knight is not hanging. Whereas after 2 Ne6? Qc1+ 3 Ka2 Qd2+ White's king is fatally restricted by the need to avoid dropping the knight with check. For example: 4 Ka1 (or 4 Kb3 Qe3+ 5 Kb4 Nd5+ 6 Ka4 Qe4+ 7 Kb5 Qb4+ 8 Kc6 Ne7+ 9 Kd7 Nxg6 and Black eliminates all threats and wins) 4 . . . Qe1+ 5 Kb2 (5 Ka2 Qxe6+ wins) 5 . . . Nd3+ 6 Kc2 Nb4+ (three menacing adults approach a helpless child) 7 Kb2 Qe2+ 8 Ka3 Nc2+ 9 Kb2 Ne3+ 10 Ka1 Qd1+ 11 Ka2 Qa4+ 12 Kb2 Nec4+ 13 Kc3 Qa3+ 14 Kc2 Qa2+ 15 Kd3 Qd2+ 16 Ke4 Qe3+ 17 Kf5 Qe5 mate.

2 . . . Qc1+ 3 Ka2 Qc2+ 4 Ka1

(Courtesy of Cyrus Lakdawala, *Rewire Your Chess Brain*)

8. Helpmate

1 . . . Qh8

2. Qb3 mate

CHAPTER 13 · *Riddles*

From page 199, **the Exeter Book riddle number 4**:

The bad part is, this riddle from the Exeter Book is a tough one.

The good part is, you can justify almost any guess on God's green earth. Here is a list of proposed solutions:

A bucket of water
A bell
A dog
A lock
The devil
A team of oxen
A sword
A millstone
Necromancy (the art of communicating with the dead)
A flail (a threshing tool)
A hand mill
A pen
A phallus

SOLUTIONS TO TWELVE RIDDLES FROM HISTORY

1. A shadow

2. Time

3. Seven

4. Water

5. A pen

6. A stamp

7. Woman (woe and man). Yes, very heteronormative and sexist, but please blame Jane Austen, not me.

8. Spider (spy, plus "d" plus "er")

9. To the mooo-vies!

10. Windmill

11. One. As *Mental Floss* explains, this "is a classic trick question. If the narrator is going to St. Ives, anyone he or she meets is going in the opposite direction. So the narrator (one person) is going to St. Ives, and all the wives and cats and kittens are irrelevant misdirections (in the literal sense of the word)."

12. A match

From page 225, the solution to *The Telegraph* puzzle used in recruiting codebreakers during World War II.

ACROSS: 1 TROUPE, 4 SHORT CUT, 9 PRIVET, 10 AROMATIC, 12 TREND, 13 GREAT DEAL, 15 OWE, 16 FEIGN, 17 NEWARK, 22 IMPALE, 24 GUISE, 27 ASH, 28 CENTRE BIT, 31 TOKEN, 32 LAME DOGS, 33 RACING, 34 SILENCER, 35 ALIGHT.

DOWN: 1 TIPSTAFF, 2 OLIVE OIL, 3 PSEUDONYM, 5 HORDE, 6 REMIT, 7 CUTTER, 8 TACKLE, 11 AGENDA, 14 ADA, 18 WREATH, 19 RIGHT NAIL, 20 TINKLING, 21 SENNIGHT, 23 PIE, 25 SCALES, 26 ENAMEL, 29 RODIN, 30 BOGIE.

SOLUTION TO ONE CRYPTIC FROM HISTORY

ACROSS: 1 MUNICIPALISE, 9 INCUR, 10 MERRIMENT, 11 HEINOUS, 12 EVERTON, 13 PALLIATIVE, 15 CARE, 18 CONE, 19 OESOPHAGUS, 22 NEWPORT, 24 BATHBUN, 25 ENDOSCOPY, 26 NURSE, 27 CHEMOTHERAPY

DOWN: 1 MACMILLAN, 2 NARCOTIC, 3 CAMUS, 4 PARLEYVOO, 5 LOITER, 6 STENT, 7 MISHAP, 8 STANCE, 14 THEFTBOOT, 16 ARGYBARGY, 17 PHOTINIA, 18 CANCER, 20 SUNSET, 21 POSSUM, 23 WIDTH, 24 BOYLE

1. Doodlepalooza

Palm Sunday
Fairy Tale
Pause Button
Capital Letter
Sales Tax
Check Point

The highlighted letters spell "Artist."

2. The first MIT Mystery Hunt

a. This is Messier 3, or M3, for which the clue answer only uses "3." The answer is one that many higher-level amateur astronomers would know offhand.

b. Tweedledum's rank is "4." This is from the chess game in *Through the Looking-Glass.*

c. "WELCOME." This is a quote from Shakespeare's *Hamlet.*

d. "THE." "First word of The Bible" is a bit of a trick question. The first kneejerk idea would be to take the word "IN" from "In the beginning . . ." in Genesis 1:1. But the first word of the two-word phrase "The Bible" is "THE."

Incidentally, the solution to the meta-puzzle in that first MIT hunt was this:

ROOM 13-E124, "WELCOME TO THE MONKEY HOUSE"

The room was a reserve reading room. The goal was to find its copy of Kurt Vonnegut's novel *Welcome to the Monkey House.*

(Solutions courtesy of Bradley Schaefer)

3.

Bobcat

by Justin Graham

Answer: BASSISTS

The animals are all bands with animal names (Beatles, Def Leppard, Eagles, etc.). Each fun fact references a well-known song from one of the bands. Match the songs (fun facts) and bands (animals) and order by the path of animals in the picture. Index into the song title using the number next to the Fun Fact. Put the letters in the order of the path in the picture.

Band	Fun Fact	Song	Letter
Beatles	. . . after eating one of Mackintosh's confections.	10 Savory Truffle	F
Byrds	. . . just a few kilometers above the troposphere.	8 Eight Miles High	L
Pitbull	This animal shouts out a warning when a tree is falling.	5 Timber	E
Eagles	These animals operate an inn on the West Coast.	15 Hotel California	A
Turtles	These animals are glad to be all in the same place.	2 Happy Together	A
Blue Öyster Cult	This animal set itself on fire on your behalf.	6 Burnin' For You	N
Phish	. . . marshmallow all over their noggin.	9 Fluffhead	D
Three Dog Night	. . . express their happiness to the entire globe.	13 Joy To The World	D
Def Leppard	Please spill your sweetener on this animal.	3 Pour Some Sugar On Me	U
Gorillaz	. . . . organized themselves into a euphoric cooperation.	11 Feel Good Inc	C
John Cougar (Mellencamp)	This animal likes rosé homes.	4 Pink Houses	K
Monkees	These animals worship flights of fancy.	1 Daydream Believer	D
Scorpions	. . . . shake you as if you were in a tropical storm.	14 Rock You Like A Hurricane	U
Counting Crows	. . . monarch of precipitation.	7 Rain King	N
Whitesnake	Look out! This animal is starting to do it another time.	12 Here I Go Again	N

This yields the message FLEA AND DUCK DUNN. These are the names of BASSISTS (the solution).

SOLUTION TO THE MISSING CYCLIST PROBLEM FROM THE INSERT

The secret is that the thirteenth man is created from the bisected features of the other twelve men. So the face, for instance, in the fourth man becomes a face for both the fourth and eleventh man.

Hints to the Original Puzzle Hunt by Greg Pliska

1. The "The Puzzle of Puzzles" Puzzle

The clue answers have something in common. Ask yourself why the title is what it is.

2. Data Error

Twelve cells each contain a unique pair of letters, leaving two letters unused.

3. Rubik's 3 × 3 × 3

Here are some of the first words to get you started: green BERET, red CHINA, blue BONNET, orange BLOSSOM.

4. Flatfoots

One way to get started is to try to identify the missing words from the context. Here are some clues for each flat:

1) What word completes the phrase, borrowed from the French, "__ monde"?
2) SECOND is a past-tense verb meaning "placed a bet."
3) LONG is a part of Ukraine recently invaded by Russia.
4) MOST and LOON are both plural nouns. In the singular, they form the title of a Disney film, *The ___ and the ___.*
5) Start with "FIVE Rivera." What famous Broadway performer is that?
6) What notable religious book fits alphabetically between *Beowulf* and *Black Boy*?

ANAGRAM: Your answer is a crime show from the '90s.

5. Signs and Symbols

If you're stuck, try figuring out the L with the plus sign. What does that sign indicate in chemistry? Once you have an idea what the answers have in common, you can work backward to figure out which items in the group are clued by which image.

6. A Perfect Match

ROBOT + BLOCKS = ROBLOX, and the two squares with those words belong in the very center of the 3 x 4 array of squares.

7. We Aim to Please

The path you take in each maze will form the shape of a letter.

8A. The Latest Fashion

The number of the time tells you which letter you need from the corresponding designer's name, while the number of outfits tells you which letter to take from the fabric type.

8B. Real Numbers

You can search for songs by each artist that have numbers in them and see if any match the initials in the left column. For example, Ariana Grande has a song called "Seven Rings," which fits with "7 ___". The R fills in the blank, and forms part of the final message.

9. Remix

The rule for #4 is to reverse all but the first letter of each word. So PNOITATIPICER was originally PRECIPITATION.

10. Border Crossings

The second pair shows Tokyo, JAPAN and Sana'a, YEMEN. The letter you get from JAPAN/YEMEN is N.

11. Coming to Terms

The top row of the KenKen is 482516739.

12. Greeks vs. Romans

The first word of the Black knight clue is ANOTHER.

13. Who Are We?

Several of the riddles involve strings of letters that appear in words that are given. For #5, you're looking for a pair of real people with the same first name, and the last names Black and White.

14. Japanese Puzzle Boxes

The second word in each set is, respectively, MANDARIN, PERPLEX, and BAOBAB. The sets are Languages, Synonyms for Puzzle, and Trees.

15. Thirders and Halfers

The Thirder answers spell out three separate clues, each of which hints at a two-letter abbreviation. The Halfer answers spell out two separate clues, each of which hints at a three-letter answer.

16. Transatlantic

Don't get discouraged! There are many online guides to solving cryptic crossword clues. Your first step should be to ignore the "surface" meaning of the clue—what it appears to be about—and try to find the two halves. Does the beginning or the end of the clue read like it might be a traditional crossword-style clue? That might be the definition for the answer, meaning the other half of the clue involves wordplay. For the wordplay, look for indications that you scramble up letters (like "reformulated") or hints that you take part of a word or pair of words ("contents" or "initially").

17. Skyscrapers of Hanoi

Consider the building names, like CITIC or Willis. Does the word have a particular property, and are there answer words that share that property? Or is the word a member of a set, and are there answers that are also members of that same set?

18. Big Secrets (the metapuzzle)

Consider what things come in sets with this many members. You might also want to pay special attention to the flavortext.

Solutions to the Original Puzzle Hunt by Greg Pliska

1. The "The Puzzle of Puzzles" Puzzle solution

Each clue can be answered with a reduplicated word. The first letters of those words spell the answer **DOUBLE BOND**.

> 1 Dik-dik
> 2 Once, once
> 3 Up, up
> 4 Bora Bora
> 5 Lang Lang
> 6 Extra! Extra!
> 7 Baden-Baden
> 8 Out, out
> 9 Nae nae
> 10 Dee Dee

2. Data Error solution

There are twelve cells in the puzzle where the across and down letters do not match. These "mismatched pairs" are placed symmetrically in the grid and include 24 of the letters of the alphabet. (Within each pair the letters are alphabetical, across preceding down, and the pairs themselves are then placed alphabetically in the grid.)

The missing pair of letters, **IO**, is the answer to this puzzle.

3. Rubik's 3 × 3 × 3 solution

Each face consists of words which can precede that face's color in a common word or phrase, like WHITE ELEPHANT and GREEN BERET.

The leftover trigrams can be rearranged to spell HARRY POTTER WIZARD WITH SURNAME BLACK, which clues the answer SIRIUS.

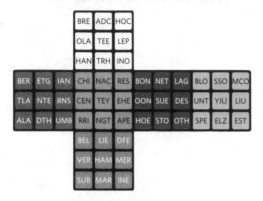

4. Flatfoots solution

The answers to each flat are given below. The bold words form the clue OH! NEED CRIME FOES HIT TITLE, which anagrams to HOMICIDE: LIFE ON THE STREET.

1. **oh**, eau, owe, haut
2. New Ager, wagered, **need**
3. Crimea, **crime**
4. hounds, bounds; foxes, **foes**
5. Chianti, tai chi, Chita, itch, **hit**
6. Bible, **title**

5. Signs and Symbols solution

Each rebus stands for the symbol of one sign of the zodiac. The indicated letters spell the message ITEM LEFT OUT, which is the missing twelfth animal, the CRAB.

1.	VI (six) R gin	VIRGIN (2)	I
2.	TW in S	TWINS (1)	T
3.	scale S	SCALES (5)	E
4.	R a.m.	RAM (3)	M
5.	L ion	LION (1)	L
6.	arch ER	ARCHER (5)	E

7.	F is H	FISH (1)	F
8.	go AT	GOAT (4)	T
9.	S, C or pi on	SCORPION (3)	O
10.	B.U. (Boston University) LL (Cool J)	BULL (2)	U
11.	(3)water (H2) bear ER	WATER BEARER	T

6. A Perfect Match solution

The grid below shows the assembled pieces. The portmanteau words created are:

1. Britain + exit = Brexit
2. lollipop + icicle = popsicle
3. three + repeat = threepeat
4. Labrador + poodle = labradoodle
5. bunny + Dracula = Bunnicula
6. Yellow Pages + help = Yelp
7. shark + tornado = Sharknado
8. American + track = Amtrak
9. robot + blocks = Roblox
10. clam + tomato = Clamato
11. 14 + night = fortnight
12. apple + martini = appletini
13. spiced + ham = Spam
14. June + 19th = Juneteenth
15. sunflower + artichoke = sunchoke
16. spoon + fork = spork
17. pocket + monster = Pokemon

	THIN			FLOOR		NAIL		PLUS	
LETTERS		BRITAIN	EXIT	LOLLIPOP	ICICLE		THREE	REPEAT	MOUSE
	LABRADOR			BUNNY		YELLOW PAGES		SHARK	
	POODLE			DRACULA		HELP		TORNADO	
TEN		AMERICAN	TRACK		ROBOT	BLOCKS	CLAM	TOMATO	BALLERINA
	14			APPLE		SPICED		JUNE	
	NIGHT			MARTINI		HAM		19TH	
IN		SUN-FLOWER	ARTICHOKE		SPOON	FORK	POCKET	MONSTER	CAN
	PAIR			STAR		MOVIE		YIELD	

The outer ring of words reads: thin floor nail plus mouse ballerina can yield movie star pair in ten letters. This clues a final portmanteau, BRAD + ANGELINA = **BRANGELINA,** which is the answer to this puzzle.

7. We Aim to Please solution

The shaded squares, which show all the cells traverse, spell out the letters **NECKTIE**.

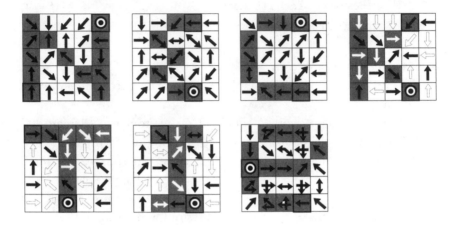

8A. The Latest Fashion solution

The completed chart is shown below. Extract a letter from each designer's name according to the time they went on, and extract a letter from each fabric based upon the number of outfits shown in it. Those letter pairs, in order, spell the answer **NEW CLOTHES.**

Time	Name	No. of Outfits	Fabric
1:00	NIKITA	5	TAFFETA
2:00	KWAME	1	CORDUROY
3:00	SALMAN	2	COTTON
4:00	BAUTISTA	4	CASHMERE
5:00	MEIFENG	3	MUSLIN

Here, thanks to test solver Joshua Kosman, is one possible solving trajectory. Numbers in parentheses here indicate which of the instructions is used to support each inference.

Salman showed either 2 or 4 outfits (1). Bautista showed either 2 or 4 outfits (4). Nikita and Kwame's outfits total 6, and they can't be 2 and 4 so they're 1 and 5 in some order. Meifeng, then, showed 3.

The one showing five outfits did it at either 1:00 or 2:00 (3), and that's either Nikita or Kwame. So Nikita and Kwame's consecutive appearances (2) was either at 1:00 and 2:00 in some order, or at 2:00 and 3:00 in some order. In either case, Bautista can't have shown at 2:00, so he showed at 4:00. Therefore he showed 4 outfits and Salman showed 2.

Salman showed his two outfits immediately after the person (again, either Nikita or Kwame) who showed 1. That's only possible if Salman showed at 3:00, the 1-outfit designer showed at 2:00, and the 5-outfit designer showed at 1:00. The person showing cashmere did it at 4:00, three hours after the 5-outfit designer (3). With Nikita and Kwame in the 1:00 and 2:00 slots in some order, Meifeng showed her 3 outfits at 5:00.

The 1 outfit at 2:00 was corduroy (1), Salman's 2 outfits at 3:00 were cotton (1), and Bautista's 4 outfits at 4:00 were cashmere. That leaves 5 outfits at 1:00 and 3 outfits at 5:00; they were taffeta and muslin, respectively (5). The designer showing 5 taffeta at 1:00 was Nikita, not Kwame (2), leaving Kwame in the 2:00 slot.

8B. Real Numbers solution

The title and artist for each song is given below, along with the missing character. These letters and numbers spell BASEBALL POSITION 7 8 or 9, which clues the solution OUTFIELDER.

CLUE	TITLE	ARTIST	MISSING CHARACTER
1 S F, 3 S ___	1 Step Forward, 3 Steps Back	Olivia Rodrigo	B
9 I T ___	Nine in the Afternoon	Panic! at the Disco	A
___ O 69	Summer of '69	Bryan Adams	S
___ O 17	Edge of Seventeen	Stevie Nicks	E
3 L ___	Three Little Birds	Bob Marley and the Wailers	B
__ 1 B T D	Another One Bites the Dust	Queen	A
50 W T ___ Y L	50 Ways to Leave Your Lover	Paul Simon	L
___ O 1000 D	Land of 1,000 Dances	Wilson Pickett	L
99 ___	99 Problems	Jay-Z	P
2 ___ O 3 A B	Two Out of Three Ain't Bad	Meat Loaf	O

G 3 ___	Gimme Three Steps	Lynyrd Skynyrd	S
___ G B (500 M)	I'm Gonna Be (500 Miles)	The Proclaimers	I
___ 5	Take Five	Dave Brubeck	T
___ W D 4 U	I Would Die 4 U	Prince	I
25 ___ 6 T 4	25 or 6 to 4	Chicago	O
19th ___ B	19th Nervous Breakdown	Rolling Stones	N
___ N A	Seven Nation Army	White Stripes	7
___ D A W	Eight Days a Week	Beatles	8
D 63 (___ W A N)	December '63 (Oh What a Night)	The Four Seasons	O
7 ___	7 Rings	Ariana Grande	R
L P N ___	Love Potion No. 9	The Searchers	9

9. Remix solution

Each rule is given below, along with the untransformed clue, the answer, the transformed answer, and the extracted letter.

The eleven transformed answers are all shades of blue, and the extracted letters spell the name of noted blues singer **BESSIE SMITH**.

1	CORNCTRLONDELTHEESCBLANKTAB		
	Clue: CORN ON THE BLANK	Answer: COB	
	Rule: Prepend a computer keyboard key	Transformed: COBALT (3/6)	B
2	TINGERXHOSECIGIITXASLISSGROMBSOSE		
	Clue: SINGER WHOSE BIG HIT WAS KISS FROM A ROSE	Answer: SEAL	
	Rule: Move first letter one place forward in alphabet	Transformed: TEAL (2/4)	E
3	GLYDEDOWNHYLLLYKELYNDSEYVONN		
	Clue: GLIDE DOWNHILL LIKE LINDSEY VONN	Answer: SKI	
	Rule: Change I to Y	Transformed: SKY (1/3)	S
4	PNOITATIPICERMGNIXIRNIAADNSWON		

	Clue: PRECIPITATION MIXING RAIN AND SNOW	Answer: SLEET	
	Rule: Reverse all but the first letter	Transformed: STEEL (1/5)	S
5	USAUTRALIANILWIDOGDOROFRMAMFAOUSERMEYLTRSTEEP INLIE		
	Clue: AUSTRALIAN WILD DOG FROM FAMOUS MERYL STREEP LINE	Answer: DINGO	
	Rule: Move first letter after third, followed by duplicated second letter	Transformed: INDIGO (1/6)	I
6	LZUNDMZUASUREEZUUALLING4ZU40SZUUAREYZURDS		
	Clue: LAND MEASURE EQUALLING 4840 SQUARE YARDS	Answer: ACRE	
	Rule: Change second letter to ZU	Transformed: AZURE (5/5)	E
7	PRESIDENTPOFPMOSCOWPORPSTPPETERSBURG		
	Clue: RESIDENT OF MOSCOW OR ST PETERSBURG	Answer: RUSSIAN	
	Rule: Prepend P	Transformed: PRUSSIAN (4/8)	S
8	WODRIGHTTHTAIGHTCNAIGHTFOLLWOIGHTHIEVIGHT MASTREIGHTROIGHTNEVREIGHT		
	Clue: WORD THAT CAN FOLLOW HIVE MASTER OR NEVER	Answer: MIND	
	Rule: Reverse last two letters and append IGHT	Transformed: MIDNIGHT (1/8)	M
9	PEOIBTOXPERITEATMENTPEAITRGET		
	Clue: BOTOX TREATMENT TARGET	Answer: WRINKLE	
	Rule: Remove 2nd letter, surround it with PEI, append that string to front	Transformed: PERIWINKLE (4/10)	I
10	ANBCYDOEFMESTICFEGHLINE		
	Clue: ANY DOMESTIC FELINE	Answer: CAT	
	Rule: Take two letters alphabetically after 1st letter, insert after 2nd	Transformed: CADET (5/5)	T
11	HAPPOBBITSHAPPOMEIAPPNLAPPORDOAPPFTAPPHERAPPINGS		
	Clue: HOBBITS HOME IN LORD OF THE RINGS	Answer: SHIRE	
	Rule: Insert APP after the first letter	Transformed: SAPPHIRE (5/8)	H

10. Border Crossings solution

The country pairs (and their disaggregated capitals) are shown below.

In each pair there is exactly one letter that is in the same position in both country names. Those letters, in order, spell the answer **UNITED NATIONS**.

Letter	Country 1	Country 2	Capital 1	Capital 2
U	**U**KRAINE	**U**RUGUAY	KIEV	MONTEVIDEO
N	JAPA**N**	YEME**N**	TOKYO	SANAA
I	CH**I**LE	HA**I**TI	SANTIAGO	PORT-AU-PRINCE
T	**T**ANZANIA	**T**HAILAND	DODOMA	BANGKOK
E	GR**E**ECE	SW**E**DEN	ATHENS	STOCKHOLM
D	EL SALVA**D**OR	SOUTH SU**D**AN	SAN SALVADOR	JUBA
N	**N**EPAL	**N**IGER	KATHMANDU	NIAMEY
A	CHIN**A**	LIBY**A**	BEIJING	TRIPOLI
T	AUS**T**RIA	VIE**T**NAM	VIENNA	HANOI
I	**I**NDIA	**I**TALY	NEW DELHI	ROME
O	M**O**ZAMBIQUE	S**O**UTH KOREA	MAPUTO	SEOUL
N	FRA**N**CE	GUI**N**EA	PARIS	CONAKRY
S	HONDURA**S**	BARBADO**S**	TEGUCIGALPA	BRIDGETOWN

11. Coming to Terms solution

When the two puzzles are solved, there are several cells that are the same in both grids. Highlighted below, these give the numbers 4, 9, 1, 2, 15, 12, 9, 3, 1, 12. Converting these numbers to letters spells the answer **DIABOLICAL**.

4	5	7	3	6	8	1	2	9
2	9	1	7	4	5	6	8	3
3	8	6	1	9	2	5	4	7
9	7	8	6	2	4	3	1	5
1	2	5	8	3	7	9	6	4
6	3	4	5	1	9	8	7	2
5	4	3	2	8	6	7	9	1
8	1	2	9	7	3	4	5	6
7	6	9	4	5	1	2	3	8

4	8	2	5	1	6	7	3	9
9	6	1	8	3	7	5	4	2
5	3	7	9	4	2	8	6	1
7	4	9	2	8	3	6	1	5
1	2	6	4	7	5	3	9	8
3	5	8	1	6	9	4	2	7
2	9	3	6	5	8	1	7	4
6	1	5	7	2	4	9	8	3
8	7	4	3	9	1	2	5	6

12. Greeks vs. Romans solution

The diagram below shows the moves that each piece makes.

The path taken by the Black knight spells out ANOTHER NAME FOR THE ORACLE AT DELPHI, which clues the answer **PYTHIA.**

The path taken by the White knight spells out VILLAIN WHO RACES WITH BEN-HUR IN FILM, which clues the answer **MESSALA.**

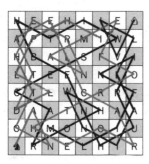

13. Who Are We? solution

The solutions to the clues are given below, along with explanations. When strung together, the answers spell out the clue ABOLITIONISTS JACKSON AND CRANDALL, whose first names are **FRANCIS** and **PRUDENCE**, the two solutions to this puzzle.

1. ABO   metABOlism, seABOrne, lavABOs; also found as blood types
2. LIT   synonyms (drunk, exciting, not pitch-black, fine writing); TIL reversed
3. ION   potION, billION, passION, erosion
4. ISTS   It's surely this simple (initials); as a suffix, means "adherents"
5. JACK   Jack Black (actor), Jack White (musician); card between 10 and queen
6. SON   A classic riddle
7. AND   FANBOYS is a mnemonic for the conjunctions for, and, nor, but, or, yet, so
8. C   Each part of the verse is a meaning of C or c
9. RAND   South African currency, senator Rand Paul; erRAND, RANDomly
10. ALL   ALLigators, swALLows, shALLows, gALLeries, digitALLy

14. Japanese Puzzle Boxes solution

The table below shows the eight categories and the items in each column. The letters extracted at the end spell the answer **VANNA WHITE**.

Dressings	Languages	Ungulates	Synonyms of Puzzle	New York Cities	PDA Manufacturers	Trees	Arm Parts
	JAPANESE		PUZZLE			BOX	
	MANDARIN		PERPLEX			BAOBAB	
	ARABIC		FLUMMOX			BALSA	
	PUNJABI		CONFUSE			LAUREL	
	PORTUGUESE		BAFFLE			ALMOND	
RUSSIAN	RUSSIAN	BUFFALO	BUFFALO	BUFFALO	PALM	PALM	PALM
GREEN GODDESS	TURKISH	GIRAFFE	BAMBOOZLE	ALBANY	APPLE	MAPLE	ARMPIT
CAESAR	BURMESE	LLAMA	BEMUSE	NEW YORK	BLACKBERRY	ASPEN	WRIST
RANCH	GREEK	CAMEL	BEFUDDLE	SYRACUSE	MOTOROLA	CYPRESS	RADIUS
VINAIGRETTE	GERMAN	ANTELOPE	BEWILDER	ROCHESTER	NOKIA	CHESTNUT	SHOULDER

15. Thirders and Halfers solution

Here are the reassembled clues and their answers:

Thirders

1. French Sudan, today (4)   MALI
2. Lakers' owner Jerry (4)   BUSS
3. Desegregation pioneer Leona (4)   TATE
4. Surgeon Antoine- Hippolyte (4)   CROS
5. Participate in karaoke (4)   SING
6. Endorse a check (4)   SIGN
7. NWA definite article (3)   THA
8. "America" lyric contraction (3)   TIS

Halfers

1. 500, in Roman numerals (1)   D
2. Symbol for carbon (1)   C
3. Opposite of acid, chemically (4)   BASE
4. Event for Cinderella (4)   BALL
5. Nam _____ (fish sauce) (3)   PLA
6. With "out," an ump's call (3)   YER
7. Took a chair (3)   SAT
8. Big coffee server (3)   URN
9. Winter time zone in Nova Scotia (3)   AST

10. Royal title for Haile Selassie (3)	RAS
11. Golfer's shout (4)	FORE
12. Paddington or Fozzie (4)	BEAR

The answers can be put together, in order, to form five more clues:

Thirders

1. MALIBU'S STATE	CA
2. CROSSING SIGN	RR
3. THAT IS	IE

Halfers

1. DC BASEBALL PLAYER	NAT
2. SATURN ASTRA'S FOREBEAR	ION

Those strings, reassembled, spell out the answer **CARRIE NATION.**

16. Transatlantic solution

The five clues with extra words are:

9A (these), 12A (answers), 14A (make), 26A (another), 29A (clue) = These answers make another clue.

The clue is: STATE BOND AUTHOR SHORTENED ELEVEN

State bond author shortened (11) = CONNECT | I + CUT = **CONNECTICUT**

Across

1 MA + GP + IE
4 bUNK EMPTied
9 ST + ATE ("these" = 1st extra word)
10 anagram
11 ADAM + ANTI + NE
12 double definition ("answers" = 2nd extra word)
14 AU + THOR ("Make" = 3rd extra word)
15 MERING(U)E (regimen anagram)
18 lean grit Spoonerism
19 FE(RR)ET
21 WI(F)I
23 CHAR + LA + TANS
26 anagram ("Another" = 4th extra word)
27 O + CHER
28 TRAP + PER (reversal)
29 EL(E)VEN ("clue" = 5th extra word)

Down

1 MASC + A + RA (MAC's anagram)
2 GUA(m) + RANTE(d) + E
3 IG + ETA + ROUND
4 UN(in)TENDED
5 KOOK palindrome
6 initial letters; &lit
7 (gr → TW)IDDLE
8 double definition
13 Mail Elinor anagram
16 GOR(BACH)E + V
17 DI(S + HON)OR
18 GAW + KSAT (reversal)
20 T(EST R + U)N (rest anagram)
22 F(L)ORA
24 homophone ("rued")
25 reversal

Crossword grid:

1 M	2 A	3 G	P	I	E		4 U	N	5 K	E	6 M	P	7 T
A		U		G		8 S	N		O		A		W
9 S	T	A	T	E		10 P	O	T	P	O	U	R	I
C		R		I		E		K		I			D
11 A	D	A	M	A	N	T	I	N	E		12 B	O	N	D
R		N		R				D		13 M			L
14 A	U	T	H	O	R		15 M	E	R	I	N	16 G	U	E
		E		U		17 D		D		N		O	
18 G	R	E	E	N	L	I	T		19 F	E	R	R	E	20 T
A				D		S			R		B		E
21 W	I	22 F	I		23 C	H	A	24 R	L	A	T	A	N	S
K		L		25 S	O		U		L		C		T
26 S	H	O	R	T	E	N	E	D		27 O	C	H	E	R
A		R		O		O		E		I		E		U
28 T	R	A	P	P	E	R		29 E	L	E	V	E	N

17. Skyscrapers of Hanoi solution

The answers to the clues (given below) can be sorted into the rings according to rules, as noted below, that are related to the names of the skyscrapers. When the answers have all been placed properly, the extracted letters can be read left to right, top to bottom, to spell the clue WORLD'S TALLEST IS FOUR SEVEN, which clues the world's tallest building, the BURJ KHALIFA.

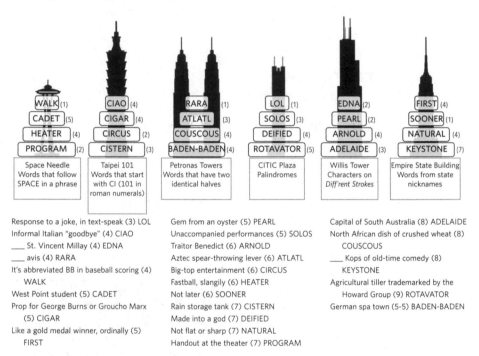

Space Needle	Taipei 101	Petronas Towers	CITIC Plaza	Willis Tower	Empire State Building
Words that follow SPACE in a phrase	Words that start with CI (101 in roman numerals)	Words that have two identical halves	Palindromes	Characters on *Diff'rent Strokes*	Words from state nicknames

WALK (1)
CADET (5)
HEATER (4)
PROGRAM (2)

CIAO (4)
CIGAR (4)
CIRCUS (2)
CISTERN (3)

RARA (1)
ATLATL (3)
COUSCOUS (4)
BADEN-BADEN (4)

LOL (1)
SOLOS (3)
DEIFIED (4)
ROTAVATOR (5)

EDNA (2)
PEARL (2)
ARNOLD (4)
ADELAIDE (3)

FIRST (4)
SOONER (1)
NATURAL (4)
KEYSTONE (7)

Response to a joke, in text-speak (3) LOL
Informal Italian "goodbye" (4) CIAO
___ St. Vincent Millay (4) EDNA
___ avis (4) RARA
It's abbreviated BB in baseball scoring (4) WALK
West Point student (5) CADET
Prop for George Burns or Groucho Marx (5) CIGAR
Like a gold medal winner, ordinally (5) FIRST

Gem from an oyster (5) PEARL
Unaccompanied performances (5) SOLOS
Traitor Benedict (6) ARNOLD
Aztec spear-throwing lever (6) ATLATL
Big-top entertainment (6) CIRCUS
Fastball, slangily (6) HEATER
Not later (6) SOONER
Rain storage tank (7) CISTERN
Made into a god (7) DEIFIED
Not flat or sharp (7) NATURAL
Handout at the theater (7) PROGRAM

Capital of South Australia (8) ADELAIDE
North African dish of crushed wheat (8) COUSCOUS
___ Kops of old-time comedy (8) KEYSTONE
Agricultural tiller trademarked by the Howard Group (9) ROTAVATOR
German spa town (5-5) BADEN-BADEN

18. Big Secrets solution

The puzzle answers (plus A.J. and Greg, as described) can all be associated with the Major Arcana (major = big, arcana = secrets) in a traditional* deck of tarot cards.

The intro text to this puzzle says "A.J. approaches his work with joyful exuberance, willing to step into the unknown without fear of failure or embarrassment," which describes the Fool. The text says Greg is "a clever trickster, conjuring mental delights from thin air"—thus the Magician.

The chart below shows the other correspondences, along with the letter that is extracted from each associated answer.

* The nontraditional Rider-Waite deck swaps the positions of Justice and Strength.

No.	Tarot Card	Associated Answer	Index	Letter
0	The Fool	AJ	—	—
1	The Magician	GREG	—	—
2	The High Priestess	PYTHIA (High Priestess of Delphi)	3	T
3	The Empress	BESSIE SMITH (Empress of the Blues)	11	H
4	The Emperor	NEW CLOTHES	2	E
5	The Hierophant	FRANCIS (Pope Francis)	1	F
6	The Lovers	BRANGELINA	3	A
7	The Chariot	MESSALA (Ben Hur's rival charioteer)	4	S
8	Justice	OUTFIELDER (David Justice)	3	T
9	The Hermit	CRAB	3	A
10	Wheel of Fortune	VANNA WHITE	3	N
11	Strength	DOUBLE BOND	1	D
12	The Hanged Man	NECKTIE	5	T
13	Death	HOMICIDE LIFE ON THE STREET	1	H
14	Temperance	CARRIE NATION	6	E
15	The Devil	DIABOLICAL	8	C
16	The Tower	BURJ KHALIFA	2	U
17	The Star	SIRIUS	3	R
18	The Moon	IO	1	I
19	The Sun	CONNECTICUT (WNBA team)	2	O
20	Judgement	PRUDENCE	3	U
21	The World	UNITED NATIONS	13	S

The extracted letters spell out what kinds of people make for excellent puzzle solvers: **THE FAST AND THE CURIOUS**.

Acknowledgments

FROM A.J.:

The book I wrote immediately before *The Puzzler* was about my quest to thank one thousand people who had even the smallest role in making my morning cup of coffee. I'm not going to thank a thousand people here. But honestly, I'm going to come close. This is because I could not have written this book without the help of so many generous people: puzzlemakers, solvers, readers, editors, and ex-CIA agents. So here goes:

Thank you to my brilliant and creative editor, Gillian Blake, who has one of the best puzzle-solving minds I've ever seen, even if she applies most of her solving skills to fixing manuscripts instead of filling in crosswords.

Thanks also to my excellent agent, Sloan Harris, without whom this book wouldn't exist. He was the first one to suggest that I write about my obsession.

I'm deeply indebted to the team at Crown, including but not limited to Amy Li, Caroline Wray, Dyana Messina, Cozetta Smith, Melissa Esner, Amelia Zalcman, Maggie Hart, Simon Sullivan, Ted Allen, David Goehring, and Nikeeyia Howell. I know all the elements—the art and the contest, among them—made this a brainbuster.

I'm grateful for Greg Pliska, who is a great puzzlemaker and collaborator, and also much higher ranked than I am on Learned League. And to Sara Goodchild, who contributed a cryptic that makes me like cryptics again.

Thanks to Victor Ozols, who is a researcher, but also a friend, joke contributor, and font of wisdom. And Annika Robbins, for tireless image-chasing and diagram-making. Also, Niko Ramirez, the future of puzzling, and Jesse Rifkin, for his research and insights into punmanship. Also to the graphically gifted Colin McGreal. And the remarkable Nancy Sheed. And to Joseph Hinson and Nathan Torrence.

Much appreciation goes to my generous friends and colleagues who weighed in on the manuscript and gave me helpful notes on everything from the emotional arc to the history of the British rock band The Vapors, including: Peter Griffin, Neely Lohmann, Alex Rosenthal, Peter Gordon, Stuart Gibbs, Stephen Friedman, Brian Raftery, Paul Shapiro, Kevin Roose, Mollie Book, Andy Borowitz, Shannon Barr, Richard Panek, Stuart Halpern, Candice Braun, Jake Kheel, Gary Rudoren, Sam Aybar, Adam Dorsay, Nando Pelusi, Kaja Perina, Richard Panek, Jim Windolf, and Logan Sullivan. Special thanks to Keiran Harris and Chloe Harris, who read it out loud and did impressions, no less.

The puzzle community has been unbelievably supportive and patient with answering my sometimes ignorant questions, including: Peter Gordon, Tammy McLeod, Andrew Rhoda, Jerry Slocum, Tom Johnson, Andrew Young, Marc Breman, Scott Barry Kaufman, James Altucher, Tom Wujec, Paula Tardie, Ed Scheidt, Mark Setteducati, Nate Cardin, Rob Stegmann, Jeff Saward, Alexey Root, Justin Kalef, David Feldman, Sara Lichterman, Art Chung, Deb Amlen, Francis Heaney, Bret Rothstein, Josh Jay, Steve Canfield, Pat Battaglia, Tom Johnson, Ellie Grueskin, Michelle Ann Crowe, Russ Roberts, Julia Galef, John Schwartz, Jordan Harbinger, Matt Gaffney, Joe Posnanski, David Kwong, Lauren Rose, Ben Bass, Klaus Schmeh, Eric Berlin, Spencer Greenberg, Chris Ramsay, Sam Ezersky, Peter Norvig, Cornelia Rémi, Karen Kavett, Michaela Keener, Nicolas Ricketts, Kay Whipple, Mike Reiss, Beryl Jacobs, Willy Ramos, Scott Nicholson, Phillip Cohe, Cully Long, Paul Bloom, Tom Cutrofello, Michael Sloan Warren, Brendan Emmett Quigley, Sydney Weaver, Jesse Born, and Harry Foundalis.

Thanks to Jay Kernis and Martha Teichner, my field trip buddies. And to the team who joined Greg Pliska in writing *The Puzzler* contest: Tanis O'Connor, Guy Jacobson, Matt Gruskin, and Max Woghiren.

Thank you to Will Shortz, who is as great a puzzlemaker as Sam Loyd, and much more trustworthy. And while we're on the topic, a special thank-you to the *New York Times* online puzzle team. In the past few months, they have gotten punctual, and started to put up the next day's crossword at 10:00 P.M. instead of 10:01 P.M. I appreciate you saving me a minute every night.

As always, I'm grateful to Rob Weisbach for giving me my first break, without which I would not be a writer today.

And, of course, thanks to my family: My mom and dad, who got me all those maze books and the (unsolved) Rubik's Cube when I was a kid. My nieces and nephew, who have been co-solvers and cheerleaders: Andrea, Ally, Natalia, Adam, Isabella, and Micaela.

And thanks most of all to . . .

My son Jasper for being my chess tutor and TED-Ed riddle guide.

Zane, for being an awesome puzzle-solving and puzzle-creating collaborator.

Lucas, for being one of my best editors and sounding boards.

And thanks to Julie for being the love of my life (I tried to come up with an anagram for that, but only got "movie fly floe," so I'll stick with the non-anagram version).

FROM GREG:

My parents, Ed and Luisa Pliska, deserve the first thanks for raising their children to be inquisitive and to follow our inspiration, wherever it may lead. This is not only good life advice, but also turns out to be an excellent approach to puzzle solving. My late father gets extra credit for putting up with my earliest crossword constructions, made up largely of the most obscure words I could find in our unabridged dictionary.

No good puzzles get made without great test-solvers checking them, and I am lucky to have three friends and puzzling partners who are ace test-solvers: Joshua Kosman, Guy Jacobson, and Felicia Yue. They have made all of these puzzles better, and if there are still errors or ambiguities, the fault lies with me.

Without Will Shortz's American Crossword Puzzle Tournament I would never have discovered the joyous and clever community of puzzlers, including the National Puzzlers' League and my teammates at the MIT Mystery Hunt. And it was Will who introduced me to the Wonderful World of Words Weekend at Mohonk Mountain House, which is where I've met so many word mavens who have become friends and colleagues, including A.J. Jacobs. Thanks, A.J., for being foolish enough to invite me along on this magical adventure!

I also have Will and the ACPT to thank for the most important puzzler of them all, my wife, Jessica, without whose patience and support none of this would have been possible. She's solved the puzzle of how to put up with me and is the best solving partner for how to raise our two remarkable children, Margot and Nicky.

Image Credits

9 Courtesy of Stan Chess

17 Courtesy of Inkubator

19 Permission from © Ratselmeister | Dreamstime.com

20 Courtesy of Peter Gordon

29 Credit: Daniel Karmann/dpa/Alamy Live News

31 Courtesy of Jeff Varasano

35 Credit: Emma Weaver

40 Credit: Lucas Jacobs

58 Courtesy Clipart Library and Openclipart

61 (top left) Sam Loyd

61 (top right) Courtesy of Getty Images/Daniel Zuchnik

61 (bottom) Sam Loyd's Famous Trick Donkeys

62 Courtesy of Lilly Library, Indiana University, Bloomington, Indiana

66 Courtesy of Alan Mays, *May I See You Home?*

67 (bottle cap) Courtesy of Lee Helzer, lonestarbottlecaps.com

67 (boxed rebuses) Graphics by Lucas Jacobs

81 By permission of the British Library

85 Courtesy of Stave Puzzles

89 Courtesy of Division of Medicine and Science, National Museum of American History, Smithsonian Institution

90 Courtesy PA Images/Alamy Stock Photo/Sean Dempsey

100 Courtesy of Gregory Wild-Smith

103 Courtesy of Mike Boudreau

109 (top) Courtesy of Adrian Fisher

109 (bottom) Courtesy of Michelle Boggess-Nunley

114 Graphics by Annika Robbins

118 Image by Colin McGreal, colinmcgreal.com

126 Courtesy of Inanna Donnelley

128 Courtesy of Jim Sanborn and the CIA

131 Credit: Suzy Gorman

141 Courtesy of NASA/JPL-Caltech

145 Currier and Ives Lithograph. Courtesy of Library of Congress.

146 Courtesy of Josh Mecouch (illustrator; @pantspants) and Sarah Adams (writer; @sarahgadams)

148 This image is actually a reproduction of the original *Last Supper*. I used it here because Da Vinci's original is faded and harder to see.

151 Used with permission of J. Boylston & Company, Publishers.

156 The Baskin-Robbins trademark is owned by BR IP Holder, LLC. Used under license.

156 Courtesy of Toblerone

156 Courtesy of Tour de France

156 Courtesy of Oracle Corporation

157 (top) Courtesy of the Pittsburgh Zoo & PPG Aquarium

157 (middle) Courtesy of Peter de Padua Krauss

158 Courtesy of Harry Foundalis

160 Courtesy of Elisabeth Bik

162 Graphics by Lucas Jacobs

163 Image by Colin McGreal, colinmcgreal.com

171 Courtesy of Thomas Snyder/GMPuzzles.com

206 Courtesy of Steven Canfield

210 Courtesy of Kagen Sound

211 Courtesy of Kagen Sound

214 Courtesy of iStock, C taehoon bae and Gunay Aliyeva

215 Courtesy of Peter Winkler

232 Courtesy of Justin Graham

239 Courtesy of WatsonAdventures.com

240 Courtesy of Justin Graham

242 (bottom left) By Nevit Dilmen, courtesy of Creative Commons

242 (bottom right) By Yves Guillou, courtesy of Open Clip Art Library

243 Photo by Lucas Jacobs (this is not part of Wei's and Peter's collection)

244 Graphics by Lucas Jacobs

245 Courtesy of Creative Commons

248 Credit: Julie Jacobs

301 Courtesy of Inkubator

302 (top) Permission from © Ratselmeister | Dreamstime.com

306 Image by Colin McGreal, colinmcgreal.com

311 Courtesy of Thomas Snyder

About the Author

A.J. JACOBS is a journalist, lecturer, and human guinea pig who has written four bestselling books—including *Drop Dead Healthy* and *The Year of Living Biblically,* which spent three months on the *New York Times* bestseller list—that blend memoir, science, humor, and a dash of self-help. He is a contributor to NPR, *The New York Times,* and *Esquire,* among others. He lives in New York City with his family.

ajjacobs.com
@ajjacobs

About the Type

This book was set in Baskerville, a typeface designed by John Baskerville (1706–75), an amateur printer and typefounder, and cut for him by John Handy in 1750. The type became popular again when the Lanston Monotype Corporation of London revived the classic roman face in 1923. The Mergenthaler Linotype Company in England and the United States cut a version of Baskerville in 1931, making it one of the most widely used typefaces today.